Drogiej Pani Józefie,

  w dowód szczerego uwielbienia,

      Lia Kmiel.

Hollywood, 1939.

UNDER FIVE EAGLES

ISADORA DUNCAN AND ESSENINE

Lido   August 14th, 1922

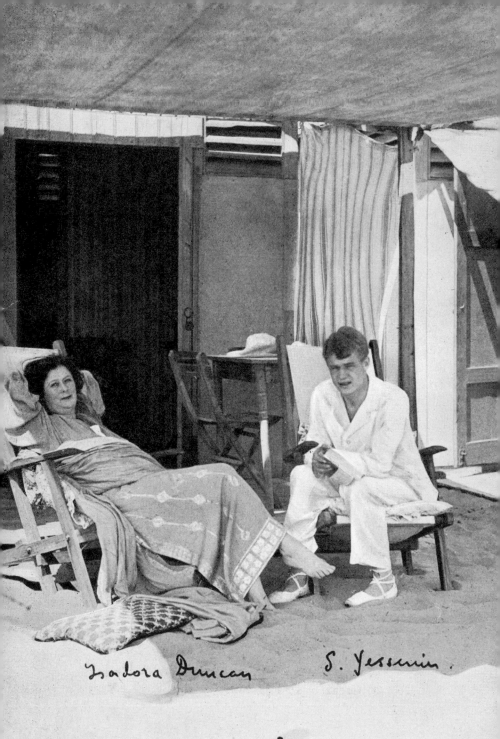

Isadora Duncan   S. Yessenin

Lido, August 14, 1922

Lola Kinel

UNDER FIVE EAGLES

My Life in Russia, Poland, Austria,
Germany and America,
1916–1936

PUTNAM · LONDON
42, Great Russell Street, W.C.I.

First Published . . . *April, 1937*
Reprinted . . . *December, 1937*

Printed in Great Britain by
Wyman & Sons, Limited, London, Fakenham and Reading.

To
VICTOR AND RITA

CONTENTS

Part III. AUSTRIA AND GERMANY

Part IV. AMERICA

ILLUSTRATIONS

Instead of an Introduction

I DID not want to write this book. The people who wanted me to write it are my milkman, a woman who works in a police department, the man who runs the circulating library where I get my books, and sundry other folk, including some of my friends.

The reason why I never thought of writing a book like this is my age. I am still in my thirties, which is assuredly the worst age for writing anything about oneself. Autobiographical books ought to be done either when one is still very young and egocentric—and the Preoccupation with Self is both amusing and excusable—or when one is quite old and life is behind one, so that one can review both one's achievements and one's follies in a mellow mood of reminiscence. As it is, I have long since lost the belief that I am unique, original, tragic, and misunderstood. Yet I certainly am not ready to review all my follies and achievements, for I haven't any—achievements, of course.

However, the milkman's, laundryman's, and other folks' opinion is quite different. It is not really an opinion—merely a reaction to my occasional moments of loquacity. Leading a very quiet life, with only a small daughter and a cat for companionship, I am given to these conversations with comparative strangers.

And so I talk to anyone who happens to be handy. As is only natural, there crops up occasionally in such conversations my mention of having been here and there, of having seen this or that. And the reaction

on the part of my listeners seems invariably to be :
" You ought to write a book." The conversation with
the milkman, for instance, ran something like this :

" Are you sure this is raw milk ? "

" Certainly. Pure, raw, guaranteed milk."

" Why doesn't it get thick, then ? "

" You mean sour ? "

" Yes, I mean sour."

" What you want is buttermilk. Now just leave a
note in the bottle next time and I will leave the best
buttermilk."

" *I do not want buttermilk*. I want thick, stiff, sour
milk."

" Clabber ? "

" I guess so. Though it's a funny name to call it.
In Russia the cook used just to leave a bowl of milk in
the warm kitchen overnight and in the morning it
would be thick. Now why doesn't this milk turn thick ?
You are sure it isn't pasteurised ? "

" Well, Mrs. S., I will tell you how it is. It's raw all
right. But it's too clean."

" Too clean ? "

" Yes. You see, all guaranteed milk is kept very
clean. Pure. The cow's udder is washed and the
utensils are all sterilised, and the bottles too, so the
germs can't get in. And so them germs that makes
the milk sour don't get much of a chance of gettin'
in either. And that's why you pay more for it. . . ."

" Marvellous. Now could you provide me with some
cheap milk that will turn thick ? "

He looked at me brightly.

" Say, have you ever tried our yogurt milk ? It's
very good for your health and your baby. . . ."

" Look here—*Now, what I want* is just ordinary
raw milk that will turn sour and thick. And the reason
I want it is because it is part of a dish that I like. It's

a Polish dish called *zsiadle mleko z kartoflami*. And I love it.   You serve thick sour milk in soup-bowls with a small dish of mashed potatoes and bits of fried bacon on the side.   You eat these together. It's one of my favourite dishes.   I haven't had it in years, and the other day I just wanted to make some . . ."

He was a fair, fresh-coloured man with big blue eyes.   And these eyes seemed to pop out a little.

" And that's what the Roossians eat ? "

" No.   The Poles do.   The Russians haven't any milk or bacon now.   The idea ! "

" And have you been in Russia too, missus ? "

" Half of my life."

" With them Bolsheviks ? "

" Oh, just about a year with them."

" Now tell me "—here he lowered his voice confidentially—" how is it in Russia ?   To hear some of them talk you would believe it's paradise on earth. Everyone's got work, no depression.   And now others claim it is awful.   How come ? "

" Well—it all depends on the point of view.   But don't you believe there is no depression.   The reason they don't call it that is because they never have any booms.   So their depression is just normal times to them.   But anyway, it's like this : If you like your three square meals a day and enough clothes and a room, or perhaps two, for you and your family to live in, and the freedom to say what you like about the government—without the fear of being shot for it— well, then you had better stay here.   But now, if you would like to live in a sort of dream, preparing a grand future for other generations—not yourself—feeling that all the hell you are going through now might help future people a little ; and if you don't mind being on starvation rations, badly dressed, ordered about

B

through your life, with a nice crowd of spies around
you all the time, in case you should change your mind
about liking that kind of life—well, then you can be
happy in Russia."

"Well . . . I declare. . . . And so you made a run
for it ? "

"Yes, I escaped."

"And your family too ? "

"Some did ; others didn't. My father did not get
out until two years later. Some other relatives didn't
get out until four years later ; some died ; my brother
never got out. He was an officer in the Russian army.
So he disappeared. The Bolsheviks don't kill people.
They just disappear."

"Good heavens ! " His blue eyes were wide open
now. "And then you came to America ? "

"Oh, much later. By and by. . . ."

"Why, you sure have been through a lot ! Gee,
you could write a book."

"I don't know about that. Say, you won't forget
to bring me the cheap milk to-morrow ? "

"You bet I won't."

The talk with the owner of the circulating library
was on a much higher plane. Quite literary, in fact.
Said I :

"I wonder how that book *From Day to Day* sold.
I just read it in Polish and it is delightful."

"Oh, quite well—quite well, for a while. By the
way, is Goetel a well-known writer in Poland ? "

"Certainly. He is very good, you know. Has
several fine novels and some excellent short stories."

"Is that right ? I have always liked Polish literature. I took it up at the university."

This statement, coming from an American, quite
overwhelmed me. Hitherto I had thought that the

only foreign literature Americans were interested in was Russian or French.

"It was fascinating—all of it," continued the librarian rather dreamily, as if he were savouring the remembrance of these hours. "Sienkiewicz's *With Fire and Sword* was stupendous. And those characters, that fellow—Pod—Podbee—now how do you pronounce him? You know who I mean?"

"Podbipienta. Like this—Pod-bee-pien-ta."

"How quaint! What a type! And then Reymont's *Peasants*. That was beautiful—his description of spring—do you remember?" And he actually went to a shelf and dug out the first volume of the *Peasants*.

It has been years since I read Reymont and untold ages since I read Sienkiewicz, and I said timidly that he knew, most probably, much more about Polish literature than I; that I hadn't read much Polish— not until I reached Warsaw after escaping from Russia, and then I read the moderns, of course.

That must have been thrilling—the escape from Russia—the librarian thought.

"Lord, no. Frightfully unpleasant. We had false German passports, my grandmother, my sister, and I— pretending to be German refugees. And the last lap of that trip we were in a German military train, in a compartment with stiff, square-necked, bristling officers, who kept on boasting all the way through how quickly they could throw their regiments from the Eastern to the Western Front—after having fed them up in Poland—and how they expected to be in Paris in six weeks, and so on and so forth. And we had to smile and pretend we were glad, while our innermost desire was to spit in their faces. They were just bursting with a special German brand of conceit— *Deutschland über alles*, you know. . . ."

The librarian gave a sympathetic chuckle.

" It may seem funny now," I said, my heart beating hard at the very remembrance of it, " but those hours on the German train were some of the worst I have had in my life, and I have been in three revolutions and am quite used to bullets."

" You really ought to use that," said the librarian.

" What do you mean ? "

" It's good material. All these experiences. It's worth writing up."

" Oh ? . . . Oh, yes, I know." I caught myself smartly. " I am really saving it all for a novel."

And I am, too. I have the situations and quite a few characters all lined up. And lots of atmosphere. In fact, everything is there, ready to be written down. Everything, that is, except the novel. . . .

Then there are my friends. They mostly wanted me to write about Isadora Duncan and Essenine. All my thrilling experiences. And all the scandals. Especially the scandals. And why didn't I stay with them any longer than I did? they wanted to know. And was Essenine very good-looking ? Very fascinating ? " Oh, a sort of blond peasant type," I would answer. " A very thick neck. Husky " " And did Isadora love him madly ? " " Oh yes, very madly," I would say. . . . " Well, why did you leave ? How did you come to stay with them such a short time ? Was Isadora jealous ? " " Oh," I would say, finally catching the drift, " no, it wasn't that at all. You see, Essenine got drunk one day and then he was very mad at me and I got fired."

In 1922, in Berlin, I was looking for a job and had put a continuous advertisement into the English paper, mentioning that I knew both Russian and English.

Then, having very little money, I went to a small
fishing village on the Baltic where life was cheap—to
await results.   A friend of Isadora's in Berlin saw the
advertisement and wired me that she wanted a secretary.   Russian was essential because she travelled in
those days with Sergei Essenine, the Russian poet.   I
got the job and travelled with them for a while—until I
got fired.

When, a few years later, Isadora's famous autobio-
graphy came out, immediately after her sensational
death, I became—in the limited circle of my bourgeois
friends—a much-sought-after person.   I was invited
to quite a few parties and was introduced to other
people, invariably with the words : " Oh, meet Miss
K.   She has travelled with Isadora Duncan."   I now
suspect that I was asked to meet some people solely
because once, for a few weeks, I had travelled with
Isadora.   It was the hall-mark of fame and renown.
If it had not been for that I should never have had the
pleasure of meeting " Mrs. Smythe, Mrs. Peabody, Mrs.
Nixkomraus," and the rest of the teaing, bridging,
gossiping crowd.   Also, most of the ladies I met
inquired subtly as to whether Isadora was " really so
eccentric, jealous, impossible, and temperamental, and
whether it wasn't true that she committed suicide."

On one such occasion, forgetting all the maxims
inculcated upon me so carefully in my youth, I said
heartily : " For Christ's sake let's leave Isadora out of
it."   It had a nice and instantaneous effect.   No one
mentioned her.   Or me either.   I was probably put
down as a rude person, of which I was glad, for it gave
me back the feeling of my own personality.

Such is the power of suggestion, however, that about
a year later—and by that time I had moved quite a
distance from my society friends, into an entirely
different community—I found myself jotting down

little reminiscences about Isadora and Essenine. My
daughter having grown into the kindergarten age, I
had free mornings, and it became a habit to sit down
and write a few pages each morning. The writing
grew into a little book. It was not meant to be a book
—not originally. It was to be an experiment in style,
in preparation for those days in my middle age when I
was to start writing novels. But it grew so rapidly
that I finally decided it was thick enough to sell.

There was, however, not much scandal in it. Mainly
because I happened to be with Isadora during a quiet
period and partly because I omitted anything that I
thought I ought not to tell. I remember I had considered the question very gravely and had put it up
before my conscience. I said, in effect, to myself :
" Now what shall I write and what shall I omit ? "
And I replied to myself : " I shall write nothing that I
could not say, were I speaking about it—instead of
writing—in a mixed, public audience."

There were, of course, little bits now and then which
I had to omit. All private secretaries carry with
them, naturally, memories of bits which it would be
a vulgar breach of confidence to divulge to utter
strangers. And, travelling with Isadora and Essenine,
I had, perhaps, more than an ordinary share of peeks
and glimpses for the reason that I was not only a
secretary, but also an interpreter, a constant go-
between, for two people who *could not speak to each
other*. For Isadora did not know Russian, and her
husband, Sergei Essenine, knew Russian only. So I
had to translate everything, from lovers' quarrels to
arguments about God or the way people slept together
in various countries. . . .

Now I am telling about it all at such length for it has
some importance. It has to do with my subsequent
attempt to sell the little book. It has very much to

do with it, for now I sometimes think that if I had happened to be with Isadora at a more violent period and had written it all up in the style of the Sunday *Examiner*, including all the bits, the little book might have been published. For it seems that is what the public wants, what it looks for in biographies of great people. The public is not averse to it in novels and other forms of fiction, of course, but likes it particularly in biographies. Perhaps because this brings the great people nearer to the heart of the great public. It bridges the gap which certainly must exist between the great and the lowly. To think that geniuses have also their bedroom scenes and find themselves in comic predicaments which can be spoken of only among trusted friends must be very comforting. " How human ! " the people exclaim, or, " The homely touch." Or, again, " Well, they are also human." This is an odd expression, one over which I used to ponder deeply when I first learned English. For it does not exist—with that particular implication—in any of the other languages I know. And I had to get used to it gradually. It used to puzzle me at first why anything that implied, as a rule, animalism pure and simple was always referred to in English as " so human." . . .

To return to the question of writing biography, I found later that the publishers, being naturally desirous of pleasing the great public on whose taste so much of their existence depends, are also in favour of a lot of choice bits, particularly about artists who have led free and eventful lives, like Isadora. And the literary agents, quite naturally, knowing what the publishers like, try to impress the importance of it on young, naïve, aspiring writers. Some agents, that is. . . .
I did not know this when I was writing the book. I

learned it all later when I went to New York—little book, code of ethics, baby, and all.

It was the very first agent to whom I offered the manuscript, with great inward trepidation, who enlightened me on the subject. She took it out of my hand, read a couple of pages, and then said sternly :

" This is good. But did you write all that happened while you were with Isadora ? Everything she did and said ? "

" Practically everything. Not absolutely, of course, for I was her private secretary. It would not have been discreet," I replied, or something to that effect.

" My child," she said—she was an elderly, stout woman with brusque manners—" you *must* tell everything. The editor will do any cutting if it's necessary. Remember—*all*. We have to know everything about great people. Nothing is too small or too trivial about them. Nothing is indecent, for it all serves to illuminate their personalities." Whereupon she went into the next room and called up a number on the telephone. Since the door was open, I could not help overhearing some of the things she said :

" I have something which would do as a serial . . . about Isadora Duncan. . . . One of her secretaries. . . . Yes. . . . Needs some editing, but is very good. . . ."

Standing in the other room, I thought : " Good Lord, is it that easy ? Good Lord, I should have done this a year ago ! Two years ago ! . . . If they pay me something in advance, I could buy Iris a new tricycle and a bigger swing. I could buy a set of Galsworthy in a limp-leather edition—with his autograph. I could buy . . ."

But the agent returned to the room, barging in on my dreams.

" I have just talked to the *Cosmopolitan*, but they don't want it. Now I shall get in touch with the

Ladies' Home Journal. Just leave this here and finish the rest of the chapters as soon as you can. I'll give you a ring."

I did not care for the lady personally, but I left elated. I stayed elated for six weeks, waiting for a call. When, after six weeks, there was no call, I rang up myself. A strange voice answered :

" Who ? Miss X ? Why, she is in Florida."

" In Florida ? "

" Yes, she went about a month ago."

" Well—when is she coming back ? "

" I don't know. It's entirely indefinite. Is there anything I can do ? I am her secretary."

" I left four chapters of a book about Isadora Duncan and I wondered what had happened to them."

The girl on the other end of the wire said she would look and see. She came back in a minute and said that nothing had happened to them as far as she knew. There were no notes or correspondence on them of any kind.

" Nothing ? Absolutely nothing ? " I said, my elation collapsing like a toy balloon.

" No." Not as far as she knew.

I cared for the fat lady agent still less after that and I went to her office, gathered up my chapters, and began to call on other agents.

In spite of her advice I did not add anything to my book. But subsequently, when I found an agent to my liking and the editor of one of the finest publishing houses finally read the book, the agent sent me a copy of his refusal, which set me to thinking. For he wrote that my manuscript's being " a quiet tale of a character supposed to be unduly turbulent rather militates against its chances as a book " ; that most of the books on Isadora, including her own, were " high-pressure stuff and, regardless of its quality, Miss Kinel's finer-textured manuscript suffers by comparison." . . . And here I had been walking up and down all Fifth Avenue, looking up agents, under the impression that a little book, beautifully written, about two geniuses, was something that just sold itself !

So now, having finally grasped the public's point of view and the publisher's point of view, I have decided to include in this book of reminiscences a few sketches on Isadora and Essenine containing nothing but the high lights of our trip and some of those funny bits so dear to the great public. Why try to explain their genius—Isadora's dance or Essenine's immortal poetry ? Those who have seen Isadora know that her dance could never be explained anyway, and those who know Essenine's poems know also that they can be enjoyed only in Russian.

I shall add these stories without any feeling of guilt, for I knew Isadora and Essenine so well. They both could always laugh at themselves and I am sure that from the Artists' Heaven they will merely look down on me and smile.

L. K.

HOLLYWOOD.
1934–1936.

Part I

RUSSIA

I

A RETURN

ONE day in the fall of 1916 my twin sister and I were in a train going through Finland to Petrograd. We were returning from abroad. We were often returning from abroad. Like many Poles, we were used to a nomadic existence ; we had relatives scattered all over the globe. We had lived in Russia, Switzerland, Poland, Germany, and America, always returning in the end to Russia, which was home. It was only a little more than a year since we had travelled the same route, through Finland and Sweden and Norway. But then it was in the opposite direction, on our first visit to America. And now we were coming back home again. . . .

The year in America had proved dull and disappointing. The people we had met seemed to be interested only in bridge and golf and led a dull, smug, conventional existence. I ruminated on this as I sat in our little compartment, looking at the lovely wooded Finnish landscape. I wondered how Russia would seem now, after an absence of fifteen months. Always it was lovely—returning to Russia : the very smells seemed wonderful, the sight of the motley Russian crowds at the stations, and the familiar speech. I hoped that this time I should not have to leave for a long while, that life in Petrograd would be more exciting than it had been in New York and in Los Angeles, more thrilling and more adventurous. . . .

Well, it was. For, please, remember the date: November 1916.

In the compartment next to us was a young *chinovnik*, a typical higher-class Petrograd bureaucrat, dressed immaculately after the English fashion, anæmic and pale, with very white, carefully manicured hands and a snobbish manner. He was impressed with our good American clothes and the fact that we spoke English. People of his tribe were always impressed by English, for English, in those days, was the language of the Russian aristocracy, whereas French was merely the language of the bourgeoisie. He tried to be agreeable and get acquainted and, though we both disliked him, in the end I gave in. I gave in because I had seen in his compartment a chessboard on which he was trying to solve problems from a little manual. Chess was harder to resist than the gallantry of an anæmic fop, and I hadn't played in ages.

We played in his compartment, and through the open door I noticed an odd-looking man walking up and down the corridor and throwing occasional surreptitious glances in our direction. He was tall, dressed in a Russian military coat, though without any insignia, and a fur cap. He had long red moustaches, completely concealing his mouth, and humorous, twinkling eyes. I lost the first game and decided to pay more attention to the second. I was winning the second game when the tall man entered the compartment and said in the most delightful, broken Russian:

" May I watch ? "

We immediately made him welcome and proceeded with the game. I won and felt that silly elation one always has on winning at chess. The odd-looking man then asked whether I would sometime play a game with him. This time, to my amazement, he spoke English, a kind of English I had never heard before. It was nicer than the American English, yet it seemed slightly artificial. The man slurred it a bit and he had a faint lisp. It was the first time I had heard the Oxford accent.

The Englishman and I played the next game and I lost rather quickly, which made me angry. I decided, privately, to look up all the openings on getting home. We played again the next day and I lost again, though after a battle. Imperceptibly, too, we got acquainted. The funny-looking man was pleasant, I thought. Aside from that accent, there was nothing foreign or ostentatious about him ; he might have been a Russian, a nice Russian. His eyes twinkled and he laughed readily. He asked about America, which he did not seem to like, and to my own surprise I found myself defending America stoutly. Although I had had a rather unhappy time of it while there, now, in retrospect, America seemed grand. "And what are you going to do in Petrograd ? " asked the Englishman. " Oh, I am going to work. I am going to find a job," I said. He smiled at that, too.

The following morning the Englishman was in our compartment, talking, when we approached a little station. I was watching through the window. The train began to slow down and people's faces at the station stopped being quick white blurbs ; they began to be faces and one face was very familiar. Before I could stop myself, I shouted in Polish, " *Tatusiu !* " (Dad) and pounded on the window. The train came to a stop and almost immediately my father was in our compartment.

He was the same old Dad, genial and handsome, with his deep, hearty laugh, and for a tiny instant I had a feeling that I was again very little and that the last five or six years, when we were almost always away and hardly saw our father at all, did not really intervene. Even this little surprise, of coming to meet us at this tiny Finnish station, barely one hour from Petrograd, was so characteristic. Always he used to surprise us. . . .

Witnessing a family reunion, the Englishman got up at once and tried, tactfully, to withdraw. But we did not let him, my sister and I. We felt that we knew him quite well and we wanted him to meet our father. They exchanged their visiting cards, those huge Russian cards customary in those days. On the Englishman's card was printed in Russian : " Artur Kirrilovich Ransom, correspondent *Daily News*." And below, in tiny English : " Arthur Ransome."

I mention him because later he became a friend, an important friend.

In a cab, on the way from the station, father gave us the latest news :

The war was going badly ; the Russian army was retreating on all fronts ; they were short of ammunition and short of food, and the General Staff was very weak. The Tsar didn't do anything because the Tsaritsa wouldn't let him. The Tsaritsa listened only to Rasputin—father whispered this last name, though no one could possibly hear us. " It is a scandal," he continued, " what goes on at the Court. If Europe knew what goes on up there, they would not believe it. We live in the Middle Ages." Petrograd, too, was short of food, father said, and flats could not be had for love or money. " We may have to live on the Vassilyevsky Ostrov. I have been in the city for nearly a month and I am still stopping with the B.'s."

We had always lived in small provincial towns, father's position being that of Government Inspector of the Monopol. The prospect of moving to Petrograd, where we used merely to visit on flying trips, had been thrilling. It seemed less thrilling now. . . . We found that our stepmother and the two little stepsisters were still in Kursk, the provincial home town. They were coming on later. . . . The *izvoschik* stopped before B.'s house.

Every time we returned home after some trip abroad, grandmother seemed a little smaller. A little smaller, yet dearer and kinder and lovelier than ever. She had grown a little smaller again, while we were away in America, and it made one's love somehow more tender.

Grandmother was trying to tidy up my room while I was sitting at the dressing-table, making up my face. In her black woollen dress, with white collar and cuffs —her habitual costume—she moved around the room in her brisk but quiet way, putting everything in perfect order. Grandmother's movements were always quick and assured and clever, but her face was beautifully serene.

"For the love of God, child," said grandmother as she watched me dab a little rouge on my cheeks, "is this what they taught you in America ? "

"But, *Babciu*," I said, "I only use a little. See, it is a powder and I use just enough of it to make my cheeks look pink, a natural pink. Then, when I powder my face, you can't tell it's rouge."

"All rouge is bad. And you don't need it. Whoever heard of a young girl using rouge ? "

"But I do need it, in winter. In summer, when I am sunburnt, I won't use it. But now I am a little pale. And I use it only in the evening."

"And why in the evening ? "

"To look pretty."

"Oh, whoever heard of such a thing ! " Grandma

o

pretended to be indignant. But she wasn't, really.
That was one of her charms. She understood one so
thoroughly and always she sympathised. And occasionally, when she looked straight at you, you felt that
she knew you really better than you did yourself.

" Now, that's enough. Come on to supper, child."

I kissed grandmother's hand and we went into the
dining-room, arm in arm, to join all the others.

The B.'s were an uncle and aunt, at whose home we
were to stay until father could find a flat. The rouble
was very low and falling daily. Food was very hard
to get ; sugar and bread were rationed, butter was very
expensive, and meat was still more so. . . .

We found out all this and more during those first
desultory family conversations at meals, where answers
can hardly follow questions, and the emotions of
meeting bubble and simmer and interfere. . . .

And where is Kocik now, we wanted to know. On
which front, and when would he come home on leave ?
Kocik (a diminutive for Constantin) was our brother.

Kocik was in Petrovsk Port, father said, on the
Caspian Sea ; he doubted whether he would have leave
soon. He had been sick, and the warm dry climate
down South would be good for him, father said
guardedly.

" Sick ! Why didn't you write ? What was the
matter with him ? "

He had been very sick, father said, not looking at us
directly, and it was no use worrying us, so he didn't
write to us.

" But what did he have ? "

" He had typhus. He was in Moscow at the time,
soon after he had joined the army, and when he did
not answer several letters, I ran up to see him. I could
not find him at first ; I went from hospital to hospital

and in each they told me he was in another. Then
when I finally found the hospital he was in, they told
me he had just died. . . ."

" Oh, my God, father, he isn't ! "

" No ! No ! I am telling you, listen ! I couldn't
write of it. They told me he had died and I could
take his body for private burial. I went into the
morgue, where they kept the bodies. There were a
lot of bodies lying around and I saw Kocik. I had
some orderlies with me and I told them to pick him
up, and when they carried him I noticed he looked
different from the other dead in the room. I put my
hand on his forehead and it was warm. He had fever."

" Oh, my God ! "

" I had him carried into a room and called the
physicians. Kocik was in a deep coma, but he wasn't
dead. He was just passing the crisis. That day I
thought I would go insane, first from the exhaustion
of hunting for him, the dreadful worry ; then finding
him dead and then discovering he was alive. . . . I
stayed with him right there for two weeks until he
was out of danger. I made a scandal. I went to
the staff and I told them plenty, and they apologised.
But if I had not stumbled on him that day, they would
have buried him with the rest of the typhoid dead. . . .
Russian management ! " (*Russkieye poriadki*), father
grumbled ; it was a favoured phrase of his whenever
his Polish sense of order was outraged by Russian
slovenliness. Father grumbled for some time, not
lifting his eyes, so that we shouldn't notice the tears
in them.

2

JOBS

OUR father had to return to the South on business, and
grandmother, my sister, and I established a little
ménage in a small, furnished flat on the Vassilyevsky
Ostrov, with but one maid.   I went to look for work.

I was going to find a very good job : a very fine job,
with very fine pay and very interesting work.   I felt
that I was fully equipped for it.   Didn't I know five
languages and hadn't I graduated from a famous private
school in Dresden and the State Gymnasium in Kursk,
and hadn't I had three months' training in an American
business college ?   And I was " very intelligent."   I
had heard that expression so often : from my parents
and uncles and aunts and teachers—all of whom ought
to have known better.   What I was actually equipped
with was the five languages, Russian, Polish, German,
French, and English, of which I knew thoroughly at
the time only Russian ; a goulash of information gained
in a dozen different schools in half a dozen countries
which never did me any earthly good ; some typing
and shorthand and the boundless confidence in my
own star which goes only with eighteen.

At the American Embassy, where I applied first, they
treated me very politely, for I had a letter from somebody or other.   But the young secretary who inter-
viewed me had the sense to try out my shorthand.
When I could not read some of my notes, he felt far
more embarrassed than I.   " I am afraid you are not
quite experienced enough," he said.   " I am sorry,
awfully sorry. . . ."   " Oh, not at all, not at all," said
I.   " How can I be experienced if it is my first job ? "

Ransome was the second try, for, seeing that I really wanted to work, he thought I might help him with his newspaper correspondence. I could help him a lot, he said, if I would go through all the Russian papers every morning and cut out such items as might be of interest to England, then translate these into English for him. There were in those days about thirty papers issued in Petrograd, representing the various political parties with all their different shadings and policies. I was quite willing, but it developed that I did not know what to cut out.

" Good Lord, aren't you at all interested in politics, Twin ? " Ransome would ask.

" I am a little. But I have been away so much that I am out of touch with all these Russian parties."

And that was that.

Then there was the American bank. Father had met the director of it and came home one day raving about American business methods. " *Zdumiewajace* " (Astonishing), he said, looking terribly impressed. " *Zdumiewajace*. A young man, barely thirty, is the head of the branch—the National City Bank of New York. Very clever young man, very able, quick and efficient. Reminds me a lot of Kocik. Oh, by the way, I mentioned to him that you had gone to school in California and he seemed very glad. He said you could call to-morrow ; he might use another stenographer."

The bank director did look like my brother, tall and slender, with a long head and witty eyes. He tried me out and, as he used ordinary business terms which I had in my manual, I made only a couple of mistakes. He said he would take me on trial for a month.

The bank was quartered in the former palace of the Turkish Embassy, and it seemed a little odd to sit at a small table and typewriter in a huge, high-ceilinged

salon with a shining parquet, and some low sofas with
cushions still lying about the corners. Diligently
every day I translated some letters from Russian into
English and took dictation from the director. Often
he would make some corrections and I had to do the
thing over again. Once in a while I could not read a
word and would have to go to ask him about it. After
a month he called me into his room and told me kindly
that I wasn't quite fast enough or experienced enough
and they were sorry to have to let me go.

But I wasn't going to be fired. I was furious.
" How can anyone ever become experienced " I asked
him indignantly, " unless one has been inexperienced
first ?   Have I not been improving ? "

I had been doing very nicely, the manager said,
considering the short time I had known English, and
considering that I had been in America only a year,
but they simply needed someone faster, a real expert
American stenographer.

" But where are you going to find one in Petrograd ? "
I demanded ironically.

" Oh, I wired to New York," the banker said.   " I
wired for one a week after you came, and he is arriving
to-morrow."

My second job was with an English firm—an English
firm dealing in steel-wire ropes and cables. The
manager was typically British, tall, handsome in a nasty
way, polite and dry in manner. He impressed me,
though I did not like him. The offices, on Nevski
Prospect, were elegant. The manager was elegant
too, and extremely well-dressed. The book-keeper, an
anæmic, flabby young Russian, inordinately proud of
his English, was also elegant. The most elegant
person, however, was the manager's secretary. She was
a Russian lady, in her thirties, of the dark and flam-

boyant type. She dressed in silks and perfumed excessively. She lived right next to the office in a superelegant apartment. Sometimes in the morning, when I arrived at the office, I would meet the manager just coming out of there. They often had " conferences.". . .

I worked in this firm until the day it closed up, unable to do any business on account of the revolution. Revolutions, it seemed, were not conducive to good business. It used to bother the English manager extremely, and he was often irritable.

The significant part about this job, however, was the fact that I was considered *very fast*, which just shows how relative this matter of speed can be. The entire office force used to admire my typing. The bookkeeper and the secretary hung around my table and watched with undisguised amazement the way I typed from my note-book, without ever looking at the keys. And the Englishman, from his throne behind the desk, cast occasional, though surreptitious glances. . . . " This is quite remarkable," he said once, when off guard. It seems that the touch system had not yet reached England and, naturally, it was quite beyond Russia, where even typewriters were still a great novelty.

My self-confidence was quickly restored. However, at night, at home, I practised strokes, transcribed notes, and improved my shorthand as much as I could. Who could tell, I thought—I might be engaged by some crazy Americans again, some day, and it was better to be prepared. Never again, I decided, would I be fired for inexperience or for being slow. And I never have been.

3

A FRIENDSHIP

RANSOME was a Bohemian. He lived in a huge room in an old boarding-house overlooking St. Isaac's Square with the famous Cathedral. It was the first bachelor room I had ever seen ; it had a desk and typewriter in one corner ; in another a bed, night table, and dresser, all behind a screen ; then a sort of social arrangement, consisting of an old sofa and a round table with some chairs around it, in the centre. And *books*. They were everywhere, heaped in rows on old dressers, heaped on chairs, heaped on the sofa and even on the floor. Among these books I found occasionally torn, soiled socks. I used to pick them up gingerly, with my gloved hand, and wrap them up in a piece of newspaper. . . .

" Doesn't anyone ever mend your socks for you ? " I asked one day.

" No. Don't bother picking those up. I wear them and throw them away when they get torn. The maid forgot to take these away."

" But then you must buy an awful lot of socks."

" I do. These Russian *prachki* (laundresses) never bother to mend things. I live like a wild rabbit."

" And look at your desk—look at all this dust. Doesn't the maid ever dust here ? "

" I would wring her neck if she did. She daren't touch my desk," he said with the air of a fanatic threatened with some danger. . . .

I thought him extremely amusing. This was two or three months after our return to Petrograd, when we had become friends. We all had nicknames by then, Ransome's being " A.K.," after the initials of his

THE BIG TWIN

Photograph by A. K.   Petrograd   1918

Russian-style name ; my sister was the " Big Twin," and I the " Small Twin."

Our first calls were very formal. We were invited to tea and had invariably strawberry tarts and tea from a huge samovar which didn't draw any too well. Like all foreigners, A.K. liked a samovar and the Russian way of making tea. The Big Twin was soon bored. She did not care much for books, she did not play chess ; she had renewed her old friendships at the Conservatory, where she used to study before our American trip, and the funny Englishman ceased to be a novelty. I began to call alone. A.K.'s calls at our house ceased rather abruptly. I think he found our people too " bourgeois," though he was not quite rude enough to say so. . . . His own Bohemianism was not a pose, but seemed real. He had, I remember, a thorough contempt for men who dressed well, or the least conventionally. He forgave women if they were pretty, but he preferred most Russian women, who do not pose and are simple, to English girls. For England he seemed to have a queer mixture of contempt, dislike, and love. He was clever, yet childish, very sincere and kind and romantic, and, on the whole, far more interesting than his books. . . .

One day I asked him how old he was.

" Thirty-four," he replied.

Quite old, I thought, and, being off guard, replied instantly to his query about my own age :

" Eighteen."

" No, Twin ! You are spoofing."

I felt a little thrill.

" Do you mean I look older ? "

" You don't look it, but you are so intelligent, so sure. . . . Good Lord, in England you would be still in a nursery—you are a child."

The compliment about my intelligence didn't flatter

me in the least. I had heard that before. What I wanted to know was just how old he had thought I was.

"Very well, then, how old did you think I was? No lying."

"Oh—twenty-three—twenty-five."

"Oh, A. K.! Really?" An ambition of my youth had been fulfilled.

4

SIGNS OF THE REVOLUTION

"But what about the revolution, what about the revolution?" you are probably thinking. "Here you have been in Petrograd already for two or three months and you have been stringing us along with all these personal, unexciting tales, and haven't said anything about it yet! We want something exciting—like bloodshed, firing. Come along now, give us the real dope."

I am coming to it. I am coming to it, but you must let me tell of it the way I saw it, the way I experienced it myself, or the telling of it will be wrong, for every one of us who was in Petrograd saw it in a different way, not being able to be in two spots at the same time. And the people who were in Moscow saw it differently and very much later, and with more bloodshed than the people of Petrograd. And the people in Siberia saw it a year later, and the way they experienced it was different again. So you see . . .

Also, the first revolution did not occur until March 1917, which was five months after my return to Petrograd. There were, of course—just to remind you, in case you have forgotten a bit—two revolutions ; the first one in March 1917, when the Tsar voluntarily abdicated ; and the second one in October 1917, when the Bolsheviks officially took control. And the difference between these two revolutions was as the difference between night and day : the March revolution being the one like a day and that of October being of the night, for on the latter day a handful of people, all of them honest and fired by enthusiasm, and at least one of them indubitably great, put the hundred and fifty million Russians back under the yoke—a yoke embellished with beautiful humane slogans about the " worker " and under the spiritual heritage of an old, bearded German professor called Karl Marx, a yoke completely different in colour and manner from the yoke of the Tsar and his squirarchy, yet nevertheless *a yoke.*

But here I am running ahead. I was going to show the bloodshed and the firing. Well, it did not come until the actual revolution in March. Until then there were merely some signs of the revolution ; in Petrograd, in particular, there were the *khvosty*—the food lines, or queues. These lines, waiting patiently in front of the small grocery stores in the side streets, became an habitual sight in Petrograd and grew with the times.

In these early days of Hunger, in the better districts, there were at first only the servants in the lines, the kitchenmaids and the like. A queue started at four or five in the morning, when it was yet pitch-dark in the winter night and the streets were still and icy cold. Those that came earlier were the first to get into the store, which opened at eight, and they had the assurance that they would get the food allotted per customer ; those that came last often went away without getting anything, for the small food stores usually ran out of all supplies before the end of the line reached the door.

There was always a little commotion, then, at the
entrance, for these patient Russian women were mis-
trustful of the grocer. Perhaps he had cheated?
Perhaps he had hidden some reserve so as to sell it at
higher prices to the fancy stores?   For the rich people
did not care how much they paid as long as they got
what they wanted.   Didn't all the restaurants still
have plenty of food?   They charged terribly high
prices, to be sure, for one meal, but they had it.

Sometimes, when our maid was ill, my sister and I
took a stand in the line, and I still remember the talk
of it.

"Did he say he was out of butter?"

"What was it he said, mother dear?   I didn't hear
it in all this commotion.   Was it butter or sugar?"

"*Akh Ty Gospodi* (Oh, my God), the *barynia* will
give me a hiding if I don't bring that bacon . . . and
here I meant to get up at four, but last night they had
company again and tea at one o'clock and how can a
body wake up at four?   It's a hard life, *Gospodi Spasi
i Pomilyi.*"

"And surely they had some cake and sweets with
their tea, did they?"

"Sure, my golden one, lovely cookies they had, two
roubles per pound I had to pay at the Universal Store."

"Two roubles for a pound!   And they ate it all up
with their tea, *nebos* (I bet you).   And you never even
saw one?"

"How could I, my dear?"

"And you still get your seven roubles wages a
month?"

"Yes, *milaya.*"

That was, perhaps, the beginning of the revolution.

And as time went on, these lines grew longer, and
the patient women servants, who stood for hours from

the dark cold of the frosty night into the noon hour of the pale sunlight, these women in shawls who stamped about from time to time and clapped their hands to keep them from getting frozen, grew more and more bitter and bewildered. At first there were lines only for things like meat or sugar or bacon or butter and eggs, but soon there were lines even for flour, for rice, and for cereals ; and then for bread, the staple food of the Russians. One pound of bread per person was allowed, then later only half a pound, and later still only a quarter-pound per day. And the bread was getting darker and darker and soon there were things mixed into the wheat—chaff and straw—and there were people who could not eat it. They became sick. It was in those days that our grandmother first became ill with " indigestion."

But on the Nevski, the restaurants and big hotels were still brilliantly lighted at night and selling dinners with lovely food. The price of these dinners rose steadily, and soon a guest was allowed only one dinner, but the rich and the foreigners, whose money stood high on the exchange, could still buy it. And the *izvoshchiki* with the race-horses still went madly on the Nevski, and the huge shining automobiles of the military went by oblivious of traffic, and the servants and the people in the lines, watching this, grew bitter and bewildered.

And in the country, in all the villages, the peasants were getting tired of the war, and faintly, dimly, like the distant rumble of thunder, their miserable grumbling would reach the big centre. Their best men had been drafted and there was no one left at home to till the soil but the women and children and the aged men. And what was this war for, anyhow ? For these peasants, almost all illiterate, could not read the newspaper headlines about the " war for democracy," the great " just " war, which was being waged. And the Germans were foreigners alike with the French and the English and the Americans.

And perhaps that, too, was a sign of the revolution. . . .

And out on the front, we heard, the soldiers were getting tired of the war. They were getting particularly tired because often there was not enough ammunition and they had to go out into an attack with just one set of bullets, while the officers still had some extra ones to fire into their backs in case of insubordination. They weren't always well fed, they said, and their wives and mothers wrote that they couldn't attend to the work in the fields. And what was this damned war for, anyhow ?

So this was, perhaps, also a sign. . . .

Then came the day when Rasputin was killed. Father came home from the city and said excitedly :

" Rasputin is dead ! I just saw So-and-so ; he was at the party in Yusupoff's palace and saw it all. They couldn't poison him—a dose that would have killed three other men couldn't kill him. Yusupoff had to shoot him, and they then threw him into the Moika ! "

This news was like a breath of relief that swept over the city. But even Rasputin's death could not save Russia now.

5

THE FIRST REVOLUTION

THERE was not much fuss about the Tsar's abdication, as I remember it. Far less than when Rasputin was killed. It was as if the people, all of us, had expected it. Things were so desperate, not only in Petrograd, but in the whole country.

"What will happen now, *baryshnia* ?" said the current maid, a scrubby, ignorant young thing. "*Gospodi pomiluy*, the Tsar is in prison. And all this revolution !"

"Why, the revolution is grand !" I would say.

It was grand. All one had to do to feel tremendously exhilarated was to go out on the streets. It was much like the feeling one had at Russian Easter time, when everyone, leaving the Greek Orthodox Church after the Easter service, embraced everyone else, strangers included, and said : "Christ has risen," and was answered : "He has truly risen," and one wasn't ashamed of tears. It was just like that feeling, only far grander. Russia was free. Russia would be a happy, free country. A democracy ! Like other countries ! Free ! No slavery, no political exiles, no subterranean revolutionary life. . . . Russia was *free* !

One walked the streets in a dream and one witnessed the most amazing sights. A small detachment of soldiers would appear and the people on the streets would stop and halt indecisively ; were they friends or enemies ? Then someone would spy a little red rag in the lapel of a soldier's coat. "*Da Zdrawvstvueyet Revolutsia !*" someone would shout, and the soldiers would shout back in return. Even the Cossacks were on the side of the people. I saw an old Cossack get down from his horse in the middle of the street, obstructing the traffic, to let a small street urchin pin a small red cloth to his coat. Bits of red cloth, wool, cotton, silk, anything red, had to be used, for there was a shortage of red ribbons. . . . "*Svobodnaya Rossya !*" (Free Russia !) How we revelled in this phrase !

There were some sporadic skirmishes, of course,

between troops which were still loyal to the Tsar and the revolutionary troops, but they were rare, or ceased almost instantly. I remember one particularly.

A gorgeous sunny day, with the snow soft and crunchy underfoot. There must have been a strike of the street-cars, for I remember I walked. I started out about ten, from the Vassilyev Island, where we lived, walking toward the centre of the town. I changed my mind halfway and went to St. Isaac's Square, where A. K. had his room. The distance was at least four miles, perhaps more, and I walked fast and at a good stride, and by the time I reached A. K.'s room I was exhilarated with the long hike, in a truly revolutionary mood. He was on the point of going out to see what was going on, and asked me to join him.

We went toward the river and soon noticed a large detachment of soldiers walking to one of the bridges. With a correspondent's " nose for news," A. K. decided to follow them. We had to walk rapidly to keep up with their steady fast march. Just as we were approaching the bridge, right behind the soldiers, we saw a detachment on the other side, approaching the same bridge. A. K. was excited. The soldiers in front of us walked a little slower, in a more compact group ; the others came straight on. When they were about two hundred feet away from us, they halted. Our soldiers halted too. The soldiers in the front ranks of the other detachment began to kneel down. Almost simultaneously they opened fire. The bullets began to whistle with the characteristic swishing sound, the crackle of the report coming a bit later. A. K. and I watched intensely. It was like a show, only more vivid. The bullets came faster—one going right between our two heads. Holding my hand, A. K. watched with shining eyes.

All of a sudden he shouted : " Christ, Twin, I forgot

you were here ! " and, pulling me by the hand, he began to back, still watching the fight.

" I don't want to go. I want to watch ! " I said stubbornly. But he pulled harder and began to run, dragging me along.

" Oh, A. K., I want to watch some more," I begged, hanging back. Instead of arguing, he raised me in his arms and began to run. Only when we had left the bridge and turned the corner, where we were free from the bullets, did he let me down.

There were other small fights all over town, none of them very serious, for even the most loyal soldiers went over to the revolutionists. One got so used to the occasional sound of firing that one did not pay much attention, and the feeling of witnessing something very grand, something tremendously moving, where individuality did not count, helped one, too, in disregarding the danger.

When, years later, people would ask me : " Weren't you afraid that you might be shot, wounded? . . . Wasn't it frightening ? " I always felt embarrassed in confessing to my lack of fear, for I had a sort of private reason for not being afraid. I seldom tried to explain this to anyone, for I knew it would sound idiotic, but the fact is that I had the conviction that I —Lola Kinel —was entirely immune from bullets and death. So deeply rooted was this feeling that I was actually not even conscious of it. It was there, a subconscious protection, that was all. I know this now, for since then, on many occasions, I have been frightened, I have run away, and I have known physical fear in its most abject forms. But not during the first revolution.

In the small fights that I witnessed, I never wanted to lie down prone on the ground —which is, of course, the surest way to avoid being hurt. I felt it was not

D

necessary. For others perhaps, but not for me. I remember one particular instance.

It was on the Liteyny Prospect. A small group of soldiers and workers were engaged in a fight with a handful of police—the most stubborn supporters of the old régime. The police appeared suddenly from around a corner and opened fire at once. Instantly the people on the street, the passers-by, were gone. It was amazing how quickly people cleared the streets in those days. I remained, flattened myself against the wall of a house, and watched. The bullets sang and a soldier close to me fell funnily, sideways, holding on to his chest. Another, a few feet away, lifted his arms high in the air, flapping them twice like wings, and then he too fell on his back. But the rest of the soldiers and workers pressed on and soon the police turned and began to run. The fight was over in a few minutes.

I detached myself from the wall. The soldier that had flapped his arms like wings was quite dead. He had a hole in his throat and the blood was gathering in a pool. I thought mechanically : " He couldn't breathe, that's why he flapped—he had no air." An old man emerged from the doorway of the house where I was standing and said to me reproachfully :

" You got to lay down flat, *baryshnia*, with your face down, or you might get hit." I walked on, without giving him a reply.

Only once did I lie face downward. I thought it frightfully humiliating, but that time I had to obey.

I had gone to call on father at his office, which was on the tenth floor of a business building on the Nevski. We were gossiping when there came the *tra-tra-tra* noise of machine-guns and the dry singsong of bullets, and the shattering of glass panes. . . .

" Down on the floor ! " father shouted, and we all obeyed.

Like all the rest, I guessed at once what was hap-pening. I knew that the soldiers and workers must have discovered a " nest " on the roof of the building, and were routing it out.

It was a rule, in the first days of the revolution, to put a handful of police with a machine-gun on the roof tops along the big prospects (boulevards), with a view to making a panic, by shooting down the workers as they came in their demonstrations. They were even stationed on the roofs of churches, the Government thinking that the people wouldn't dare to fire back on a holy church. But nothing could stop the revolution, and, though these snipers managed to kill a few soldiers and workers, most of them were caught and killed. Most of them didn't think of changing their uniforms and so they didn't dare to come down from the roofs. The populace would have torn them to pieces if they had, for they were always the staunchest supporters of the old régime. So they stuck to their roofs, hiding behind buttresses and chimneys ; the workmen from below would pick them out the moment they showed so much as a hand, and a volley of shots be dispatched toward the roof.

The building in which father had his office was about ten stories high ; his office was on the top floor, below the mansard. As volleys of shots were directed toward the roof, many struck our windows. Within ten or fifteen minutes from the beginning of the fight, all the panes in the dozen or so large windows were shattered and the floor was strewn with deflected bullets.

It was all of three quarters of an hour before the fight finally ceased, and it seemed like an eternity. At last, when everything quieted down, with that intense still-ness peculiar to an after-a-fight mood, father let us all get up. No one was hurt, not even scratched. Those of us who had been close to the windows shook off the bits of glass. Father sent one of the clerks to investigate and he returned with the story that three policemen had been on the roof and the workers had gotten all of them, and their machine-gun too.

I decided to go home.

" Be careful," father said. " Why don't you wait and go with me ? I am leaving early." But I preferred to go alone. I still felt humiliated. I wanted also to know what was happening on the streets.

On the street below I saw soldiers and workmen carry away some wounded. The usual knots of people, talking, discussing, and commenting in their Russian way, were standing about. I went home.

6

THE TWO "DEMAGOGUES"

" WHERE are you going ? " grandmother asked, seeing me dress for the street.

" I think I will go and hear this Lenin. I am curious," I said.

Father, who was reading a bourgeois paper, lifted his eyebrows derisively. " Since when have you become interested in Socialism ? " His tone was ironic, but I knew the anxiety behind it. So many young people were drawn towards Communism; so many students who had been democrats and liberals now listened to the Communists and were ready to join them.

" I am just curious," said I. " So many people hear Lenin."

" That demagogue ! " father said, and grandma added a little anxiously :

" I wouldn't go into those dreadful crowds ; all these soldiers and workers—who knows what might happen to you ? Please don't go. You can read his speech in the paper to-morrow."

And so I didn't go on that day. I went on another, however, without telling anyone at home, so as not to worry them.

The crowd around the Krzesinski Palace that day was so big that I could not get close enough to hear. Soldiers, workers, all the common people, were pressed tightly around that famous balcony, their mouths open, their eyes glued to the small figure standing up there, their brows puckered in unaccustomed hard thinking, trying to catch every word. I was too far away to hear even one consecutive sentence, and, rising on my tip-toes, I merely caught now and then—over the shoulder of a tall soldier—a glimpse of Lenin's characteristic face, a gesture or two. The tall soldier in front of me said with good-natured contempt : " *Ish, baryshnia, tuda zhe pripiorla.*" (Hey, miss, so you, too, came shoving along.) After ten minutes of this futile standing and tiptoe gazing, I turned and left.

Lenin was the " demagogue who had come through Germany in a sealed car." The bourgeoisie of that day believed firmly that it was all engineered by Germany, who had paid Lenin money for disorganising Russia, and for quite a while they did not pay much attention to this small, funny man who spoke daily to the common people from the balcony of the palace which the workers had taken quite unceremoniously from the former mistress of the Tsar, the prima ballerina Krzesinskaya.

Lenin spoke very plainly and simply, and most of his speeches were reported quite faithfully, I believe, in all the papers. He told these common people who came to listen to him that all the power should go to the

Soviets ; that the soldiers should fraternise with the enemy and make their own peace ; that war, even under a Socialistic government, was a capitalist war, as long as it was on the side of capitalist countries ; that all banks and property should be nationalised and a workers' government take control.

And the soldiers and workers and cooks and maids and small artisans and common tramps, and all the motley people of Russia who live much of the time on the street, listened to him spellbound, as he hammered these simple ideas into their heads. And these speeches and simple ideas were printed in the Bolshevik papers and reprinted in the others. And why the bourgeoisie, so terrified by it all six months later, did not pay any attention to him in those early days of April and May, will remain one of the mysteries of history. . . .

About a month after Lenin's spectacular arrival, another demagogue arrived from New York, via England, where he was incarcerated for a few weeks. His name was Trotsky. He, too, was a popular speaker and his favourite place of oratory was the Cirque Moderne, a huge circus which he crowded to overflowing with admiring throngs. Less plain and succinct than Lenin, he was nevertheless tremendously popular with the people, a very emotional, fiery man. He did not interest me as much and I never went to hear him, though I had seen him a few times, passing by in an open car or an open truck, surrounded by students, soldiers, and workers. With his proud carriage and his goatee beard, there was something Mephistophelean in his appearance.

His name began to be linked with Lenin's, and his fame, in those days, was almost equal. With these two names, the term " Bolshevik " became daily more formidable and Lenin's simple slogans,

Vsia Vlast Sovietam !
(All Power to the Soviets !)
Zemli, Chleba i Mira !
(Land, Bread, and Peace !)

which expressed so exactly what the masses, the
common people all over the country, wanted and felt,
began to appear dangerous.

The term " demagogue " is not mine, of course. It
expressed the attitude of the bourgeoisie, to which I
belonged by class. Yet, in a sense, the bourgeoisie
was right. Lenin and Trotsky were brilliant demagogues, far more brilliant than the bourgeoisie or the
moderate socialists at first realised. Demagoguery is
part of every great revolutionary's equipment. And
how great and determined these two were, neither the
bourgeois, nor the other socialists themselves, and least
of all the military groups and reactionaries, ever
realised.

The entire period, the first four or five months after
the first revolution, was, indeed, full of brilliant oratory,
and it should actually be called the " talkie period "
of the Russian revolution. People who had never
had free speech and a free Press, who had been dammed
up for three hundred odd years, were suddenly allowed
to speak. And as Russians are inveterate speakers
anyway, the thing became an epidemic. But whereas
they used to speak mostly in the privacy of their
homes (on politics, I mean) or at secret meetings or
secret clubs, now they could speak anywhere. They
spoke on the streets and in trains and in tram-cars.
People always forgot their stops, because they were
for ever engrossed in discussions.
The Government, too, the so-called " provisional
Government," assembled hastily from the more liberal

elements of the former ministry, was full of fine oratory.
The Government was very much elated at that period,
full of pleasant speeches about Free Russia and Democracy and the Allies and the War. The new Government was all for continuing the war ; it was to be loyal
to the Entente, to the pledges of the old Government.
Only the working men and soldiers did not talk much.
They mostly listened and thought their own slow
thoughts. Anyway, they had no trained speakers. It
was about that time that they began to form their
Soviets of Workers' and Soldiers' Deputies. Everyone
knew about them, but somehow people did not pay
much attention. Anyway the soldiers did not speak
much ; they listened mostly. Only once did they rise
in speech : when Miliukov, the head of the provisional
Government, and his Minister of War, Guchkov,
pledged themselves definitely to the continuation of
the war, the workers and soldiers made a rousing
demonstration. They paraded the streets with the
banners " Down with Miliukov," " Down with Guchkov," and the two prominent cadets had to quit.
Then the Government and the Soviets both elected
Kerensky. Kerensky was a Social Democrat, a lawyer
who became popular because of his gift of oratory. He
was particularly good at the elation stuff. Really,
he beat them all. I have never heard him, but
father did, repeatedly, and he would return home
and say, " What a speaker ! An orator ! Positively
inspiring ! "

But Kerensky was more than an orator ; he was an
actor, an actor with melodramatic leanings, and in
choosing his career he had surely made a grave mistake.
If he had become an actor, he would now be still adored
by the Russian *émigrés* in the big centres of Europe, instead of being the most hated and despised man in the
Russian revolution. For Kerensky loved to inspire his

audience and he loved to be adored—adored, if possible, by everyone, like a woman. And Kerensky, also like a woman, was gentle. He did not like to have enemies. Enemies are awkward—they might do something to one particularly in a revolution. So he was friendly with the Soviets and their Socialist leaders, and with the Liberal bourgeoisie, and with the representatives of the Entente ; and, as much as he could be, with the soldiers —until the soldiers, with the peasants' instinct, turned away from this gesticulating, screaming, weak man, with his beautiful but pitiful phrases and his hysterical outbursts, and the end was that the actor-orator lost face with everyone. If he had been a Chinaman or a Japanese, he would have committed suicide ten times. Being a Russian, he went on a lecture tour and wrote his memoirs.

I did not tell A. K. about my attempt to hear Lenin. It was sheer contrariness, for A. K. was very enthusiastic about the Bolsheviks and I did not want to give him any satisfaction on this point. My neutral attitude both puzzled and irritated him.

" All the young people I know are working for the revolution. How can you be so indifferent and stand aside ? " he would say.

" I don't know whether the Bolsheviks are right, A. K.," I would reply. " You are very romantic. You are just carried away. You don't know anything about Socialism or economics."

He would grow almost furious at this—as far as was possible with his kindly and childlike nature.

" Then you are against them ? "

" I don't know. I want to know first all about them. Perhaps they are fools or dreamers. I am just standing aside and looking on."

" Exactly ! When you should be working furiously

for one side or another. The revolution needs people like you, young, intelligent people. You could easily get a job in the Smolny. They are bound to need secretaries who know English."

" No, thanks, A. K. I don't want to go to the Smolny," I would say politely and obstinately, and our political discussion would end in a discord. . . .

Once, after vainly trying to get at my attitude, when I tried to explain that I could not generate enthusiasm when there was none, A. K. said quite cruelly :

" You are interested only in yourself, Twin, you are utterly selfish."

I was cut to the quick. I knew it was not mere selfishness, but I could not explain. I was egocentric, of course. But that I did not know. No egocentric knows until he (or she) has ceased to be so, not until he can see himself as others do and can detach himself from his pitiful ego. In some it takes years, in others it comes with a snap ; still others do not lose their ego until the day of their death. . . . No, I didn't know it then. Even the term was not in use. It did not come into use until years later when Jung and Adler and all the other psychologists took the poor human being apart and showed him why and how he got that way, and had no enthusiasms, and could neither love nor hate properly, nor take part in any social scheme. Until then all the egocentrics just ran around merrily with the other people, carrying their little vicious circles around with them like a dead and precious weight and puzzling or repelling their friends with their curious aloofness. . . .

No, I was not selfish. I just did not care, for I was not quite alive. I didn't care whether a stray bullet took me or missed me ; I didn't mind much when there was no food, and, if there was some, I always shared it with those about me. I simply lacked some spark.

The revolution was spreading in an ever-increasing, grand show, but I could not take any part in it myself —either for or against. I remained aside, a curious and aloof spectator. . . .

7

A VACATION, AND TERROR

IT was midsummer, in the little town of Gdov on the great Gdov Lake, famous for its fish. The office in which I had currently been working as an English correspondent had folded up for lack of business, and, having saved a little money and being tired, I decided to take a vacation. I was very thin from lack of proper food, and everybody advised me to go to some tiny village where food was still plentiful. My sister worked in a relief agency for some refugees and could not go along, so I had to go alone.

I hired a room with a fisherman's family. Their little cabin, the last one of the tiny street, was standing on the bank of a small river which flowed into the lake. It was a very quiet spot, rustic and somnolent, and but for the rumble of the cannonade on the front, which was very close and which sounded like distant thunder, one felt as if transported into an entirely different world.

The banks of the stream, sandy and white, alternated with long patches of thick rushes which sometimes encroached into the tiny river, leaving only a few feet of clear space in the centre. It was an ideal place for rowing, so I hired a row-boat by the week.

The little town was filled with soldiers, reserve troops and some of the troops which were being withdrawn from the front. But they usually thronged the main

street, the street with the small shops and tea houses,
and out here, on the outskirts, one did not see many of
them. It was very quiet.

Every morning I would untie my little boat and go
downstream until I reached the lake. I would pull my
boat out on a sandbank and take a swim. I had forgotten to buy a swimming suit and, as none could be
bought in the village, where everybody swims naked, I
just used one of my old American knitted union suits.
I thought it would do, until one day I discovered that it
wouldn't.

On returning from my swim one day, just as I was
tying my boat, the fisherwoman met me and said
anxiously :

"Say, *baryshnia*. Is there something wrong with
your body ? "

" No," I said, rather surprised.

" The reason I am asking is the boys around here
saw you swim and they keep on telling us you wear
something when you go in the water. Some garment
that covers you all up."

" *Nu da*. It's instead of a bathing suit."

She repeated the words, a little puzzled : " *Kupalny
kostium ?* (Bathing suit.) And what is it for ? "

" To swim in, of course."

This seemed a little beyond her. And after a while
she said kindly :

" Well, I was just curious. I am glad you are all
right, *baryshnia*. It would be a pity, with your pretty
face. We all thought that perhaps you are all spotted
with moles, like some people, so you covered yourself
up."

So after that I didn't use my union suit. I didn't
want them to think I had moles or that I was ugly in
some manner. I forgot the habit of prudery acquired
in America and I swam again without clothes, which is

far pleasanter. And the boys stopped watching me.
For a young nude girl was no novelty to them, of course.
It was the girl who swam in a garment that aroused
their curiosity.

The fisherman's wife gave me my breakfast and my
supper, consisting of milk and black bread and fried
fish, and sometimes an egg and even some butter, and
tea with sugar. But my main meal I took in the little
town proper, at a table d'hôte in a boarding-house.
Before the war this boarding-house probably housed all
the bachelor intelligentsia, maiden schoolteachers, and
the unmarried doctor and post office clerk. There
were still many of these people left. But now that
Gdov was an important military point, with a great
many of the reserve troops stationed in it, there were
also many officers. There was a famous cavalry divi-
sion and about a dozen of the officers came to this table
d'hôte, where we met at two each day. They looked
like the old-time officers, elegant and beautifully
groomed, a trifle snobbish and condescending in their
manner, but there was something about them, nevertheless, which had subtly changed. They seemed lost,
these elegant young men, and their swagger was a little
forced. Out on the street when the soldiers met them
they now often omitted the salute, and this made the
officers feel funny, I think. Nor did they mention in-
ternal politics during the two weeks that I boarded
there. The word " Bolshevik " was never mentioned.
After Petrograd, where Bolshevism was the most glaring topic of conversation, it seemed odd. They talked
about the war a little, and their own military affairs,
and they gossiped—local gossip. And a few of the old
maids that were at the table hung on their words with
ill-concealed adoration, just as they used to in the old
days, I suppose.

One day one of the officers, a handsome fellow with a black moustache and oily brown eyes, was telling something that happened in the next village where a small detachment of infantry had passed. It seems they were returning from the front and they were a discontented lot. They had not had any leave in a long time. As they passed the little wooden schoolhouse, in the middle of the hot afternoon, one of them saw the schoolteacher through the window, sitting at her books. There were no children, for school was out, but there was the young teacher, sitting all alone, bending over her books. The soldier went into the schoolhouse and raped the young teacher. And, hearing her cries, his comrades followed him and raped her too. She was more dead than alive when the soldiers left, but she had just a little strength left—just enough strength to hang herself. She hanged herself on the hook from the chandelier, on her silk garters. Blue garters, they were, the officer said, and that's how they found her the next day. The soldiers confessed it then.

" I would shoot every one of them, if it were in my regiment. Every damn son of a bitch ! But they don't dare nowadays. Court-martial is going to be revoked. Soviets—meetings—there, that's your revolution." He spread his hands in a gesture of helplessness. A discussion arose. Even then the word " Bolsheviks " was not used. The officer called them " they."

I did not listen much. Hearing the story of the girl teacher, I felt a little sick and I could not finish my cutlet. She was only nineteen, they said. That was my age, too. I went back to my room in the fisher's hut. . . .

It was two or three days later, I think, that I conceived the grand idea of going for my swim at night. It was a hot and still night ; the moon was full, and I felt I

could not part with this night. I could not return to
my small and stuffy room in the fisherman's house. I
untied my boat then, got inside, and let myself drift
downstream. I used only one oar, as one would a
paddle, and the boat went slowly with the current.
The little stream looked deep and mysterious at night,
with silver arrows where the moon struck it and black
shadows beneath the rows of reeds at the edges.
Within a few minutes the last hut was out of sight and I
was alone in the world, a beautiful, dark, mysterious
world with a limitless sky, the stars, and the round, full
moon.

It was about a mile to the lake and it took me half an
hour or more to get to it. The little river made a deep
turn here, before it finally flowed into the lake, and then
it spread itself in a wide estuary and joined the lake like
a big, real river. It was quite impressive there, at the
end, at least one hundred feet wide ; the thick rushes
ended abruptly on the right side and there was a huge,
flat sandbank.

That night, when I made the turn at the bend and
saw the lake, I gave a gasp. It was a huge, endless, and
limitless plate of glass—soft glass, shining in the moon.
Only here, near me, where the quiet little river joined
the glass, could one see any motion, could one guess at
all that it was water. I felt I could not spoil this magic.
It would be like a sacrilege, and I decided I would swim
in the river instead of the lake. I rowed to the sandbank, pulled the boat out on the sand, undressed, and
dived into the water. I swam until I was tired, then
turned on my back, floated lazily about, returned to the
sandbank, and lay down on my back. The night was
so warm that I did not feel chilly at all. I lay breathing deeply, in perfect contentment. I thought I would
stay there until I got dry and then dress and row back
home. I thought it would not be more than half an

hour before I got dry, the night was so warm. And so I lay still and closed my eyes.

Presently a slight breeze came up; it moved the rushes delicately and I felt it on my hands and face and my whole body. I lay there, musing. I was almost dry, too, and I turned to dry my back. Stretching my arms out in front of me, I lay prone, my face buried in the warm, fine white sand. It smelled of water and weeds, of the hot sun from the day before—the indescribably lovely smell of clean sand. . . . I lay quite motionless, and then, through the thin sound of the breeze, I heard a sound from the river. It was a very familiar sound—at first very faint, coming and disappearing again, then a little stronger. I lay very still then, taut, listening. . . . Oh, I knew the sound so well—it was of soldiers singing. They sang in a chorus and, judging from the sound, there must have been at least five or six of them. And because the voices ebbed and grew stronger and sometimes became almost faint, I knew they were on a boat, coming down the river, and it was because of the turns and twists of it, when it was obstructed by the wall of rushes in a bend, that the sound was so broken. Yet it grew stronger all the time, slowly but inexorably, and as I listened I thought of the girl teacher and of what I ought to do. If I ran to the other end of the sandbank, I might reach the little path that led back to the village before they saw me, before the boat made the last bend. If I ran hard, I might just do it, just grabbing my clothes and running as hard as I could. But also I might not, and if they saw me run it would be worse. To see a naked girl run away would be just the very thing to rouse them. If I stayed still, they might not even see me, for the sand was white and I was naked and white and so flat on the ground. . . .

And even while I thought of this, while I argued with

myself, I felt a terror gripping me from head to foot, like an iron load, and I found I could not move. I could not move a finger and I stayed lying on my face, while the sound of the voices came nearer and nearer. Through my fear I could hear the separate voices, one high tenor and one low bass and several intermediary voices, and soon, though it was ages of terror, the voices burst out loudly, terrifyingly—the boat had turned the last bend. They were within thirty feet of me and then the song stopped abruptly—as if cut by a knife. . . .

In the sudden, terrific stillness I could hear the gentle splash of the water as it licked the sides of the boat. Then one man's voice said slowly :

" See the body ? "

" Perhaps she isn't dead yet," another voice said.

" Looks dead to me. I'm afraid of bodies."

" Better not get mixed up in it. Turn around, rebyata (fellows)."

" Let's get back. That's best. And we don't know a thing about it, if they ask in the village. Seen nothing, heard nothing, so help us God."

There was a splash of the oars and the sound of the boat again churning the water as it was turned around rapidly, and in the sound of it I could not hear much more of the conversation. I heard the oars splashing methodically and rather fast as the boat began to pull away. I remained motionless, listening. For a long time I was immobile, prone on the sand, even after the last bit of sound had died away, the last faint splash of the two oars. . . .

I should have laughed, I guess, as I got up and began to dress, but I did not. I felt weak and I had to dry myself after all, for I was covered with cold sweat from head to foot.

For the remainder of my vacation days I did not go

E

swimming at night. I sat out on the wooden bench in front of the little house, eating sunflower seeds and listening to village gossip. Once or twice I went horse-back riding with the officer with the small moustache whom I had met at the table d'hôte. We never talked of Bolsheviks. We pretended that the world, the Russian world, was the same as it had been for the last three hundred years.

8

ROMANCE

It started inauspiciously, as so many of these things do. One evening I went to see A. K. I wanted to return some books and I also wanted him to read a poem. Poem is not the right word, though the thing had rhymes and a sort of childish rhythm, for it was the story of a quarrel we had had which I had put into verse. It was my first attempt at verse in English and I wanted Ransome's opinion, and, because it was very personal, I was also curious to see his reaction. " I wonder how he will look when he reads it . . ." I mused as I walked up the two flights of stairs. " He will sit in his deep chair and his eyes will twinkle. . . . He will say : ' Hi, Twin, what have you got there ? Let me see it.' And then he will read. He will read and his twinkle will disappear. Perhaps he will grow pale. I should like him to grow pale ; I should like him to be miserable."

And, thinking thus, I knocked on the door and went in. Deep in the recesses of the huge room, A. K. was sitting at a small table with another man and they were playing chess. Now he would not read the poem, I shouldn't see him grow pale, and everything had gone wrong ! I could have cursed the whole world, instead of which I had to say primly : " How do you do ? How are you ? " to two Englishmen who jumped up from their chairs and were also being polite.

" Please don't let me interrupt you," said I after the introduction. " I brought you back the books, A. K., and may I have some to take with me ? "

But A. K. had already seen the small white roll in my hand and he did say : " Hi, Twin, what's this ? Something you wrote ? "

" Oh, it's something I wanted you to read. It's not important," I lied.

" That's splendid, Twin. . . . You aren't going ? "

" I am. Go back to your game. I'll just take a few books."

" But you must leave the story. Oh, of course. . . . I want to read it."

I left it then, though my lovely plan was all spoiled, and, after I had chosen a few books, I took my leave and was about to go when the other man asked rather shyly :

" Do you play chess too ? "

" I do. Not as well as Ransome, though," I said, not looking at this man much, for I was still so angry at his being there, at his being in the way.

" May I have a game with you sometime ? " he asked.

" Why, yes," I replied vaguely, and then I looked at him fully and saw that he was beautiful ; young and tall and slender and dark, with brown eyes that were both clever and shy, and with an imperious chin.

" When shall we play—to-morrow ? " said the young man, speaking with a sort of desperate shyness.

" To-morrow is fine," said I, and left.

.   .   .   .

D. was twenty-four and working for the British
Embassy. He was well-bred in that unobtrusive,
charming English way. He was a linguist and had
travelled quite a bit and had read enormously. And
he was just a boy, shy and very charming and utterly
different from the Russian boys I knew.

We played chess the following night and many a
night afterwards. We would play two games and then
D.'s housekeeper would serve tea or cocoa and we
would talk. We talked about books—Dostoevski,
Tolstoy, Ibsen. About *Peer Gynt* and about God.
About religion and life. . . . But we never talked of
Bolshevism. Around us the first social revolution in
history was being waged, but we did not see it. They
were just a lot of desperate workers and soldiers and
some of these mad Russian demagogues. We had our
own interests—chess and books and ourselves, mainly
ourselves. . . .

9

THE OCTOBER REVOLUTION

ALL revolutions, of course, happen on the streets.
That is, to outsiders—those who don't take any part
either for or against them. And the main difference
between the first revolution and the Bolshevik upheaval
in October was that in March one felt happy only when
out on the streets, while in October one tried to keep off
them.

On the night of October 25–26th, small patrols of
armed workers and soldiers, sent out by the Revolutionary Committee, headed by Comrade Trotsky, took over
the telephone, the telegraph, the armoury, the Peter and

Paul Fort, and the State Bank. They also stationed guards at all the bridges and the railway stations. That was the October revolution.

The people of Petrograd were not aware that the greatest of all revolutions in history, the first social revolution, was taking place that night. The theatres and cabarets were full as always ; the trams ran ; the starved, thin nags of the *izvoschiki* trundled their passengers home in the wee hours as usual. But in the morning people woke in a city shrouded in an ominous silence, with streets that were empty save for small detachments of soldiers and workers on trucks. And we all knew. We knew instantly what had happened then, before the few newspapers came out to tell it all in detail. And I think most of us felt that behind these still, empty streets there was something both terrible and serious. The first revolution gave the Russian people their freedom ; the second meant the beginning of a new order. The second revolution meant business.

" What, was this all ? " you will probably ask. No, it wasn't quite all, though this was the main event. There was a show, after all—the show of taking over the Winter Palace, where the ministers of the Provisional Government were still sitting. They were sitting in an interminable session on that dreary October night, surrounded by a vacuum, as it were, and waiting for a rescue.

On hearing that the Bolsheviks were taking over all the important institutions, and that all the Petrograd regiments were on their side, Kerensky, the head of the Government, fled from the Palace in the direction of the front, to bring back some " trusted soldiers " and save the revolution. He fled in his car, followed by another belonging to the American Embassy and flying the American flag, and giving him immunity—a fact which later was explained very variously in their respective

memoirs by himself, Miliukov, and Trotsky. He did
not bring back the trusted troops and barely saved
himself from his own soldiers, who were more than
willing to give him up to the revolutionaries, by escaping in the uniform of a private. The ministers sat
waiting. . . .

In justice to these ministers, most of them elderly
civilians, they showed extraordinary bravery. Twice
they refused any parley with the Bolsheviks, who sent
their delegates to offer them a safe conduct and freedom
if they were to submit. The ministers felt this would
not be dignified ; also, they still hoped for rescue from
some quarter. There were a few bunches of young
cadets, mere boys from various military schools,
stationed in the Winter Palace. And there was the
famous Woman's Death Battalion.

The Bolsheviks had a number of troops stationed on
the huge square in front of the Palace, others on the
side streets, facing the various exits. And, across the
Neva, the old battleship *Aurora* had its guns pointed
at the Palace, and so had the old Fort of Peter and Paul.

At one time the Woman's Battalion made an attempt
to attack the soldiers and break through their ranks.
But both they and the young cadets, who tried to help
them, were beaten back. Towards evening of that
day, when it was clear to the Bolsheviks that the
ministers refused to surrender, they opened fire from
the square and from the cruiser *Aurora*. The ministers
gave up. The soldiers entered the Palace and led them
away.

The detonations from the heavy guns of the cruiser
were all I personally knew of the battle of the Winter
Palace. I was working in the newspaper office which
was not very far from the Palace Square, but the boom
of the guns shook our building and was very impressive,
and it was only fifteen years later that I read in

Trotsky's description of the revolution that most of
these shots had no shells. And the empty shot has an
even bigger boom than the one with a shell.

On the third or fourth night, when almost all sporadic fights had ceased and the young cadets, who
fought to the end, were either killed or had surrendered,
I went out for a walk. The streets were empty, almost
deserted. It was very cold ; there was no snow, but
an icy wind was blowing from the Neva. Once in a
while a truck rumbled by, filled with soldiers, their
bayonets raised. . . . There were small pickets everywhere ; sometimes they were soldiers, more often a
soldier and a worker standing together, their guns
resting beside them. They had lit small fires for
warmth.

Out in the Smolny, I knew, there was feverish
activity ; the handful of men who were behind it all
had gained their victory and were facing their gigantic
task. Here on the streets everything seemed mournful
and grim. The joy of the first revolution was gone,
never to return, and Russia, which had had a glimpse
of liberty after three hundred years of autocracy, was
going back under another yoke.

10

THE " DAILY NEWS," ALIAS " EVENING POST,"
ALIAS " MORNING STAR "

I, TOO, can say I have worked on a newspaper. Its
name was the *Russian Daily News*. That is, until the

day it was shut down for the first time and began to have other names. But that is at the end of this story.

The *Russian Daily News* was the only English paper in Petrograd. The editor's name was Mr. Vezey— Custis Vezey. Short, with a close-cropped, square head, he looked like an American business man, not the least like an editor or even a journalist. He was the chief editor. Yet he was also the sitting editor, which was unusual. All Russian papers of that period had extra editors on their staffs, pure figureheads at insignificant salaries, whose names were printed at the top, but who were there chiefly for the purpose of sitting in jail whenever the government censors held it necessary to stop an issue, to close the paper, or to use other repressive measures. Hence the name " sitting editor." However, as the *Russian Daily News* was an English publication, published officially for the British colony and financed unofficially, by the British Government, Mr. Vezey did not think it necessary to have an extra editor for " sitting " purposes.

But it was our night editor who ran the thing. He was a stocky young boy with a curly black head, by the name of George E. Sokolsky. I called him " Sok." Sok was an American. He was of Jewish-Polish origin and he was the first person of the New York East Side intelligentsia I had met. He seemed quite extraordinary.

He was always in and out, talked a great deal, and never seemed to work ; yet he wrote most of the copy. He it was who first enlightened me on such things as " blocking in," " layout," and " type." He seemed to be also the chief reporter and he bossed the compositors and everybody else. Between ourselves, we called the paper the " Russian News of the Day before Yesterday," for so much of our copy was always a day late, consisting of translated excerpts from the Russian dailies.

The rest of the staff consisted of several nondescript young men who gathered news, wrote some copy, translated clippings from Russian papers into English, did some proof-reading, and ran errands. My official position was that of secretary to the two editors, though in between times I also translated from the Russian, read proof, and did some other dirty work.

Sok stayed at the office until one, when the thing went to press. Once in a while I was asked to stay longer to do some extra work, and in intervals between intensive writing Sok and I talked. Sok was going to write the greatest American novel. It was going to be about a Jew. Why the greatest American novel was going to be about a Jew I now don't quite remember. Sok explained that no one had yet written a thing like that and he knew just how to do it. He also told me about Emma Goldman, and slowly I gathered that he had been one of her disciples. That would have put him on a par with the wild and fanatic Russian students, the political *émigrés* I had occasionally met. Yet somehow he was entirely different. There was a shrewdness about him, a knowledge of practical affairs and hard common sense, which, permeated with humour, gave his radicalism an entirely different colour. He had none of the Russian socialist's contempt for comfort and riches. On the contrary, he liked comfort and he knew how to achieve it.

He invited Rita and me to dinner at his place one day, and we were quite overwhelmed. Together with two secretaries of the American Embassy, he occupied a lovely, roomy, almost luxurious apartment which obviously had belonged to some wealthy Russians. What overwhelmed us more than anything was the food. Like all the other foreigners connected with some embassy, Sok's two chums used to get in the diplomatic bags all sorts of lovely things—white flour and cocoa and coffee, and even canned stuffs. And so we had a really gorgeous meal. The conversation with these three young Americans doesn't stand out in my memory very well ; it was bright and skipped back and forth over everything. Sok talked a great deal on birth control, about the best preventive methods—" sure-fire " methods, as he put it—and I listened very solemnly, quite impressed. He certainly seemed to know everything, though he looked so young and even childish, with his black curly hair, his slightly yellow complexion, and his narrow, piercing black eyes.

Sometimes, when there was extra work, or when something more than ordinary was happening at the Smolny or about town, I had to stay longer too. When Sok and I remained in the office alone to get the latest news, there were moments when I felt a sort of thrill, when I felt that I was part of that curious thing, THE PRESS. On those nights Sok would sit right close to the telephone, and the moment one of the reporters phoned, he would give me a sign with his hand to be ready and I would quickly insert a fresh sheet into the typewriter. And as he listened to the reporter over the wire, he would dictate to me the ready copy, all in trim, quick newspaper style, down even to paragraphing it. This filled me with admiration. Sometimes he only made quick little notes which no one but himself could read, and dictated the story to me later. Whichever way it happened, it always had to be fast, so as to get into the press-room at once. Occasionally I heard him yell into the phone and even use bad language, and always, it seems to me, he used to ask : " Have you verified it ? " or " Are you sure ? " And sometimes he would say : " All right, I'll let it ride, though I shouldn't." And then when he got through he would

roar and say : " Christ, what a paper ! They don't even
verify. All we print is rumours ! " Then my feeling
of being part of an impressive, modern organization
would evaporate dubiously. Why was it wrong to
print rumours ? Or why should one always verify ?

The *Russian Daily News*, it seems, printed anything
and everything, all sorts of rumours, but particularly
rumours which could have bolstered up the courage of
the bourgeoisie. For, although this was all after the
October revolution, when the Bolsheviks had finally
grasped the power, the city still was full of the opinion
that it was only " for a few weeks." " The Bolsheviks
can't last more than a month or two." . . . " Why,
they don't know anything about administration or
government." . . . " And they have no people." . . .
" Even the Mensheviks and the other moderate
Socialists are against them." And our little paper,
being sponsored by the British Embassy and the Anglo-
Russian Commission (at whose headquarters, as far as
I could judge, official and unofficial English and Russian
gentlemen met daily and exchanged compliments and
assurances that everything was going to be all right in
the end, while they ate food which was slightly better
than the rest of the population, especially the workers,
ate), was read avidly by all the bourgeoisie.

For a time, after the October revolution, the Bolsheviks did not pay any attention to the English paper.
It reached only the small English-speaking colony anyway, and though they gradually closed all the bourgeois
papers and the " counter-revolutionary organs of the
Press," the *Russian Daily News* went on blithely printing
its daily crop of rumours. But as the Russian papers
all disappeared from the stands, the demand for the
English paper increased and our circulation leaped
ahead. And then someone had a brilliant idea of
issuing half of it in Russian. Why should only the

English-speaking people of Petrograd have the benefit
of rumours ? Why not all the Russians, too ? Hitherto
we had only had some Russian advertisements and here
and there a line in quotation.   Now half the issue was
in Russian.

Things went humming.   I was very much impressed
with all this activity.   And I worked much harder, too ;
I did a lot of translating and proof-reading in addition
to all the correspondence. It was a busy life. Although
I did not have to be at the office until ten o'clock, I had
to get up at about eight, for it took fully an hour to
reach there—if you contrived to get on a street-car.
Getting on a street-car in Russia in those days was an
entirely different thing from getting on a street-car
anywhere else in the world.

The little paper, the only " bourgeois " paper in those
days, became very popular.   When the newsboys got
their copies out on the streets you could see people on
every side hurrying to buy a sheet and reading it right
then and there, with a crowd around each lucky pos-
sessor, reading along over his shoulder, commenting,
exclaiming. . . .   Our rag became the Paper of the Day.

It remained so until the day when a little delegation
called on us from the Smolny.   It was just a small delegation, half a dozen or so of Kronstadt sailors, and the
moment we saw them at the door we knew instinctively
what to do.   Mr. Vezey went at once into the compositors' room and I, having the best knowledge of
Russian, was told to meet the sailors.   The Kronstadt
sailors, who made most of the official arrests for the
Bolsheviks, were well known for their curt and businesslike methods and so the little call had its thrill.

The half-dozen of us in the room were quite alive to
all the possibilities.   The sailors filed in, all big,
strapping fellows, with their sailor caps well on the
backs of their heads and their guns in their hands.

" We want your editor," they said simply.

" I don't know if he is in," I said innocently.

" Go and find out," one of them said, and I went into the other room. Mr. Vezey had already left by the back door and, giving him a minute's time to make his getaway, I returned and said truthfully that the editor was not in.

Sok then came bravely forward and I told the sailor that this was our night editor.

" Tell him," said the sailor plainly, though rather politely, " that we have come to close your paper for counter-revolutionary propaganda and printing false news."

I translated. Sok looked thoughtful and seemed to bow to the inevitable. The sailor produced a little scrap on which the order was typewritten and signed by someone ; we signed a receipt and they left.

After that there was a brief conference, at which, following the methods of the Russian pre-revolutionary Press, it was decided to call the *Daily News* the *Morning Star*, and it was under that name that the little paper was issued the next day. The policy, of course, was not changed.

I don't remember all the different names the paper had after that. I don't remember how long it ever stayed under one name, either.

The Bolsheviks would close it for " counter-revolution " and we would go on blithely printing all the news we heard. Mr. Vezey was very careful in his movements and always went into the compositors' room whenever strangers called. I don't know why the Bolsheviks did not close the paper entirely at first, as they did the big Russian dailies ; perhaps the fact that it was backed by the British Government made them still a little wary. Perhaps they simply did not think it important enough, for in those early months of their power the

Bolsheviks were dreadfully busy. They issued streams of decrees, though some of them were just scraps of paper and never were enforced or became valid. It was the first Communistic government in the world and there was no precedent for anything ; they had to build it from the bottom as they went along. So, once in a while, if they telephoned or sent someone to " close the paper," we changed the title and went along. This kept up until one day we printed some news which seemed to annoy the Bolsheviks more than usual. This time when they sent the sailors there was a slightly different air about it all. They did not even ask for Mr. Vezey any more, nor did they want to talk ; they just asked the way to the compositors' room and after they got there they smashed the linotype, broke all the machinery, and then left.

Within five minutes the *Daily News*, alias the *Morning Star*, alias the *Evening Post* and all the other heavenly bodies, ceased to exist. In the language of the Bolsheviks, we were completely " liquidated."

This was early in February and it was the last job I had in Russia. Excepting for Sok, I don't know what happened to the staff of that dinky paper. When I saw Sok he was just on the verge of leaving Petrograd. He seemed very much agitated and he said he was going to Siberia. Fifteen years later, while in New York, I read an article about China in the *New York Times* Sunday supplement signed by " George E. Sokolsky." Rather curious to see what time had done to the curly-headed, lively Sok, I called him up. He came to see me and I saw with amazement what fifteen years had done to him : always of a yellow complexion, with slightly Oriental eyes, he had grown completely Chinese. He was twice the size of that young boy who was then merely inclined to be fat. He even seemed taller. He seemed even shrewder and cleverer than before and his small eyes still twinkled. He told me he had just returned from China.

" Have you spent all these fifteen years there ? " I asked.

" Yes. This is the first time I have been back. I am not used to it yet."

" How does it strike you ? "

" The people are terribly ill-bred. I can't get used to their manners."

I laughed.

" They quarrel in public. Married people argue in the presence of their friends. At parties. My wife can't understand all this. She is Chinese, you know."

I listened curiously.

" In China no man would argue with his wife, even if there were a reason. It would give away the fact that he is not the master of his own house. He would lose face."

II

A DAY IN PETROGRAD IN THE WINTER OF 1917-18

I GOT up at eight, and fifteen minutes afterwards I had my breakfast. I could hardly wait long enough to get to it. It consisted of one small slice of black bread with a dab of red caviare and one cup of tea with a teaspoonful of sugar. Sometimes there was no sugar, only honey. I could have consumed it all in two minutes, but I never did. I took my time over it. I took fully six or eight minutes and I chewed every small bite very thoroughly. The salty, tangy red caviare tasted so good, and, even after one washed it down with the tea, there still remained the flavour of it. The bread was coarse, very dark, and often had things in it—chaff and bits of straw and, sometimes, pieces of grit. It tasted marvellous.

I took another piece of bread like this, with red caviare, for my luncheon at the newspaper office. I cut it in half and folded it, making a little sandwich. And I also took a teaspoonful of sugar in a piece of paper, and then I wrapped this all securely in some newspaper and put it in the pocket of my dress. I carried no bag. My handkerchief and a little money I put also in an inside pocket of my dress or skirt. If one of your hands was occupied, you were apt not to get on to a street-car at all. I then put on my coat, cap, and gloves and walked the few blocks to the street-car stop.

There were always people waiting for the car. We stood in a small, compact group near the track, waiting. If it was very cold, fifteen or twenty degrees below zero (Celsius, not Fahrenheit), we would stamp our feet occasionally and rub our hands.

When we saw, in the distance, the street-car approaching, swaying slightly on the track, we all became a little excited. For that was when the big moment came, the moment, in Shakespeare's language, of " to be or not to be," the moment when we wondered whether we should get on or stay behind, to wait another twenty or thirty minutes in the biting cold for the next car.

We would all strain toward it a little, gauging— gauging carefully—its speed and its momentum, trying to guess where *exactly* it would stop. Then we would move on toward that imaginary stopping place. Sometimes the whole group guessed identically and moved to one spot ; occasionally the opinion was divided and there were two or even three groups. There we would stand, a little excitedly, our eyes glued on the swaying rumbling street-car. . . .

When it was about fifteen feet away, some of the boys and men in the group would run toward it. Women rarely did, for this was a dangerous thing to do. For one thing, it was usually slippery on these stop places, for the snow, trodden by so many rubbers, would become like a hard sheet of ice. For another, if you missed getting on the street-car on the run, you were sure to be left behind, for you could never hope to run back in time to get on in the proper way. For the street-car did not stop until all the people on the street climbed on, as do the street-cars in normal countries. It couldn't, for it was always already full when it came to a stop, and by no possible means could it take on all the people who were waiting. So the conductor just made a perfunctory stop for a minute or so ; then the bell rang and the car went on again. And in this interval of one minute or less, there were a few lucky ones in the crowd who could get on.

You will wonder how we could get on if the car was already full. Of course one did not " get on " in the Western sense of the word, for the car was full indeed, full to overflowing, with people jamming the inside and the two platforms and standing on the steps, holding to the two rails. One did not get on, as I said —one tried to get a hang-on, that's all ; if one could only hang on to something, a piece of a rail, or someone's arm or shoulder, and remain like that for the next four or five blocks, one was on ! To be or not to be !

The street-car, then, would stop, and all of the waiting people, converging into a tight, forceful knot, would push inside by sheer force the people who were hanging on to the rail and standing on the steps. These people would protest, of course, but they were pushed nevertheless, and they pushed, in turn, the people on the platform, who, in turn, pushed those inside the car. As all these were forced up and in, the few of the

r

waiting group who were lucky enough to be quite near the steps, those lucky ones who had gauged the stop place right, would grab the rail or an arm, wedge one foot on to the step, and then hang on with all their might. For the street-car would be off, and off with a tremendous impetus, and it took all one's strength and grit to remain hanging on. If by any chance one lost one's grip or let oneself be pushed off the step, one was hurled down on the cold ice with terrific force, especially if the street-car happened to round a corner. For somehow Russian tram conductors never seemed to slow down on corners. One would be lucky to get away with only a broken arm or leg.

Of course this getting on, remember, would take less than a minute, and only four or five out of the entire group waiting could get on at all ; the rest would remain waiting. Always the older or more careful would remain, or the very young ones. In time one never really saw old people or children try to board a car ; it was a sheer impossibility. No old person could even dream of the feat. Boys of fourteen or so would be the youngest ones to try it. Personally, I can say with pride that I got on usually at the first try, since I could gauge so well the exact spot where the rear platform would stop, and could run to it if necessary. Also, I was very slim. I would stand right in front, let the heavier people, the men, do the pushing, and then, spying a piece of rail, I would grab it quickly with both hands and hang on like that. Sometimes I would hang on just by my hands for several blocks, without a foothold, being wedged firmly between the bodies of other people. And after the first half-dozen blocks or so, the seemingly impossible would happen, and the people inside would be squeezed still tighter, and a few of us at a time would push our way upwards on to the platform and there stand with a tremendous feeling of relief. The first five or ten minutes, when you finally got on to the platform, were of sheer animal relief and relaxation. It was warm, standing in this tight, breathing mass of humanity. It smelt bad, but it was warm. And you did not have to hang on to the ice-cold rail and feel the cold air swish in a blast behind you, getting inside of your coat, freezing your very marrow.

One could not allow more than five minutes for this rest, however. There was the task of pushing on ahead through the whole length of the car to the front in time to get out at your stop. One could mount the car only at the rear and get off only at the front.

Less dangerous than hanging to the rail on the steps with the car rounding corners at full speed, getting off was nevertheless a heavy task. About a mile from one's destination, ten or a dozen or more blocks, one had to start elbowing one's way to the front. One said " Pozhalusta " (Please) and " Mnie wykhodit " (I have to get off) numberless times, and while the jammed crowd jammed itself to the side, one inched oneself through, unbelievably slowly and laboriously. Sometimes one's dress or even coat was torn in the process and one's feet were sorely trod upon. Finally the front was reached, a block before the stop.

" But if taking a street-car was such a horrible ordeal, why didn't you walk ? " you might ask. Well, for two reasons, or even three. True, the distance to my office was about three miles. I know, because sometimes, when I could not get on the first car and the second was late, I did walk. The main reason, however, why one did not want to walk was because it made one more hungry. Walking is, in cold weather, tremendously stimulating, and hunger is not a pleasant feeling. It can actually be annoying. At least standing in the car, jammed so full, one did not spend energy.

Also, it was warm ! And that was the second reason one did not like to walk. The popular notion that you get that wonderful feeling of glowing warmth when walking briskly through the snow fizzles out when it has to be done on an almost empty stomach. The first mile you might feel a little warmer ; the second, you begin to feel hungry ; and the third, to feel hungry and tired and cold. And the alternative of the dreadful street-car with its jammed humanity, with the daily adventure, morning and evening, of hanging on to the rail and pushing one's way through, is paradise.

At the office I would work hard until one. At one we were served tea, the tea being still furnished by the office, but not the sugar ; then we unwrapped our food and ate our lunches. That second caviare sandwich also was delicious. It had to last me until six or seven, when I quit the office and went to my father's place. There, daily, my sister and I had our only filling meal. It consisted of soup made from dried vegetables, potatoes in one form or another, tea with a little sugar or honey, a little piece of bread, and red caviare. Once in a great while there was meat—horse meat. When it was from a young horse it was good ; but when from an old carcass, it was indescribably tough. All this food was good, however—delicious. We were so hungry, and it was well prepared. Dunia, the maid, brought along from the provinces by my stepmother, was an excellent cook. She had been in the family for years and what she did with potatoes defies description : potato cutlets with mushroom sauce ; potato patties fried in cottonseed oil ; potato bread ; potato dumplings, and so on—all this outside of the ordinary ways of cooking them.

After this meal, which was about seven o'clock, I returned to the room which I shared with my sister, dressed a little better, and walked to D.'s place. We played chess and talked until twelve or one. Then D. took me home. I went to bed at 2 a.m.

That winter in Petrograd was the happiest time of my youth. I enjoyed my work, especially Sok's stimulating personality, and I was very happy with D. A little hunger did not matter. The revolution didn't matter. My days were very full and the future could take care of itself.

12

A CRISIS

THE game of chess was finished, the cocoa was drunk, the sandwiches were eaten, and D. and I were discussing Life. No, Wells's *Research Magnificent*. We both liked the book tremendously, and its idea of personal courage, for an aristocracy of spirit, of character, appealed to us immensely. We talked of it and then began to generalise about quests and principles, about life ideals and goals. Said I :

" I really don't think I have any set principles. Just a general desire to live fully, to experience every side of it, all of life. . . ."

Didn't I have any at all ? D. wanted to know.

" I don't think so—beyond just being honest and not hurting anyone. But that's ethics ; one does this instinctively—but no set principles, like a definite road with fences that would interfere with any experience...."
And, thinking that this was as good a time to say it as any, since I was bound to tell it to him anyway, I added : " I know quite a bit—except of course, the

biggest thing. . . . The biggest thing is to bear a child."

I said it casually. I tried to be sophisticated—child that I was. Then I saw D.'s eyes and all my silly sophistication vanished. He had grown white and looked sick.

" Do you mean ? . . ."

" Yes. . . . Why ? Why do you look like that ? "

" Christ ! " he said, and got up from his chair. And I got up too.

" But why ? "

" Oh, my God ! " he said, and then, fiercely : " Who is the man ? " And then : " Not that it matters."

I do not remember all that we said then, not the words or the whole sentences. We stood in the middle of the room, talking away at each other and growing angrier by the minute. I knew the revelation would be important to the boy, but I never thought he would grow so miserable and so angry. His beautiful dark eyes were blazing and he was white with pain and indignation, and the gist of it all was that though I was " without principles " he still " had a few " and would be damned if he pushed me further " into the gutter," and I grew angrier and angrier and refused to be treated that way, I refused to see that I was worse than he or worse than I had ever been before. He couldn't treat me like a Mary Magdalene, said I, but I couldn't make him see my side, I couldn't make him see it at all. And I left saying that I was through. . . .

A week later D. wrote and we patched it up and started anew. But it was to be only a friendship, D. wrote, and because I loved him I consented. With a little ironic bitterness in my heart, I slowly learned from D. about the English code of honour and sex morality, the inexorable morality of his class in those days : the

girls were always chaste before marriage, and most of
the boys. Of course, there were always some cads
among men—there had been a few in his year, at
Cambridge, who ran around. . . . He, D., never did.

So pathetic it all seems now in retrospect, after all
these years when even the rigid English code went
topsy-turvy, when both England and America and all
Western Europe had their jazz age—now, when even
the jazz itself is long dead and forgotten. . . . But in
those years during the war, just before the revolution,
Russian youth had its own jazz age—oh, so different
from the Western ones, without the gin and the whisky
and the dance band, without the fanfare and the smart-
ness. Quietly and unobtrusively they threw the old
morality to the winds and just lived as they pleased.
Not all of them, but many, and when a few years later
the Bolsheviks issued their new decrees about marriage
and divorce which so shocked the Western World, they
hardly invented anything new ; they simply legalised
something that had been going on for almost ten years.
As to artists, they had lived like that, freely, even long
before. . . .

I tried to explain this to D., but he would not listen.
He had those principles. These principles, it seemed,
were sacred things, just as England was something
sacred. " Home," he called it. These sacred things,
I gathered, the Englishmen carried with them when
going to live abroad, as they did their tweeds and pipes,
their charming manners and clever brains, and things
like the funny rubber bath which A. K. carted around
and which used to provoke me to gales of laughter. . . .

And in the end, I knew, it did not matter who was
right and who wrong. In the end it mattered only who
was the stronger, who was the stronger of us two. D.
was stronger than I ; I could not shake his beliefs ; I

could not shake him at all. Perhaps I loved him even more for it, just as I loved his strong, jutting chin, his fine eyes, and his whole beautiful, chiselled face. . . .

13

REVOLUTIONARY LOVE

IN the room my sister and I had at that period, there was no telephone, and whenever I wanted to call up someone I had to go to a neighbour. He was an acquaintance of my stepmother's, a Menshevik by the name of Nikitski, and so the calls were not purely unofficial. Sometimes we talked a bit.

Nikitski was a man in his forties, spare, not very tall, with a good head, a goatee beard, sharp grey eyes, a thin, determined mouth, and a lofty forehead. Quite the typical intellectual. His hair was always closely cropped—a habit, he explained, from his days in prison in Siberia, when, in fact, it was totally shaved. For Nikitski had served his time, both in Siberia in jail and abroad as an exile. He was an economist and wrote in Gorky's paper, the *New Life*.

Sometimes when I telephoned the room was full of other men, who all talked and gesticulated in the manner of all Russians. They, too, were Mensheviks ; some of them rather famous, like Dan and Martov and Sukhanov. Of all of them I recall Sukhanov best. He was just like his name, which means something like " dryer," the name Sukhanov being derived from the word *sukhoy*, which means " dry." He spoke fast and nervously.

As I usually called the Embassy and talked to D. in

English, the presence of these Russians did not disturb
me, and they, with the indifference to such matters
which most Russians possess, probably never even
knew I was in the room ; but went on discussing and
arguing.

Nikitski's apartment consisted of a bedroom, a small
living-room, which also served as his dining-room, and
a tiny kitchen, where Annushka reigned. Annuskha
was his old nurse, a wrinkled old woman with a round,
kind face, invariably wearing a grey shawl, who took
care of him when he was a child and now took care of
him when he was a middle-aged revolutionary, an
important economist and party member. But to her,
I think, he was still the little boy.

One afternoon when I came to telephone, old
Annushka, who opened the door for me, did not let
me in ; instead, blocking the entrance into the room,
she whispered confidentially :

" To-day you can't come in, dear *baryshnia*. It's
Thursday."

" *Nu* what if it is Thursday ? " said I impatiently.

" Thursday is the day when the mamselle comes.
Thursday between two and four."

" What mamselle ? "

" The mamselle that he sleeps with, my dear. Between two and four on Thursdays. Now after four,
milosti prosim, you are quite welcome, *baryshnia* ; you
can come and telephone to your heart's desire."
Annushka whispered and then closed the door.

It amazed me—the fact that even Nikitski had a
mistress ! He looked so dry and austere, with his thin,
determined mouth and his hard grey eyes. He did not
look as if he ever could make love to a woman—nice,
romantic love. Then an overpowering curiosity consumed me to see how his mistress looked, how this

"mamselle" looked. Perhaps she was French, I thought. Surely she ought to be a particularly attractive woman, perhaps a little plump, vivacious—a pert Frenchwoman, I thought. . . .

Accordingly, on the following Thursday I went across the yard up to Nikitski's flat. I went at five minutes to four, thinking that I might encounter her on the stairway. Just as I was on the second flight of steps, Nikitski's door opened and a woman came out. She passed right by me—tall, shabbily dressed in a black skirt with a grey shawl around her, with a dry, colourless face and straight, mouse-coloured hair, she looked like a neglected seamstress.

I went right in, since Annushka had seen me and had beckoned invitingly, but as I fumbled in the telephone book, ostensibly looking for a number, I thought with horror : " This is a mistress. This woman is a mistress. Oh, my God ! "

A few minutes later Nikitski emerged from his bedroom and, buttoning his coat, nodded at me and went at once to his desk. As I looked at his straight, rigid back, and his ascetic head, I thought : " So this is how a revolutionary loves—between two and four on Thursdays. Very regularly. They do not believe in love, of course ; in romance. . . . Love is just a ' physiological function ' which one has to practise, *nolens volens*. . . ." I had often heard of it. And now I had seen it.

14

A MEETING

I was walking on the Zabalkansky Prospect when I met him, and I was the first to recognise him as an acquaintance. In a semi-military uniform, with a revolver at his belt, in high Russian boots and with a new assurance in his manner, Blanc looked so different from the *émigré* student I had met on the ship on our first trip to America that I stared at him in silent amazement. . . .

" Lola ! "   He ran forward and took both my hands.

" I thought you were in California."

" We returned in nineteen-sixteen.   And you ? "

" I got back last spring, after the revolution."

And then we both stopped and just looked at each other and became instantly appraising, silent, on guard. . . . That's how it used to be in those days.   One weighed one's Russian friends if one had not seen them for some time ; one wondered on which side of the fence they were—and the purely personal relationship often could not bridge the political one.   Not that we had ever been intimate friends—just the sort of odd friendship one develops on board ship.   In New York he had called once or twice ; then California separated us. We never even wrote or exchanged addresses.

He began to walk at my side and I found that I could not say anything.   There was no need to ask on which side Blanc was : his new swaggering manner—somehow a little ridiculous with his typical face of a Jewish student, a face that was intellectual and not insensitive —showed it conclusively.   And it was he who broke the silence.

" Lola, aren't you with us ? "

" You mean with the Bolsheviks ? "

" Yes, of course."

" I am not."

A long silence. In the middle of the sidewalk he turned squarely to me, his blue eyes with the very pale, reddish eyelashes looking earnestly into mine.

" I wish you would let me explain. It's going to be a new world."

" Yes. Over a ruined Russia."

" We didn't ruin it. The old régime did."

" I know that. But you want to destroy the little that's left."

" But it's going to be different. We are starting from the beginning."

" A beautiful beginning. Why did you stop the Constituent Assembly ? What about the peasants ? "

" We will educate them ; they will turn Bolshevik too."

" At the point of the gun."

Another long pause. I thought it was time to say good-bye. . . .

" *Pozhalusta*, won't you walk with me to the station ? I am on duty at the Nikolayevsky Station."

" Very well. But let's not discuss that part any more."

" Lola, if you would only let me explain. . . . I could in a few hours. You don't know the situation ; the reactionaries have poisoned you with their lies."

" I am not a reactionary. I just believe in democracy, social democracy. What's the good of helping humanity by killing and starving and persecuting ? It's nonsense, a contradiction in itself. I, too, believe in Socialism ; but not Communism. African savages are all Communists. But we aren't savages."

" Yes, but your Socialists, these democrats and Mensheviks, never get anywhere. They are weak.

They believe in war, a capitalistic war. They still support the capitalists of the Entente."

We were in the throes of it, the interminable Russian discussion ; only now it meant something. I knew that the moment I would turn Bolshevik, if I could convince the leaders of an honest desire to help, I could get work, and a better food card—perhaps a job in the Kreml . . . in Moscow. . . .

" Oh, let's stop, Blanc. It's no use."

We went into the station. It was crammed full of people, all sorts of people : soldiers, peasants, remnants of the bourgeoisie trying to escape from the hunger city, going South where there was still food and the Whites were gathering an army. The trains were full—not only inside, but on the platforms. There were people on the roofs, clinging for dear life, desperate with fear and with hope. . . . I thought of my sister who was doing social work in one of these big stations ; who had seen sights like these for almost a year. . . . I turned to say good-bye to Blanc. Suddenly, taking hold of my hand, he said in a low voice :

" Have you enough to eat ? You and Rita ? "

" Plenty," I lied, out of sheer stupid pride and obstinacy.

" You see, this is not my regular job. I am really in charge of a food train. I have a fine bunch of Letts." He lowered his voice still more. " I could get you something now and then."

" I see." I did see. In my mind I saw it all, for I knew how these food trains operated. A detachment of Letts under a revolutionary officer went into the villages and requisitioned food for starving Petrograd. When the peasants hid it or refused to deliver the ordered quota, they were lined up in a row and every tenth one of them was shot. It was a very efficient method : the villages gave their quotas obediently.

And because the Russian soldiers refused to fire on their people, the soldiers sent to requisition food were usually either Letts or Red Finns. . . . I thought of all that and I saw Blanc, a Jewish revolutionary officer, commanding a group of Letts who shot Russian peasants when it was necessary. I saw it all, instantly, much quicker of course than it can be told, and I said stiffly :

"*Spasibo* (Thank you). We don't need anything."

He tried to look into my eyes and, bending closer, said again : " I could bring you something now and then."

"*Spasibo*. We are fine. We don't need anything. Good-bye."

" I am leaving next week with my train."

" Good-bye."

" What is your address ? "

" What for ? "

" We don't have to be enemies even if you don't believe in Bolshevism."

I gave him my address and left.

About a month later one morning my sister and I were at breakfast. For breakfast we had tea. We could drink two or three or even four cups. There was plenty of hot water and plenty of tea, but there was nothing else.

There came a sudden knock on the outside door. For a moment we sat in frigid silence. A knock in those days often portended evil and one had always a feeling of fear. Our friends were instructed to knock in a certain manner, so that we knew at once whether it was a stranger or not. One of us finally summoned sufficient courage to ask :

" Who is it ? "

" Is this where the *Baryshni Kinel* live ? " The voice was a man's—common but cheerful.

" It is." We opened the door a little, leaving it on the chain. The man was a soldier with a sack on his shoulder. He had an open, kind, naïve face. We opened the door entirely.

He came in quickly, threw the bag on the floor, and with a cheerful : " Comrade Blanc asked me to deliver this," he turned about and fled, without giving us even time to thank him. It looked as if he had orders to fly. . . .

The bag was full of food—bacon, bread, flour, even a lump of country butter. We sat over it on our haunches, for a moment utterly unable to speak—it was all so lovely. I don't think I even thought of the peasants from whom it was taken, or that some of them might have been shot. . . .

15

I DO SOME QUEER SHOPPING

OF course by now I am quite aware that the Russian Revolution was a very " mighty event in the history of mankind " and that generations hence children will read books about it with the same curiosity and awe with which we read of the revolution in France. And the more distant the future, the greater will be their awe, unless all history by then has been debunked of some of its traditions, and books about the great events will be written in a different manner, somewhat on the order of Hendrik van Loon's. All I know is that, personally, I shall never feel quite bamboozled by this aura of historical magnificence, nor whisper to my grandchildren about the great and wonderful things I have witnessed. I was too close to it when the people who made it were not yet great, but only, I suppose, in the process of becoming so—when they were, in fact, just Russian revolutionaries up against all kinds of difficulties and problems. Quite unwittingly I have even assisted one of them in applying one of the " chief levers in the success of the Great Social Revolution "— does that sound historical enough ? Like so many things, it started in a small bookshop, or, rather, several.

It was in the spring of 1918, during that monotonous period when there were no jobs, except Bolshevik jobs, when all the foreigners had left, when the Bolshevik Government had left for Moscow, and one vegetated with nothing to do, not much to eat, and a general feeling of utter hopelessness.

A. K. came down on one of his flying visits from Moscow, hungry, bubbling with enthusiasm for the Bolsheviki as usual, and in a tremendous hurry.

Having eaten a bit of *kasha* and drunk his glass of tea, A. K. said :

" Twin, will you do some shopping for me ? I have got to catch the night train back to Moscow to-night ; I promised to attend to this and I don't know how I can manage it—I have so many other errands to do."

" Why, certainly, A. K. I shall be glad to do it for you," I said, thinking that anything was good that would break the monotony a little.

" Very well. Here is the list. It's books, so I know you will enjoy it. Just take a cab and go from shop to shop." And, handing me a closely written long list of books and some money, he departed.

I took a cab and went on a round of bookshops, mostly antiquarian, as some of the books on the list were quite old. I spent an entire day getting those books and, although I could not get them all, I got a good two-thirds, and when I returned home I had a

cabful—parcels and parcels of them.   Some of the titles
had puzzled me a little and I wondered why A. K.
wanted old stuff like that, anyway.   Was he going to
write an old-fashioned romance *à la* Conrad, or what ?
For the titles of these books were quite funny : *The
Mexican Rebellion, Partisan War, Guerrilla Warfare,
Tactics,* and so on.

However, I had no time to puzzle it out further, or
even to look through the books themselves, all tied into
clumsy parcels with cheap brown string, for A. K. was
already calling for them and was in a great rush to get
back to the station.

" Oh, how jolly, Twin ! " he exclaimed.   " Where
did you find so many ?   By Jove, you have done well !
Trotsky will be so pleased ! "

" What ! " said I.   " Trotsky ?   What do you mean ? "

" The books are for Trotsky.   He couldn't get
anything in Moscow ; the best book-stores are all up
here, you know, so I promised someone I would look
around.   Trotsky is building a Red army, you know,
and, not being a soldier, he doesn't know much about
it.   So he is trying to learn all about it from books.
And he is clever enough to do it, too."

" Oh, great Scott, A. K. !   You are a pig, asking *me*
to help your silly Trotsky with his army.   Oh, A. K. !
I will never forgive you this."

But A. K. roared and chuckled and went away,
highly pleased with himself and his little trick and
leaving me all disgruntled.

And that, as far as I know, was the beginning of the
famous Red army.

G

16

A LETTER AND A POSTSCRIPT

ABOUT once a month we received a letter from my
brother. The letters were affectionate, and quite
amusing. He was stationed in Petrovsk Port, on the
Caspian Sea, in charge of the supplies for his company ;
for his health did not permit him as yet to take part
in the campaign.

He described his work and the place. He wrote that
he liked his men and we could read between the lines
that he must be very popular. Cheerful, witty, without sarcasm, he exercised his authority with a sort of
charming ease. The men under him obeyed him
willingly because they liked him and because they
trusted his judgment. It had been like that in the
bank in which he worked before joining the army,
where both his superiors and all the men under him
liked him equally well ; it had been like that in the
Russian gymnasium and later at the University of
Zurich, which he attended for a while and where he was
always a sort of natural popular leader. He knew
how to be firm, however, when it was necessary.

It was sometime in the winter of 1917–18 when we
realised that things down there in the South weren't
quite right. In his cheerful, amusing manner he wrote
then that his men, too, were getting restless ; they were
hearing a lot of " this Soviet propaganda " and getting
their heads full of nonsense. But, he added, he had had
a talk with them and had pounded some sense into
them. They promised not to do anything without
asking him first ; they trusted him absolutely ; they
were grateful for all he had done, and so forth. So, the

letter ended, he hoped for the best. Of all the officers in that regiment, he added, he had the best standing with his men. They were, at bottom, good-hearted fellows.

We knew from previous letters that he had done much more than was officially his duty : he had organized a library for his men, a sort of club where they could gather ; he wrote letters for all those that were illiterate, and looked after them like a big brother.

When the next letter came we opened it with more than usual curiosity. We were all sitting around the table in the dining-room of father's flat and one of us read the letter aloud. I have lost it since, but I still remember the contents so well, particularly the ending :

To-day we had a veritable show. You should have been here. From morning on the men were busy with discussions. I did not interfere. I pretended not to notice. I knew they would come to me in the end, with all their troubles. Sometime in the afternoon they sent a " delegation " to me and told me they were having a meeting and they had made some resolutions and they wanted me to hear them. I went to them, got up on a box, so they could see me and I could face them squarely, and asked them what they wanted. They looked very sheepish and hee-hawed and stamped their feet, and finally one of them brought me a little dirty scrap of paper and said that was their " resolution." On the scrap it said that at this meeting, on such and such a date, they, the soldiers of this company, etc., etc., had decided to form a soviet and depose their officer. And would I kindly depose myself and not give them too much trouble about it.

I read it and looked them squarely in the eyes. They all looked at me. I said : " I have been a good officer to you, haven't I ? "

" Yes, sir ! *Rady staratsia !* " (Glad to obey—a Russian soldier's slogan.)

" You have never had any reason to distrust me or my judgment ? "

" No, sir."

" Very well.   This is my answer."   I tore the scrap deliber-
ately into small bits and threw it away.   Then I dismissed
the men and walked away.

The letter continued with family matters.   But at
the end there was a curious postscript :

PS.   I don't want you to worry.   If things get too hot here
I shall try to go down to Persia and join the English.

This was the last letter we had from him and it was
not until a few months later that we heard that the
massacre of the officers by their revolting soldiers had
been particularly fierce in that region.   Twice my
father sent couriers down there to find out, if possible,
what had happened, but none of them ever returned.
. . . The letter with the postscript remained the only
haunting memento of his fate.   Perhaps it is best
so. . . .   It is best that we never knew what was his
last " show " with his fellows.

17

I TURN BOLSHEVIK

I DON'T know exactly when this happened.   I know it
was one of those horrible, dreary days in that spring of
1918 when Petrograd began to turn into a doomed city.
    D. was gone.   All the Embassies and Consulates,
except a few which were established temporarily in
Vologda, had left.   All the foreigners were gone and all
those Russians who could had escaped.   Some went
south, to join the White forces ; others to Siberia, to
Norway or Sweden.

The Bolshevik leaders had left the Smolny and moved to Moscow to establish the central government there. They had moved because of the danger of a German attack. The Germans were in Riga and had pushed on to Pskov, only a day's ride from Petrograd. Although we did not talk of it much, everyone knew it, and the realisation did not add anything to the dismal feeling of living in a dead and doomed town.

None of us had a job now ; no bourgeois could hold one—only those who joined the Bolsheviks could work. Hunger was worse, too ; our food cards were cancelled. I remember my sister and I used to tighten our American corsets as the day wore on and drink lots of tea to kill the empty feeling. Sometimes, when it was not too cold, I used to go out and wander around the streets, looking for food. Once in a while I stumbled upon a little shop where a few old canned foods were still for sale, or perhaps some dried vegetables or dried fruits.

The streets in those days had an empty, dead look and there were many dead horses—horses which had died from starvation. They never remained there for long ; while they lay there, yet breathing, dogs, starved into impossible thinness, would converge upon them and, if no one bothered to take away the poor horse, they would start on a feast of their own. Perhaps it was because they were weak themselves and this was the most vulnerable spot, but somehow they always used to start on the horse's belly. The sight of the entrails and the blood and the dogs' snouts all messy and bloody always made me feel sick. I could not bear to look on. I would return home, go back to my books, and read. I read more than ever, books on Socialism and all the newspapers. Although all the bourgeois papers had been shut down as counter-revolutionary, the Left Socialist and Menshevik papers were still allowed to continue. Of these the most notable was the *Novaya Zhizn (New Life)*, the chief mouthpiece of the Mensheviks, under the editorship of Maxim Gorky, who, in those early days, was still against the Bolsheviki.

The *New Life* was filled daily with long, fiery editorials, full of invective against the Bolsheviks and their Dictatorship of the Proletariat. I read them and agreed with them all. They expressed everything that I felt or knew on the subject : that the masses were not ready for Socialism ; that it was absurd to expect any co-operation from disgruntled peasants and disorganised soldier deserters ; that the policy of the Bolsheviks was simply suicide for Russia and thus suicide for the revolution, and so on.

I read these articles daily. . . . I agreed. Then, suddenly, one day, I disagreed. Now I don't know how it happened : whether it was the cumulative effect of weeks of inactivity and dreary hopelessness, just standing by and watching, or the memory of the endless, futile discussions I had witnessed in Nikitski's rooms—the endless pacing back and forth of all these Menshevik leaders ; the endless talking and talking and analysing and criticising of these men who were all so clearly dry theorists, devoid of the power of action. I don't remember what exactly made me change my point of view. But I remember the enthusiasm with which I sat down to write my own article, at one white-hot streak, almost without plan, piling up argument on argument as to *why* all the other Socialists, all the intelligentsia, all the professional men, should now join the Communists ! The main argument was that only by joining now, full force, could they expect eventually to change some of the ruthlessness and barbarism of Communism—only that way could they democratise it. For, I wrote, the Communists were, after all, the only party in power and, with the support of the masses, the only active agency in governing Russia. If we could not fight them, we could join them and influence them by sheer numbers ; there were thousands and thousands of fine democratic, liberal Russians who just stood aside, talking away their time, unable to decide which way to turn. And so on and so on and so on— five or six thousand words of impassioned appeal to stop sabotage and inactivity, to help the Bolsheviks fight the chaos and the hunger, and thus save Russia and the revolution.

This article, I felt, would save the country. When it was completed, I went straight to Nikitski's rooms.

" I just wrote this," I said, " and I want to ask your help in getting the *Novaya Zhizn* to accept it. I know you have influence there. It is very important." All this rather breathlessly.

Nikitski, I knew, was one of their chief economist writers and had quite a bit of pull.

His dry face screwed up in a smile and his eyes twinkled : " And I never knew that we harboured an author in this house."

" I am not an author," I replied with dignity. " This is a political article and it is frightfully important. I don't know how to write ; you may have to correct it— I don't care. Please read it and you will see that I am right. My only wish is that it should be printed in all the Socialist papers."

" That's certainly a large order," he said, still smiling ; then added politely : " I shall certainly read it," and put the manuscript on the table.

I left with my enthusiasm a bit dampened by his attitude, yet fully convinced that, once he read it, he would see the truth of my arguments and all the Mensheviks would see it too. If only they printed it, I thought, we could save Russia yet ! I would write many more. . . .

One day passed. Two, three. Four, five, six. There was no call or word from Nikitski and, though I scanned the *Novaya Zhizn* carefully every day, there was no sign of my article. Gorky still wrote wrathfully about the stupidity of the Bolsheviks, calling them blockheads and what not (he was allowed to do this because he was of humble origin, a worker himself, therefore an aristocrat in the new valuation of things. Bourgeois editors, for the same words, were put in prison and their papers stopped). Then, perhaps a week later, father said casually at dinner :

" I met that Nikitski fellow on the stairs to-day and he asked me to tell you to call on him to-night. . . . Something you wrote ? " Father smiled at me, with a question in his eyes, but I kept my mouth shut. It was too early to tell. My conversion to Bolshevism would probably shock him. Perhaps it would be best for him to see it in the paper, in print. Then he would also be persuaded by my wisdom and join too. Father was a cadet, he liked Miliukov and the conservative liberals.

When eight o'clock came, I went up to Nikitski's flat : Annushka opened the door and asked me to wait, as the *barin* was not yet home. Annushka had not yet learned the Communistic language and still called her Socialist employer " master " and not " comrade." She brought me a glass of tea with a little honey and I sat down on the leather divan. Presently I became drowsy and leaned against a pillow. When I opened my eyes, Nikitski was standing at the foot of the divan, smiling.

" I must have fallen asleep," I said in confusion.

" Like a sleeping princess. Dear *baryshnia*, you have real talent. Stroyev and I talked it over and we want you to write a story, and he is going to show it to Gorky."

A little stupid from sleep, I could not comprehend it

all. Nikitski, still standing at the foot of the divan, his hands resting on the arm of it, rocked back and forth on his toes. His eyes smiled quizzically, enjoying my puzzled state.

"But my article? About Bolshevism and sabotage?" I cried.

"I *am* talking about the article. Beautifully written. Remarkable syllogisms."

"But is the paper going to print it?"

"Oh, no, no. We aren't interested in that. But we want you to write a story—a sketch, anything. Do it now, soon, no matter how short. Stroyev wants Gorky's opinion."

"Oh, but my article!" I almost cried. "Don't you realise what it means? Can't you realise that all this continuous criticism, this sabotage, is only augmenting the chaos, the hunger, the agony? It is too late now to criticise them. The Bolsheviks are in power and the people follow them. It is a *fait accompli*. And all you other socialists just keep on talking. Talk and talk. If all the intelligent people, all the doctors, engineers, teachers, would join their ranks, they could later, perhaps, influence them and make their rule democratic. I could write ten more articles like this, develop all the ideas. If you would only print this one first. Surely, coming from a paper supported by Gorky, it would find response among all the intelligentsia?"

It was a long, impassioned speech, but as I went on I saw it was hopeless. Nikitski was not listening to the arguments—just watching me talk, as if I were a marionette that had been wound up. I felt tears coming up, but I fought them back bravely. Finally I stopped and got up. Nikitski took my hand :

"We can't use articles of this sort. Now you bring me a story. The *Novaya Zhizn* has its own policy and I cannot discuss it with you. But you write very well. Very good syllogisms."

Full of resentment and anger and suppressed tears, I left. As I ran down the two flights of steps, one word kept intruding into all these emotions—" syllogism." What did it mean, anyway ? It was a new word to me. . . .

A week later some of my resentment evaporated and I wrote a story. It was entitled " Hunger " and dealt with a reporter of the bourgeois Press who fell asleep one day from weakness and hunger and had a nightmare. The nightmare was full of allegorical persons, skeletons, Bolshevik slogans, and both Trotsky and Lenin were there, too. I did not write it with any enthusiasm, but as one does a composition assignment in school, and when it was finished I took it to Nikitski and Nikitski took it to the *Novaya Zhizn*. A week or so later Stroyev, the editor, a thin man with a gentle face resembling pictures of Jesus, asked me to call on him and told me that Gorky said the story was very bad but my talent was good and I should go on writing.

I went home in a mood of I-told-you-so and did not write any other stories. It wasn't at all what I wanted; what I wanted was to write articles about the idiocy and crime of sabotaging the Bolsheviks. Yet since no one wanted to print them, there was no use in doing it. I also thought of my own personal problem of joining the Bolsheviks. I dreaded telling my decision to father. He would be terribly upset ; so would the rest of my family. I was putting it off, for I thought I would arrange it all through Ransome on his next visit from Moscow. I had had a note that he was coming down. I knew he would be glad. He had always wanted it, he would probably know exactly, too, where I should fit in best.

But when Ransome came, he had with him a proposal which completely changed all my plans.

"Look, Twins," he said almost immediately, "you speak German, don't you?"

"We do."

"And does *Babushka* know German too?"

"Oh, grandmother speaks beautiful German. And beautiful French. But why?"

"Now listen. If you and your *babushka* can pretend you are German, I think you could get out of Russia; you could all three get to Poland."

"But how?"

"Mirbach, the German Ambassador in Moscow, is arranging with the Bolsheviks for the transfer of all German war prisoners to Germany. Some of these trains will go through Petrograd. The only trouble is passports; if we can get over that and I think we can, you will board the train here and, when you get to Poland, you will just get off. No one will stop you there. Now let me talk it over with your father."

It was terribly exciting and within a few weeks it was all arranged just as Ransome had explained it, and one day in June we went to the station at which the prisoners' trains had stopped, to start on our journey to Poland. I forgot all about the Bolsheviks and saving poor Russia and my pragmatic turn-about. All I wanted was to get out.

18

SIX HORSES AND ONE MAN

THE train consisted of cattle-cars, the kind on which there is usually marked in chalk : " Six Horses and One

Man." Instead of six horses and one man, however, each cattle-car was filled with about forty or fifty German war prisoners. They were not allowed to leave the cars and a guard stood at each door to see that they didn't. The sliding doors were open and we saw them, crowded, sitting on bales and small bags—weary, patient, and unkempt. Some of them had travelled from as far as Siberia, others from the Volga region.

We were allowed one suitcase each, and after father had deposited them in one of the cattle-cars we went back to our group, a little distance from the train. We talked Polish, in low voices, so the guards shouldn't hear. From now on we should have to be " German."

The parting was like most partings in the war—very casual and slightly humorous, for the things that were in our minds none of us could voice. We weren't at all sure whether we should ever see each other again, and, if so, when. And so it was best to pretend that the thing was just funny, slightly irregular. The fun didn't last very long, for one of the guards approached us and told us to get in. Grandmother clung to our father, who was her eldest and favourite son; he kissed her hands once more ; we all had a quick embrace, and then climbed into the cattle-car. The heavy sliding door was shut. There was a tiny square window in the door, the only one in the entire car. Father lifted my little stepsister up so she could look in through the window. She was a charming little girl, just six, and we had always been great pals. She looked at me with her dark blue eyes fringed with dark eyelashes and said plaintively :

" I want to go with you. Can't you take me ? "

" No, darling, I can't. You have to stay with papa and mamma."

She pressed her little face close to the small pane and I could hear her thin, childish voice through the glass :

" If you were a fairy, you could make me tiny and I could crawl into your pocket."

" I am sorry I am not a fairy."

The box-car gave a little jolt and began to move. It moved so slowly that for a long while I could still see father walking alongside, with his little daughter in his arms, throwing kisses to me. Then they fell back . . . we were actually leaving.

Herded close together, body to body, we sat on our respective bags, scarcely speaking. Ransome had warned us to speak little, and only German, to avoid suspicion ; but I think now that even if we had spoken our own Polish, or even French, it would not have stirred the curiosity either of those war prisoners or of their guards. They hardly spoke between themselves and it was a strangely quiet crowd huddled into this space of " six horses and one man."

At night it began to rain, and through the holes in the roof the water came down into the car in thin streams. We moved grandmother's suitcase away from the water and sat on, huddled together. It was impossible to sleep, sitting erect on hard bags, but we must have dozed now and then. In the morning we reached Pskov. It was the forepost of the German army.

Everything there smacked of military discipline ; the station was crowded with busy soldiers and swaggering haughty officers.

The prisoners were ordered out and convoyed, this time under German guards, to a long row of barracks and tents. The tent we were taken to was bare except for plain bunks, made of shelves, in tiers three deep, each with a coarse blanket. Grandmother gave one look, then turned and, in her beautiful German, addressed the soldier who had conducted us there :

" What is this ? "

" This is the *Entlausungsstation* (delousing station), *gnädige Frau*," he replied. " You will stay here for two weeks, get deloused, inoculated for typhus, and then go on to Germany."

" Please lead me to the commanding officer," said grandmother.

The soldier started to answer, then changed his mind and went ahead toward a small building, grandmother, sister, and I following closely. We were led into a small whitewashed room with a big desk at which the commanding officer sat. The soldier saluted and said :

" *Herr Kapitan, diese Dame möchte mit Ihnen sprechen.*" He then stood aside.

The captain, a blond, stiff-looking German, rose, and then sat down again. I believe if he had had chairs in his room he would have asked us to sit down. There was something about grandmother that always commanded instant respect. She was so quietly dignified and proud and her blue-grey eyes looked so straight at one.

" What can I do, *gnädige Frau ?* " he said politely, though rather stiffly.

" *Herr Kapitan*," said grandma, " neither my granddaughters nor I have ever had any lice. We are clean. We have just come from Petrograd where there is no typhus. We are not ill, but if I have to stay in this tent for two weeks, then I shall surely become ill and may die. And I am an old woman and I want to go home to die in peace."

Sister and I held our breath, never taking our eyes off the officer. Surely on this small pause hung the decision. The officer, in turn, looked at grandmother. It was as if he waited for her to say more. Then, perhaps, he could argue. But grandma did not say

anything. She had said what she wanted, and waited
for the officer to see the wisdom of her remark. She
just looked at him, waiting, with quiet dignity. And
the officer lowered his eyes, coughed, and said :
" *Wohin fahren Sie* ? "
" To Lodz."
" The military express train for Warsaw is leaving
in an hour. I shall arrange for you to go on it. You
understand I am making a great exception."
" *Ich danke schön,*" said grandmother, smiling.
Something inside me danced as I thought : " If he
only knew we were Poles ! "
We all smiled. It seemed a little incredible. The
officer smiled back and then demanded our passports.
The formalities had to be attended to, he said, whereupon we handed him our lovely false passports, which
were duly examined, and supplied, each, with a little
green slip and a pink slip testifying that we had been
deloused and inoculated. An hour later we sat in a
coupé of a fast *D. Zug* (express train).

In twenty-four hours we got into the station at
Warsaw.

It was that easy ! When I think of the hardships
all the rest of our relatives in Russia had to go through
during the first two years of starvation of 1919 and 1920,
the terror and disease and the slow, tortuous returns
home, I feel a little ashamed. . . . Of course it was
grandmother. Grandmother's lovely personality was
at the bottom of it all. All her life she had always told
me that one should trust to God and everything would
always turn out well in the end. If you only had the
real faith, the complete trust, nothing could go wrong.
Now I don't know just how much of a hand God had
in all these affairs, but I do know for sure that her
belief in the better side of people, her own sweet,
unswerving trust in the ultimate triumph of good,

has always made people want to do things for her,
so perhaps she was right after all.

Not that this trip from Pskov to Warsaw was all
sugar and cream. It had its bitter dregs. As the
hours went by it became increasingly hard to pretend
to be German and, so to say, like it.

There were three German officers in that compartment with us. I don't remember their faces, but I
remember their manner. It was arrogant, stiff, and
haughtily patronising. It was a military train and
probably they thought it a piece of impudence on the
part of the camp commandant to put three female
civilians into their compartment. They ignored us
at first, completely. Then, having taken a better look,
they thawed a bit. They ogled my sister and they
ogled me, and with each look their eyes grew kindlier
and oilier. They began to talk : they asked grandmother whether she wanted the window raised or
lowered, and whether smoke disturbed her, and, finally,
where we were travelling to.

" I live in Lodz," grandmother answered briefly.
This was true, for, although grandmother usually
peregrinated continually between her children's families
scattered all over Russia, her home town was
Lodz.

" There are quite a few Germans in Lodz," said one
of them, a fact which we did not dispute. As a matter
of fact, it helped us ; it helped to carry on the decep-
tion. But the conversation developed and soon there
were aspects which I had never expected.

How was it with the Bolsheviks ? the officers wanted
to know. Very bad ?

" Very bad," grandmother consented.

Oh, well, they were fools, ignorant, stupid savages,
these Russians, the officer continued. Russia could
never be the same again. All of Poland was going

to be German forthwith. The Poles would like it
better, too. They would have *Kultur*. . . .

"Undoubtedly the Germans could teach the Poles
a lot," grandmother said diplomatically.

"You should see what we did for Poland," the
officer said. "We have laid miles of new tracks,
telephone connections, a new highway, the one to
Brest-Litovsk. This summer we will finish with
France. . . ."

I could not hold out any longer. What was the
news from the front ? I asked. I was consumed with
curiosity, for since the October revolution we had
known practically nothing of Western affairs.

"Oh, *Deutschland* is winning," said the officer—this
in June 1918 ! "Now that we have no trouble on the
Russian frontier, we throw most of our men on the
Western Front. Every six weeks we send a few
regiments to Poland, to feed them up ; then back
to France in three days. We have a marvellous
system ; all the fast trains are requisitioned by the
army." . . .

It was horrible. We did not know that most of this
was Prussian boasting. . . . "This, too, is a military
D. Zug," I thought. It actually seemed incredible,
for moments, to be going at this breakneck speed in a
narrow-gauge German *Schnellzug* over these Russian
flat landscapes. It was as if something had gone
wrong. The German officer explained proudly that
they had shifted all the rails in Poland, so they could
use their own trains. What a job ! . . .

This continued, on and off, for most of the day, until
it was hard to look overjoyed with these German
victories and the *Kultur* which was being brought to
Poland, and the narrow-gauge trains. And we welcomed the night when we could retire to sleep. We
dozed, sitting and putting our heads on each other's

H

shoulders, and when morning came we were in Poland. . . .

The train stopped at a small station. German soldiers and officers and Polish civilians and peasants thronged the platform, and then we saw Polish women coming out with trays from the station building toward the train, and these trays were piled with rolls —authentic white bread—and there were small pots of coffee, and sandwiches. . . . Oh, my God, white rolls ! Now we were sure we had left Russia behind. . . .

Part II

POLAND

I

WARSAW IN 1918

WHEN we got out at the station in Warsaw we did not hesitate as to our next step. We did not offer thanks to God, Ransome, or the German captain for our miraculous escape from the Soviets ; we did not start a frantic search for our relatives ; we did not even try to find a room in a hotel, though we had heard that Warsaw was dreadfully congested and people had to sleep in waiting-rooms at stations for days. We had one unanimous idea, and it was grandmother who voiced it :

" Children," she said, " we shall check our bags and go to a restaurant." .... And I still remember the taste of that schnitzel. Having tasted practically no meat in two years except a little horse meat now and then, this seemed a gorgeous meal. It consisted of soup, meat, potatoes, salad, and a simple dessert. My sister and I felt like having one more like it, but grandmother said no. She told us to eat slowly and chew carefully. Grandmother herself ate very little. She complained that too much food hurt her. Although we did not know it then, the cancer which she had undoubtedly contracted in Russia, and of which she died a few years later, had already begun its deadly task. ...

I recall, too, looking through the big plate-glass window of the restaurant at the street, trying to discover some visible signs of the *Kultur* the German

officer spoke so much of on the train.　I couldn't find it.
What I saw was German officers usurping the sidewalks while the Polish male population walked in the
streets.　Later we found out that with the women this
regulation was not so strictly enforced.　However, the
young and pretty ones were subjected to such remarks,
compliments, and even more tangible forms of German
admiration that most of them, too, preferred the street
to the sidewalk.

There was a general feeling of depression, poverty,
and fear.　The fear was of a different sort from that we
felt in Russia as members of the bourgeoisie, a class
that was being outclassed and destroyed.　The fear was
that of a civilian population under the thumb of an
inimic, military rule.　And it was not pleasant.

Nor, as we found out by and by, was food so good or
so plentiful.　In the restaurant, at the exorbitant price
we paid in the heat of enthusiasm over our escape,
schnitzels were still to be had.　But the majority of the
people in the cities subsisted on a variety of ersatzes :
ersatz butter, ersatz coffee, ersatz tea, and so forth, and
all the left-overs which the Germans kindly allowed
them, after exporting the best of the land to Germany.
Poland was being gradually denuded of everything—
food, clothing, machinery, copper.　Anything that
was of copper was requisitioned—door handles, pots,
pans, parts of machines in factories, even the copper
leaves with which the cupola of the Russian Church was
covered.

At our uncle's, where we stopped for a while, they
used their fine old table linen for shirts for the men and
the curtains and drapes for dresses for the women.
And this had been a well-to-do house, for my uncle was
the director of a big bank.

It was, however, only when we got our jobs that we
fully understood the Polish situation.

Due to uncle's pull in banking circles, I got the job of a switchboard girl in one of the banks. All banks were under German control. My salary was two hundred marks a month. I could spend these two hundred marks in a variety of ways ; I could, for instance, pay :

1. A month's rent for a small room—and live on air.
2. Buy one shoe (a pair costing 400 marks)—no room, no food.
3. Buy a few yards of dress goods—no shoes, no food, no room.
4. Have enough food for a week—no dress, shoes, or rent !

The problem was quite exciting. It was solved by my uncle and aunt's kind invitation to stay with them until things got better. Similarly another aunt offered a temporary home to my sister. We paid part of our salaries for food.

My sister, for slightly higher pay, got a job as a pianist in a third-rate movie house. She provided the musical atmosphere from 5 p.m. to midnight for the " silents " of those days. Being extremely gifted, with a rare talent for improvisation, she seldom used music, but improvised as she went along, looking at the picture from behind the screen which was placed to hide the piano.

Even so, she used to get tired, physically tired, from playing continually for so many hours every day. On Sundays the movie started at two—it was the children's matinée hour—and occasionally I substituted for her a few hours on these days. Not being able to improvise, I played pieces which I arranged in advance to suit the pictures ; but three hours was usually all I could manage. For I, too, had my own tiredness, my own private aches—in my elbow and in my ear. There were no earphones in those days, and for the eight hours of my shift at the bank I had to hold the heavy phone handle in my left hand, using the right alone for pulling the plugs, making connections, jotting down messages. Toward the last hour of my shift each day, both my ear and my elbow were numb with a dull, seemingly never-ending pain.

My ear ached from listening for far-away sounds, from pressing the earpiece tightly to the ear, and from the constant straining to hear when trying to make long-distance connections in the days when telephones were far less perfected than they are now. The long-distance calls I tried to make were usually with Berlin, Breslau, or Dresden. It took anywhere from fifteen to twenty minutes or half an hour to make a connection, and after accomplishing this feat, after saying, " *Hallo* . . . *Hallo* . . . Berlin ? *Warschau spricht* . . . *Amtlich* . . . *Dringend* . . . *Hallo, Hallo*, Berlin," dozens of times and finally getting the German director on the line, I would listen in with curiosity to some such conversation as this :

" *Wie geht's, Herr Direktor ?* "

" *Danke, gut*, etc. . ."

Business . . . Business . . . Business. . . .

And then :

" *Meine Frau* would like to have another ham like the one you sent us last week. . . . Yes, as big as you can get it ; and five pounds of butter and some bacon. . . . Yes, very good, very good. Sugar too, if you can get it. About twenty pounds. . . . *Danke* . . . *Danke.* . . ."

" Not at all. . . . Not at all, *lieber Herr Direktor*, I will send it by the express train to-day. My *Frau* sends her warmest greetings. . . ."

" *Hallo* . . . *Hallo*, Berlin ! "

" *Hallo* . . . *Hallo* . . . Dresden ? *Die Dresdener Bank* . . . *Ja. Warschau, dringend* . . . *Amtlich.*"

Business . . . Business . . . Business. . . .

Food! Food! Food! Hams, porklings, butter, eggs, geese, flour. . . .

The wives of the bank *Direktors* in Berlin and Dresden and Leipzig and Breslau gave their orders to the *Direktors* in Warsaw just as one leaves orders with a grocer, and our *Direktor* most obligingly sent them all this food. . . . And at the table of my uncle, the *Polish* bank *Direktor*, there was ersatz butter, ersatz coffee, and rarely any meat. And Stefan, my cousin, insisted gravely that the soap the Germans manufactured in Poland was made with the fat from the corpses of Polish soldiers because all animal fats were exported to Germany. Of that, I have no proof.

2

AN URGENT CALL

IT might have been on November 5th or 6th that this happened. I don't know for sure now. And it doesn't matter, except to historians. All I recall is the fearful, heart-stilling excitement of it.

It was a call from Berlin. The connection was hard to make, wheezy with overtones, hums, and noises. Then the director of the Berlin Deutsche Bank spoke to our director. No hearty *Lieber Herr Direktor*; no preliminary greeting; just a throaty, hoarse cry:

"*Alles ist verloren!* (All is lost!) Entire army deserting. An outbreak in Kiel. . . ." His voice broke and our director could only stammer back:

"*Was?* . . . *Was?* . . . *Um Gottes Willen!*" (What? . . . What? . . . For God's sake!)

"Pack and leave. Leave at once! Leave everything!"

The connection was broken. I sat stunned, with the earphone still jammed tightly to my ear, the plug motionless in my other hand. I was in the same frozen position, trying dimly to see all the implications of this frantic call, when I saw the director himself appear behind the glass partition of the door. He was a fat, gross German, with staring blue eyes. I forget his name.

The switchboard room was a tiny cubicle with the switchboard and one chair and just one door leading into a hall. The director entered swiftly, slammed the door behind him, and, staring at me with his big, blue hard eyes, said :

"Have you been listening in?"

"No, *Herr Direktor*," I lied. It was strictly forbidden to listen in after the connections were made. But my face did not lie well enough, and with a sullen glare the director turned on his heel and left the little room. To my surprise I heard the key click in the door. Ten minutes later, to my still more intense surprise, I saw one of the German soldiers, doing guard duty outside the bank, come and station himself outside the door in the hall. Thoughts raced frantically through my mind. . . . Should I call my uncle . . . or the editors of the Polish papers? . . . If I talked Polish, they wouldn't catch me at it . . . and if they did, what could they do? . . . Jail. Surely not the firing squad! But why was the Berlin *Direktor* so excited? And ours too? Their voices were full of funk. . . . "*Ein Ausbruch in Kiel*," he had said. . . . What was Kiel . . . a small port on the Baltic. . . . My God, the sailors! And the army deserting. Could Trotsky have been right? Was this the German revolution?

While I was in the midst of these conjectures, the

girl who had the next shift at the switchboard came on. The soldier unlocked the door to let her in, but as I wanted to get out, he refused to let me through the door, saying he had orders not to.

" You have no right to do that," I said, flaring up.

" It's *Herr Direktor's* orders," he said.

" But you can't keep me locked in a switchboard room. Suppose I want to go out ? Or go to the toilet ? How long am I supposed to be here ? "

" I shall conduct you to the toilet, *Fräulein,*" he said, with German gravity. I led the way, trying to think of some plan for escaping ; but none offered itself and after spending ten minutes in the toilet pondering over the problem, while the soldier stood outside on guard, I returned with him to the switchboard room.

The moment he had locked the door behind us, I overwhelmed the relief girl with questions. She was a big, heavy girl, a young Jewess of very phlegmatic temperament.

" What was in the papers to-day ? " I asked. " Anything about Germany ? "

" Nothing special," she said. " But the town is full of rumours. They say there is revolution in Germany—the Kaiser has escaped. The people are frightfully excited. . . ."

They were ? My God, so was I ! A revolution in Germany ! And she had said : " Nothing special."

I do not recall what happened for the next hour or so. I do not recall when I got out of the bank. The excitement seemed to increase by the minute. Calls were so constant we could not cope with them ; conversations were broken off in the middle ; the German officials seemed frantic with panic ; everything was in a state of flux, and sometime in the afternoon the soldier outside just disappeared.

A little later I saw the bank *Direktor* pass by in a

civilian suit, though ordinarily he wore the uniform of a colonel. A Polish employee of the bank came and unlocked the door. I walked out. . . .

And that was the first day of Polish independence— after one hundred and fifty years of subjugation. Not technically, perhaps ; technically, it might have been on November 9th, the day Josef Pilsudski was returned by the Germans from the prison in Magdeburg, and was acclaimed by the crowds and made Chief of State. Or, perhaps, on that later day when the big moguls in Versailles signed the final treaty.

In reality, however, I think it was on that day full of rumours, enthusiasms, and fervent hopes being finally realised, when the streets were full of people and Polish boys were disarming German soldiers. What an odd picture it made—our slim, Polish youngsters, most of them undernourished, poorly dressed, and the square-headed, pink-faced German soldiers, who had suddenly lost all their assurance and swagger. The Prussian superiority complex, the *Gott-für-uns* and *Deutschland-über-alles* spirit, dinned into them so carefully all their life in school, in drill, even in church, was turned inside out and showed its lining of fear and insecurity. They gave way almost without a struggle. As to the officers, there were hardly any of them on the streets any more. To be sure, there appeared a lot of funny-looking men in ill-pressed clothes, but then, who can recognise a German officer in an ill-fitting civilian suit, with his Prussian moustaches shaved off ?

Again, as during the Russian revolution, I can only describe the streets, being just an ordinary person, without any knowledge of the behind-the-scenes activities. What struck me very forcibly, I recall, was the efficiency with which these Polish boys managed the disarming business. Some of them had guns, some

had old, funny-looking pistols ; some, I suspect, were
unarmed. But they all seemed to know exactly how to
proceed about it. The moment they approached any
soldiers they issued a short command ; then, while the
tall, uniformed men were taken aback, or merely surprised, or even smiled incredulously, the boys would
take off their guns and sling them over their own
shoulders. In the gate of a house on Krolewska Street
I saw a youngster, not more than thirteen, take a huge
German soldier's gun, inspect it right there and then,
very businesslike, and fling away his own poor piece in
the gutter ; then he put the newly acquired weapon on
his back, where it looked too big. The German looked
on, smiled and walked off.

The boys knew all about arms. . . . How did they ?
There was the " P.O.W."—mysterious initials, mysterious insignia. On that day it shed its furtiveness.
It blossomed out, the *Polska Organizacja Wojskowa*
(Polish Military Organisation)—Pilsudski's famous
troops which were started by him in a small unit in
Galicia (then under Austria), with the Austrian Government's consent. This regiment, composed mostly of
young students, had spread rapidly all over Poland,
and everywhere they drilled and practised secretly.
Now it was there, in the open. The new Poland was
terribly poor. It had nothing to start with. But it
had an army which was created for just such an
emergency as this.

One of my cousins, Stefan Kinel, whom I regarded as
a mere child, was a soldier of the P.O.W. He was just
seventeen and he had been in the secret army for two
years.

3

THE RELIEF MISSION

THE work at the Mission was far more interesting than the work at the bank. The man who offered it was also interesting. He was a fat, elderly man with the mobile face of an actor, twinkling shrewd eyes, and a bad accent. His name was Dr. Bogen.

On hearing of the arrival of foreign missions, consuls, and other officials, I had asked my uncle for a letter of introduction to the British Consul, whom he knew well. My uncle went into his study to write the note, when suddenly something occurred to him, and he turned around and said, smiling :

" How would you like to work for an American ? He is the head of an American-Jewish Relief Mission and he came to my bank this morning. He left a lot of money at the bank and he will probably pay more than a consul. Shall I call him up ? "

" Well, do . . ." I said. And so it happened that I hunted up Dr. Bogen the next day in a small hotel and was promptly engaged as his secretary. The pay was eight hundred marks. A month later he raised it to twelve hundred. That the eight hundred marks was equivalent only to about twenty dollars in American money did not occur to me then. Nor did I realise that the raise was not really a raise from his point of view— for the Polish mark had fallen correspondingly in the interval. There were, however, in those days, many things of a practical nature that did not occur to me.

Eight hundred marks was simply four times as much as two hundred and it meant a sort of breathing spell.

I stayed with this Mission for three years and I

FIELD RELIEF

Warsaw 1919

dare say I learned more about America and American methods than I have since, living in the United States for the last ten—perhaps because a group of people transported bodily into an alien environment stands out in much sharper relief than in a more homogeneous environment. Everything my employer did, the way he did it and the pace he set, seemed fantastic. Even the memory of the months spent on the English newspaper in Petrograd with Mr. Vezey and Sok paled in comparison.

The first thing Dr. Bogen did, up in his dingy room of a second-rate hotel, was to dictate telegrams. They were telegrams addressed to Baron Rothschild in London, Nathan Straus, Felix Warburg, in New York, and people like that. They were very long and very sentimental and in each he asked for money. He would ask for fifty thousand dollars or twenty thousand pounds and he would call them " appropriations," and in these telegrams he would say : " Children on streets barelegged in rags need urgently special appropriation for shoes stop," or, " Polish Jewry indescribable plight appeal to English Jewry," and so on, and transcribing these long telegrams on my typewriter I would wonder vaguely why Dr. Bogen should be in such a stew about the barelegged children, for most of the poor children in Poland ran barefoot all summer from preference and in winter they stayed indoors. I, myself, in my childhood, during the summers spent on my grandmother's estate in Poland, ran around barefoot all day because I liked it. And as to the lack of shoes—why, even as I was taking down these telegrams, my sister and I had only one sound pair of shoes between us, and another pair of slippers that leaked. The one of us that had more walking to do on each particular day would wear the pair of high shoes ; the other the slippers. But of course I did not speak of this to Dr. Bogen. Besides, with the magnificent salary I was getting I hoped to be able to get a new pair soon perhaps in two or three months' time.

The work itself was very interesting and the pace Dr. Bogen set was extraordinary ; for he, the chief director and organiser, was merely doing his scouting during these first few days. Within two or three weeks we had become organised. We had big offices on Nowo Senatorska Street, now swarming with American social workers in grey-green uniforms, with nurses, office help, and the various petitioners. We had huge warehouses where all the canned milk and hardtack and rice and flour and cocoa, which Dr. Bogen got from the American army supplies in France at nominal prices, were stored for distribution.

Dozens of milk stations were established at which needy children were given milk. It was canned milk, which was diluted with boiling water from huge boilers that were kept going all day long. Later they were given regular little meals, rice gruel and cocoa and hardtack.

Then there was the field work. A squadron of Dodge and Ford touring cars, which Dr. Bogen got cheaply from the American army supplies in France, were used for that. The country—that is, that part of the country which could be reached—was divided into sections and each car covered one section. There were three people allotted to each car—a local Polish chauffeur, an American social worker, and a nurse. Stocked with canned milk and hardtack and later things like soap, flour, linen, and other supplies, they would follow a definite route, stopping at each village and hamlet always at a certain time ; and the peasants in the place would have their boiling water ready in vats, wash-tubs, kettles, in one big hut, and when the car drove up the children would already be standing

in line, waiting. The moment the car stopped, the
nurse and the social worker would get out and carry
the cans into the house, open them as fast as they
could, dilute the canned milk with the boiling water,
and hand it out to the children. There was also another line, with the old people, the really old who could
not chew army tack ; they too were given canned milk,
like the children. But that line was very small ; it was
small because the old people had mostly died off.
There weren't any really small babies either, for such
as were born now and then died off very rapidly when
the mothers couldn't nurse them, so that most of the
children in these tiny villages were older than four.

Sitting at my typewriter and writing the reports
which the field workers made out once a week, on their
return trip to the office, I often thought I should like
to go on one of these trips. Once or twice I asked Dr.
Bogen whether I couldn't go in place of a nurse, and he
would pat me on the shoulder or squeeze my arm in his
jovial American way and say : " Sure, I'll let you go,
little girl. But we can't spare you now. You know
there isn't anyone here that could take your place.
You wait till we get some more stenographers from
New York." And I waited patiently until there came
a day when I lost all desire to go on a trip with the
field workers to see the sights.

It was a day when Lieutenant Schein, one of our
field workers who had returned from his weekly trip,
had come to me to make out his report.

The lieutenant was a non-commissioned officer, a big,
dark, good-looking man in his thirties, kindly and
happy, perpetually smiling, and with the heart of a
child. I liked him for that and I also liked him for
another reason. He never dictated his reports, as the
other men did, but just told me about the trip and let
me write it all in my own way. I enjoyed that.

I

" Back in the United States," he told me, he used to
be a salesman for the Singer Sewing Machine Company
and, as he put it, he " was always on the go. Never
had time to study much . . . so you just fix up the
report for me, Miss Kinel, will you ?   And I'll just tell
you about it in my own way."   And that suited me
perfectly.

On that day, having settled his huge bulk in a chair
near my desk, having blown his nose and coughed a
couple of times—for the lieutenant was not a very
articulate man and the formulating of sentences even
in " his own way " was always a hard task—he began
to speak of his week's tour.   Up to a point the report
proceeded in the usual manner.   Through his halting
words I could see the small villages where he stopped,
the lines of children and old people waiting patiently
for the food—those daily rations of milk and hardtack
which were their only sustenance—their thanks and
their wails as the little touring car sped away to the
next village.   I saw it all quite clearly, I had taken
down so many similar reports ; and then the lieutenant
proceeded with his account of a trip into new territory—
the farthest they had yet reached—and he said :

" We came to a place where the village was supposed
to be.   But there was no village.   No houses at all.
Fences all gone too, and the chauffeur—you know him,
Miss Kinel—nice fellow, smart—he kinda looked
around and said he didn't know it, though he had been
there before the war.   Well, I got down anyway and
began to look around, and there was some old dug-outs,
and when I looked in there was people in them dug-outs
and they was scared stiff.   We got a Jewish man to
talking and he couldn't get to understand who we
were—thought perhaps we were another army.   My
God, we couldn't make them believe we came with
help.   They were worse than scarecrows, those people

—skin and bones and filthy rags. And when I asked about children, they said most of the children had died and the few that were left were in the forest up in the trees. And—say, Miss Kinel, say—when we got them down from them trees. . . ." And here the lieutenant stopped, his big happy face puckered up like a child's ; he began to shake and covered his face with his hands. I sat perfectly still, waiting until he wiped his face with his handkerchief and calmed down a little.

"Well, when we rounded up a few," he continued, still sobbing a little, "we couldn't do anything with them ; like wild animals they were, skinny and frightened, and their lips weren't pink but sort of green, and their ears too, and the older folks said it was from the grass they ate and the leaves off the trees. That's what they mostly lived on, grass and wild berries and roots. We took some of them to Suwalki and the doctor told us their blood was that colour because of eating nothing but grass. They said most of these children died from the least little scratch ; their blood wouldn't get thick-like. They can never operate on them. And in the next place we stopped they still had a couple of shacks and some boiling water ready for the canned milk, so we fed them and then began distributing the soap, and you know half of those kids *ate it* and *they liked it*. It's the fat in it. Gosh "—and Lieutenant Schein smiled, though his eyes were still wet—" I had been through the war, you know, but them poor people in the dug-outs and the kids in the trees is the worst I ever lived through. Gosh, Christ Almighty ! " And the lieutenant wiped his face again.

So that was that. I " fixed " his report in as good and as simple English as I knew how, and in the process I lost all desire to go on a trip with the field worker and see " the sights." From subsequent reports I learned that there were sections in the Podol and in Volhynia which various armies had passed through nine and sometimes as many as eleven times, Russian, German, Russian again, German, Soviet, Polish, Ukrainian (the Ataman Petlura), Polish again, Russian, and so forth, and as each time the soldiers took away whatever they could lay their hands on, the people in these villages had nothing left for themselves, each army requisitioning whatever it could. When these people were finally removed from the ruins and dug-outs to the little cities in the interior, their children of eight or nine and thereabouts had the times and the scares of their lives getting acquainted with *the world*. None of these children had ever seen an animal ; cats, dogs, horses, cows, were all new to them, for they had none in the Godforsaken no man's land where they had spent their miserable, starved little lives living on roots and leaves.

4

INDIVIDUAL CASES

THE blind man was an individual case and I think I shall remember him all my life.

The blind man was very unfortunate, not only because he was blind and sick and penniless, but because he did not belong to any category under which we distributed help and so was doomed to starve. For that is how social work, scientific charity, operates. I couldn't quite understand it then and I am not sure I understand it now.

I remember well the first time he came in : small, emaciated, shabby, in an incredibly frayed and aged frock coat and striped trousers, with dark glasses shielding his almost sightless eyes, a cane in his hand, he walked in slowly. He was very erect and was enveloped in that tremulous, defensive dignity which is so disconcerting and pathetic to deal with in social work. For you dare not be rough and ready, you have to play up to it, to play the game of dignity, lest this awful dignity turn to dust and leave a pitiful, cringing, lost creature.

He walked slowly across the length of the room, stopped at my desk, cleared his throat, and asked if he could see the director of the Mission.

Something in his accent caught my ear and I replied in Russian. (He had addressed me in bad Polish.) At the sound of Russian he almost went to pieces, his hands began to shake and he became incoherent.

" *Gospodi* (God), how fortunate—you speak Russian —I am from Siberia—my Polish isn't much good. Please, please announce me to the director ! "

" You will have to tell your business to me," I said as gently as possible. " The director is busy," and I offered him a chair.

He begged and expostulated, as they all do, and then subsided suddenly and in tremulous accents told his story. He had been book-keeper in a bank in Omsk when the Bolsheviks came, and he fled to Moscow because he had relatives there—but they were gone, somebody had said, gone to the Ukraine, so he made his way there. It took him months, months of privation, and he was very sick with some eye infection and lost his eyesight. He could just see in glimpses and couldn't work.

" I cannot beg on the streets," he said with that dreadful dignity, " I am educated. I have been a book-keeper. Will you let me speak to the director, please, *baryshnia*, I beg of you ? "

I rose, undecided. It was the rule to send all beggars

away, for all help and all relief were distributed through the local agencies.

" I am sorry, but the director can't possibly see you," I said. " You will have to apply to the community for help ; we do not handle individual cases, we just give all the charity organisations funds for their regular work."

" But all the charity organisations have turned me away, *baryshnia*, because I am Russian, I do not belong. They have their own poor. I cannot beg on the streets. I am a book-keeper. I used to work in the bank. . . ."

In desperation I went to the director in charge and told him the story, but he was very impatient. " Send him away. Send him away," he said. " We don't handle individual cases. Why, we would be swamped —he's got to apply to the charity in his own district, wherever he lives—just like the rest."

" But they won't help him because he is a stranger. A Russian is a foreigner in Poland now ; and he doesn't want to beg," I replied.

" Well, just tell him to go. We can't do it. If we do it once, we will be swamped ; we have no appropriations for individuals, only for institutions."

And so I sent him away, though he did not go at once, but sat for a while, very erect on his chair, clothed in his pitiful dignity which gave one the awful feeling that it might crumble away any instant. And I returned to my desk, wondering how it was that we who handled hundreds of thousands of dollars for all sorts of relief of the poor could not give a few dollars to this one blind man—wondering about the system that allowed such things.

Nor was this the end ; he came again and again until I began to hate the very sight of him and then hate myself for feeling that way. I hated to watch him

walk slowly, probing with his cane, sheathed in that
dignity which prevented rough speaking, while he told
in a tremulous voice of his life as a book-keeper, the
head of a bank department in Omsk, of the horror of
the Bolsheviks and all his travails, and the horror of
going blind, and his inability to beg.

" Allow me, *baryshnia*, I cannot beg in the streets ;
I used to be the chief book-keeper in the Asiatic Bank "
— and so on and on and on, his shaking hands on the
knob of his cane ; his legs in the striped trousers ex-
tending so stiffly ; his shabby frock coat hanging almost
to the floor ; his thin beard shaking as he spoke.   He
could not take " no " for an answer, yet one could not
speak to him as one does to a beggar.

One day, unable to stand it any longer, I opened the
drawer and took out my bag.   I couldn't offer him
much—enough for some food for a few days . . . I
wondered how to do it, how to offer it.   At this
moment Dr. Hershfield, who was taking Dr. Bogen's
place at the time, opened his door and walked in.   He
saw what was going on.   Quickly he pulled out his
own wallet, took out a few hundred marks, and gave
it to the book-keeper.   The man rose and thanked
him—with tremulous dignity, as one gentleman to
another ; then walked slowly away.   Dr. H. turned to
me and explained that what he had done was wrong.
He explained why it was wrong and how it established
a bad precedent.   Once you gave some money to cases
like that, he explained, you got them on your hands,
they came again and again, and you couldn't possibly
support them all your life out of your private pocket.
They belonged to institutions and one shouldn't make
an exception.

That time, after the blind man went away, I swore to
myself that if he ever came again I would speak my
mind ; I would tell him exactly what had hovered in

my mind for days. I would hand him the gun—for I intended to borrow a gun for this next visit of his—and I would tell him that he was an exception to our rules and regulations and therefore was not entitled to relief, and since he could not beg on the streets because it was not compatible with his past life of head book-keeper, I was gladly lending him the gun. And would he please do it soon because I could stand it no longer, watching him come into the office and sit in the chair with that false, trembling dignity of his. . . .

But he never came back.

She was Russian, too. And, technically, she was also a beggar. The main difference, however, between her and the blind book-keeper was that, whereas he begged for a little money which would keep him from the streets, she begged for thousands of dollars, as many as she could get. And she got them. I have since discovered that if you do things in a big and arrogant way, you are apt to succeed much better than if you ask only for what is your just due.

She sailed into the main room of the Mission one day, brushing past the amazed office boy as a ship passes a piece of driftwood, enveloped in an aura of good but pungent perfume, stopped at my desk, and asked for the director, in French. It was the almost perfect but unmistakable French of the Russian aristocrat, and I replied in Russian as I offered a chair. She was all smiles, she was delighted at my speaking her tongue, but she never took the chair ; looking around shrewdly, she chose the right door and walked straight into the director's office. And that was that.

I sat down, amazed. Who was she ? She was a personage in the full sense of the word and she was a Russian beauty—of the old-Russian, the Asiatic type ; stately, tall, full-blown, yet with tiny, most beautiful

hands and feet, a round, fresh face, with big dark eyes,
a small, full, pursed mouth, and cream and rose complexion. Her clothes gave me a sudden, dreadful sense
of my own shabbiness.

But Dr. H. did not know any French, to say nothing
of Russian, and I was called in to interpret. The
Russian lady was Madame X., *née* Tugan-Baranow-
skaya. There were hundreds of Russian refugees in
Warsaw, she said, and more drifting in continually ;
they couldn't return to the Soviets for fear of death, and
she was going to organise relief. There were quite a
number of Jewish people among them and the American-Jewish Relief Mission was bound to help.

We didn't know just how many Jewish people there
were among these refugees Madame spoke of. I don't
think Dr. H. ever troubled to count, either. It would
not have done much good.

She said she wanted twenty thousand dollars to begin
with. She spoke rapidly, suavely, overwhelming Dr.
H. with her talk, brushing away all opposition with
smiles and flashes of her magnificent eyes ; she was a
lady who had been used to implicit, instant obedience,
and it showed in her every gesture and movement. She
did not get the help at once, for the good director had
no authority, but he wired to Paris to Dr. Bogen, and
to New York, and then wrote a long letter to confirm it
all. And in time she got her food and money and other
help. Her husband had been governor of one of the
outlying Polish provinces and she was the sister of the
famous Russian economist Tugan-Baranowski, who
lived in Paris.

When Madame finally left, Dr. H. accompanied her
as far as my room and, watching her departure, he
turned to me, twitched his nose, and said : " Whew,
what a woman ! "

.   .   .   .   .

Then there was the Russian girl. That was quite a
bit later, when the camp for the Russian refugees had
already been organised. She came into my room one
morning, having somehow slipped past the ever-
vigilant office boy, and, standing close beside my desk,
she began to speak rapidly, as if afraid that I might not
listen to her story.

" I had heard about you in the camp, *baryshnia*—
that you spoke Russian. They feed us there and we
have shelter, but they don't give any clothes. And if
I could get just some decent clothes, I could get a job
as nursemaid ; I have it promised to me. Would you
ask the *Amerikantzy* for some clothes, *baryshnia,
milaya ?* "

Although she was asking for a favour, there was
nothing of the beggar in her, nothing abject or timid.
She was tall, stocky, strongly built, with a typical flat,
round Russian face, and brown lively eyes that looked
at you with a sort of fresh frankness.

" The Mission doesn't give individual case relief,"
I began my old formula, hating myself as I spoke. . . .

" *Oh, baryshnia,* but I would repay it later ! All I
want is one shift. I can get the job, but the woman
has no clothes to give me. All I have is what is on my
back." And suddenly, without warning, she opened
her thin, worn, blue coat and I saw that underneath she
was stark naked. It was as if someone had struck me.
I forgot all the damned rules and became just a girl, a
girl like her, only a little older.

" You come to my place to-night. After six. Here
is the address," I said quickly, and I gave it to her on a
slip of paper. " Now run ! " Obeying instinctively,
quickly, she went away at once, but as she was going
through the hall door Dr. Hershfield came out of his
office. He eyed her departing form suspiciously.

" Now who was that ? "

" A girl from the Russian camp," I said, and volunteered no more than that.

He gave me a sharp look.   As a rule, I always told him all about these applicants, their little tales of woe.

" What did she want ? "

" Some clothes."

" Then come in.   I have a few letters.   You tell that boy in the hall not to let these people in.   We don't handle individuals and they can't take your time.   I want these to go off by the Paris pouch."

I smoothed my pad and poised my pencil. . . .

And in the evening, when the girl came to our room, out of the affluence of our own miserable things, the remnants of all the American clothes, now almost four years old, all patched and mended and repatched, we scraped up one chemise and a pair of bloomers and a petticoat, one blouse and an old linen dress.   No skirt—we couldn't spare a skirt, for we had only one each ourselves.   Yet to her even these shabby gifts were overwhelming.   Her eyes shone.   And later she got the job.

5

A POSTAL CARD

" THERE is a card for you—from Russia," my aunt said one day as I came to dinner, and while they hunted for the card I waited in a tumult of conjectures : father, brother, uncles, cousins, aunts—it could have been from any of those whom we had left behind us in Russia, as if beyond a huge, dead wall. . . .   For although we had been in Poland now for nearly a year, we had had no news.   We knew there was a terrible civil war and there was hunger, but beyond that there was silence. . . .

The card was found on a mantelpiece. My cousin handed it to me and I stood transfixed : it was in D.'s handwriting ! It was in Russian all right, and the postmark showed that it was six months old.

I had not heard from D. since that day he left Petrograd with the rest of the Embassy staff. Just on the slight chance that we might escape too, I gave him a Polish address. " I shall write you. I shall write you from England. I will see you again," D. had said. He was standing near the door, in his huge fur coat and fur cap ; his luggage was downstairs. He bent down, kissed me on my mouth, and shut the door. I sat down on a little stool in the hall and cried ; his housekeeper brought me a handkerchief and patted my head. I thought I should never see him again. . . .

All this came back to me while I was reading the pathetic little card. Finally I collected myself : " It is from an old friend, an English boy I met in Petrograd," I said, trying to sound casual. They were just mildly interested in that. " There haven't been any other cards for me, have there ? " I asked presently. " No, of course not," said one cousin, " we would have told you."

In his delightful simple Russian—the Russian of a foreigner—D. wrote that he had written many times, both letters and cards, and that he had had no reply, and that he thought of me all the time. . . .

The card was like a little miracle. That night I put it under my pillow and next morning I went to the British Military Mission and asked permission to send a letter through them. There was no postal communication with the Allied countries as yet and mail abroad could only be sent through diplomatic and military couriers.

The young British officers at the Mission were very polite and affable. They would be glad to transmit any message they said. No trouble at all. Certainly. They were sorry, though, to insist that it should be open. Military censorship.

I didn't like this at all. How could one send a love letter for all these boys to gloat over ? Could I send a wire, I asked ? Yes, certainly, was the reply. It would go to Downing Street and the Foreign Office would transmit it. It would get there in two days. And so I sent a simple wire and the thread of our friendship was resumed again.

If I could have foreseen the misery that fate had in store for us I should never have replied to that card. I ought to have burned it and with it the dreams which it aroused. But none of us can see into the future, and at twenty whose future is not a dream of perfect love and happiness ? And so, until D.'s first long letter came, the first uncensored, sealed letter— which was even more of a miracle—the soiled post-card became a little talisman of happiness which was preserved faithfully under my pillow at night and in my handbag in the daytime. . . .

6

A YOUNG AMERICAN

HE seemed a little naïve and helpless and so aroused my instant sympathy. Of course, all of them seemed to me naïve at first. All the American boys, I mean, who came to work for the J. D. C.[1] from Paris and from New

[1] Officially, the American Jewish Joint Distribution Committee.

York. They seldom knew any languages and seemed
to have no talent for picking up any. Polish, with its
many sibilants, gave them a sort of complex so that
they didn't even try to master it. I remember I
sometimes used to type their address on a little slip of
paper and pin it on their coat lapels so that all they had
to do was to hail a cab, show the slip to the *dorozkarz*
(cab driver), and thus avoid getting lost in the dreadful
wilderness of unpronounceable Polish streets. I
remember, too, how their general ignorance of Poland,
of its history and its position in Europe, used to
astonish me into a feeling of cheap superiority and
amazement. I wondered what they ever learned in
their American schools, outside of sports.

Captain Grey, however, was far from ignorant. I
think he was better educated than most of the other
boys. But he, too, was full of a kind of naïve wonder.
At twenty I was *blasée* and to me he seemed a child of
the New World, that American world which was a mere
infant of a hundred and fifty years, gazing open-eyed
at old, callous Europe, so wise and yet so petty, rooted
in its customs and class prejudices. . . .

Captain Grey liked to ask questions and I liked to
answer them, and so it came to pass that I began
occasionally to look on things Polish from the outside,
as it were, objectively. I saw it for brief moments
through the blue eyes of a young, intelligent, unsophis-
ticated American. The things I had always taken for
granted and had never bothered to think about became
suddenly interesting and changed their aspect.

Captain Grey was at first assigned to the food
squadron which distributed food to starving villages in
the outlying provinces. It was after the first trip, I
believe, that he began to ask me things. He seemed
extremely bothered.

" Do the Polish peasants always kiss one's hand ? "

he asked, and blushed. He used to blush readily. He was about twenty-five, of the Lindbergh type, very tall, slim, and rather shy.

" If they want to express their gratitude, yes. Or, if you are their landlord, or a member of the landlord's family, or even a guest. Why, did a peasant kiss your hand ? "

" Say, when we distributed the canned milk and other stuff, the women came up and tried to kiss my hand. It was awful . . . I . . . I couldn't shake them off."

" Oh, but you shouldn't shake them off," I said, horrified at the insult to the peasant women.

" But it's terribly embarrassing. I don't want them to kiss me. I kept on refusing and they kept on jabbering their Polish and grabbing my hand, and one young woman came up to me and, well . . . embraced me and kissed my shoulder."

I didn't laugh at this. I asked quickly :

" And did you ' shake her off,' too ? "

" Well, sure. I hate that."

" But, Captain, you must never do that. You have offended the woman."

" How ? "

" When a peasant kisses your shoulder, it is a mark of deep gratitude. As a rule they only kiss their land lord's shoulder, the people whom they know and love, for whom they work. . . . If you refuse the embrace, you insult them."

" Well . . . Gosh . . . I can't stand it. Why do they humble themselves ? "

" They do not. It's just a form in which they are used to express their gratitude. They no more think that they humble themselves by doing it than you would in shaking someone's hand heartily. It's just a form," I repeated.

"But it seems so servile. I don't want to appear superior to them."

"You do not appear superior to them. You brought them help from far-away America. Food when they are starving. In their hearts they are as proud as you. They have their dignity."

"Well, I can't stand it."

"You have to. If you keep on ' shaking them off,' as you put it, you hurt their feelings. They have been kissing people's shoulders for hundreds of years. Can't you see? It's a form."

But he couldn't see it. Nothing I said in explanation could make him feel that it was right for some people to kiss other people's shoulders, though he understood that it was merely a form, a gesture. And for the first time in my life I stopped to reflect on what was behind that mere gesture . . . the hundreds of years when the Polish peasants were slaves and when this " gesture "—now merely a form—was really a sign of humility and subjection. It took an American boy's revulsion to Polish formality to make me see this.

Now, fifteen years later, I wonder whether the peasants still kiss the shoulders of the landed gentry. The last time I saw Polish peasants was not in the country at all but in the Polish *Sejm* (parliament), where my father once took me. Paderewski—then Prime Minister —was making some sort of impassioned speech. It was about Silesia and the plebiscite. The peasant delegates—and they numbered by far the most among the hundreds of representatives—listened with opened mouths, very attentively. When they liked something they beat the tables with their calloused fists. Sometimes they guffawed audibly. They looked tremendously solid, hard, canny, and self-sufficient. They looked as if they had come into their own and wouldn't let go. I cannot imagine any one of them going back

to the land and kissing any " gentleman's " hand. . . .
Perhaps they don't. The world nowadays moves
faster than it used to. . . .

7

THEY TURN UP

ONE didn't meet people at the station with flowers in
one's hand and a telegram with the hour of their
arrival in one's pocket. There never was a letter or
any news. There was no postal communication of any
kind. And they didn't really arrive, any of them.
They just turned up. . . .

It was almost two years before any one of our relatives returned from Russia. In 1920, after the last
Bolshevik offensive, they began to arrive. A cousin
turned up in the sky-blue uniform of General Haller's
troops, with a tale of incredible adventures. A week
later his mother arrived with a group of refugees from
South Russia. Neither one knew that the other was
alive. . . . Then the trains with Polish hostages from
the Soviets, which were now exchanged, person per
person, for Bolshevik war prisoners, began to arrive in
Warsaw. Even these people could not be met,
although the lists with their names would be printed in
the papers for weeks in advance. The trains they came
on, the worst, the most broken-down trains in all the
glorious railway system of the Soviets, without windows, without water, without lights, crawled along for
weeks and weeks, at fifteen miles an hour, until they
reached the Polish border and the people were transferred into Polish trains. The prisoners were not

K

allowed to get out at stations ; the hot water—the only
thing the Russian stations had to offer on the way—
was brought to the trains by the Red guards. They
cooked their *kasha* (buckwheat cereal) on little tiny oil
stoves which they carried along, the same oil stoves
on which so many of them had cooked their food in
Moscow when their flats and houses had been requisitioned because they were bourgeois and they had had
to crowd a family into one room.

They turned up, thin, ragged, with tales of hunger
and hardships and sickness and death, all incredibly
happy to be free, to be in Poland ! For a few days
there would be nothing but an endless telling of tales.

" Where is Kuba ? "

" He is in prison. But he will get out. He is
coming with the next batch."

" And Julek ? "

" We don't know. He went south, to the Whites,
when we were still in Petrograd."

" Why isn't Pietrek here ? "

" Pietrek died. Of typhoid."

" Oh. . . ."

And so on and so on and so on. And then, after a
few days, they would start the task of adjusting themselves to the new life—the finding of work, finding of
rooms, getting some decent clothes.

One day an aunt telephoned to the office : " Your
father is here. He just came from Russia. Yes, he
came straight here."

Another exciting evening of talk, talk, talk. Although
nearing sixty, father looked quite well, not half as
emaciated as some of our relatives. His trek from
Russia was like an Odyssey. After we left Petrograd,
he was drafted into Bolshevik services as a " spec "
(specialist), being an engineer of technology with a lot

of administrative experience. He worked on the first
Gosplan and was on a business trip in Kharkov, in the
South, when the White Russians staged an attack and
took the town.   There were many Poles in the region,
more coming daily with the entrance of the Whites,
until there were several hundred.   They banded together, elected father as their informal chief, and
pooled their resources.   They travelled to Odessa,
where father chartered a small steamer and then sailed
down the Black Sea to Rumania.   From Rumania they
made their way to Poland.   The trip took six weeks.

Thus the Polish people made their various treks to
their homeland.   From Russia, from France, from
America, from Switzerland, from Siberia, from the
entire world, the Poles were returning to their resur-
rected country.   Warsaw became a beehive of
repatriates.   Within a year the population rose from
half a million to almost two.

8

A MEETING

EARLY in 1919, D. finally arrived in Danzig from England.   My first meeting with him, after two years of
separation, was not very romantic.   The *sine qua non*
of romance is secrecy.   It would have been so nice to
have gone quietly to the station and boarded the night
train without anyone knowing it—as they do in novels,
where everything can be arranged to suit the pattern. . . .

As it was, I had to get a permit to board the military
train, for there were no others in those days, and get a
visa to Danzig, which was now a free city.   It all took

pull and, worst of all, I had to give a reason. D. had
wired me, begging me to come, as he was swamped
with the work of organising an office and couldn't
possibly leave for a week. Having waited patiently for
more than a year, I could not now wait another week,
not when there were only a few hundred miles separa-
ting us. I went to my director at the Mission.

" Could you wangle me a permit to go to Danzig ? "
I asked. " I want to see a friend. I'll run over for the
week-end and be back Monday."

" I believe so," he said. " Let's go around to the
A. R. A. and see what they can do. They know all the
officials." And then, in the cab, on the way to one of
the offices, he suddenly asked : " Are you engaged to
this boy ? " " No, I am not," I answered, and
promptly lost my reputation. Perhaps not at that
exact moment, but certainly later, after my week-end
trips over to Danzig became rather more frequent. I
didn't care a twopenny damn, for I always adhered to
the Russian point of view that one's personal business
was really personal and should not be confused with
one's work.

In the train that night I could not sleep at all. I
thought of D. and wondered whether he had changed
much, what he would say and how he would look. I
never thought of how I looked myself. And I looked
very badly—not my face, that is, but my costume. . . .

I was incredibly shabby. My coat was five years
old ; when I got it in New York, it had been a lovely
green travelling coat with a big fur collar. Now the
fur was gone and the coat was no longer green : it had
three or four shades, all streaked, and all blending into
a dirty grey-green. The dress, too, was five years old.
Originally it had been a stunning two-piece suit from
Altman's ; in Warsaw, five years later, it had been re-
modelled, or, shall we say, repatched, by a cheap dress-

maker, into a warm dress I used to wear in the office on
the days when I did not wear an old skirt and blouse,
the only other outfit I possessed.   My shoes were high,
coarse Russian boots, completely concealing my slim
feet.   And the hat was a concoction of my own, made
of some green stuff supposedly to match the coat.   It
was all very terrible, but I had been shabby now for
more than two years, most of the people in Russia and
Poland were shabby too, and I was not conscious of it
any longer.

When I got out at the station in the morning, I saw
D. at once, standing at a little distance, quietly scanning the people.   I ran towards him, but he did not
know me.   He did not know me until I was quite
close. . . .

Then, for a while, we were incoherent.   We were
completely stupid.   We either talked together or we
became silent all at once.   We laughed.   Going up in
the lift in the hotel, we held hands, as children do,
and we laughed.   We would talk Russian and then
change into English, and the throbbing excitement of
seeing the familiar face, of hearing the dear voice,
dominated everything so that I could not even understand his words.   The words did not matter, only the
voice, the voice. . . .

The next day I was sick.   The splendid dinner and
the wine D. had ordered for us had proved too much. . . .
I had not had wine or food like this for a long time and
my stomach could not stand it, and so I had to frequent
the bathroom rather too often. . . .   And that same
day, too, we had our first real quarrel.

I had accompanied D. to his office and then returned
to the hotel.   In the lobby the fat, huge porter blocked
my way and pointed to the servants' entrance.   My
amazement and fury were so great that for a moment
I could not speak ; then I looked at him and said icily :

" *Was erlauben Sie sich ?   Ich wohne hier !* " and
swept past him while he stared, open mouthed. . . .

Upstairs, in my room, I stood in front of the mirror.
" What's wrong ? " I thought.   " My clothes are old
but they have no holes.   And they are clean.   Anyone
can tell I am a lady."   The fact is, I had acquired a
Russian's contempt for mere finery and never realised
just how odd I looked.   That night, however, at
dinner, when I told the episode to D. as something
funny, I saw him turn white as he stammered :
" Look . . . why don't you let me get you some things
. . . these are really too awful . . . you can't let these
damned fellows insult you this way."
" No !   My clothes are all right."
" Please do. . . .   I am just rolling in those damned
filthy marks ; we might get rid of them that way. . . .
They have some nice shops here, too.   Please do."
" No.   I hate to borrow.   Next month I shall save
enough to buy a coat ; meanwhile this will have to do.
I look all right."
" No, you don't !   In Petrograd you used to be so
chic. . . .   Why can't you let me lend you a few
pounds ? "
" No.   I am all right.   If you don't like me in
shabby clothes, then you don't care for me at all."
" But it's for your sake !   For you !   And you can
return every damn' penny when you get your
salary."
" No," I repeated in stubborn misery.
Worse was to follow.   The typewriter.   The typewriter was the *pièce de résistance* in a suitcase full of
presents which D. had brought for me from England :
there were a lovely sweater, silk hose, even two pairs of
shoes, one of which was two sizes too large, a fact which
made me furious.   But the most wonderful thing of all
was a shining, brand-new portable Corona, a thing I

had always wanted and dreamt about and could never afford to buy— my special kind of toy.

There it was, standing on the table, and D., rather pleased with it all, watching me open it, watching me insert a sheet of paper. . . .   I put my fingers on the keys and instantly took them off again.   I said in a sulky tone :

" I can't use it."

" Why, what's wrong ? "

" It isn't the right keyboard.   It has only nine keys instead of twelve.   I am used to the touch system.   I can't type on this thing."

" Does it make such a big difference ? " D. said, both amused and anxious.   " I thought it ran all right. We had lots of fun with it in the office.   Our supplies from home aren't in yet, so we used it for our letters."

" That's because none of you knows how to type.   I use the touch system and this keyboard doesn't fit in. If I try to adapt my system to this keyboard, then I won't be able to use the standard keyboard in the office.   You see, I don't look at the keys, it's all in my fingers. . . ."   And so on and so forth, a lengthy elaboration on my precious system. . . .

It never occurred to me that here was a lovely present, an evidence of D's affection which he had brought to please me, to fulfil one of my " dreams." . . . I never saw his side of it at all ; I merely sulked because the thing had the wrong keyboard. . . .   And, of course, I kept the typewriter and had lots of use from it though it did play havoc with my touch system. . . .

It was only one of many quarrels that followed, some about the most trivial things, others about matters less trivial.   D. was still chock-full of principles and, what was worse, conventions, while I, in the Russian manner, was indifferent to these things.   We saw

each other at infrequent intervals, over week-ends,
either in Danzig or in Warsaw, and though we were
intimate now, we were less happy than we had been
before in Petrograd.

" Why didn't you come up to my room ? " I would
say, greeting D. in the lobby of my hotel.

" You know perfectly well why," he would say, rising
stiffly. " Even if you don't think of form, I still do.
For your sake."

Considering that I used to return to the same hotel
from D.'s flat somewhere around the milkman's hour
and the night porter used to return my " Guten *Abend* "
with the pointed greeting of " Guten *Morgen*,
Fräulein," D.'s nice formalities somewhat lost their
point. But he could not change. He was quite rigid.
And as to myself, I was even more so. I was moody,
supersensitive, and obstinate. And the more I realised
that D.'s affection was waning, the worse I became, as
if hemmed in by a vicious circle. . . .

I did not realise all this at the time, though. I was
miserable as only the young can be. Not until the day
I met Sabira did I begin to realise things about myself.
But that was months later. By that time our affair
was on the rocks. . . .

9

SCIENTIFIC CHARITY

THERE were many aspects of social work which, at the
time, I did not understand fully : the insistence on putting people into categories and on investigating ; the
insistence on having only, or mostly, professional social
workers ; the insistence on treating it all as a science,
something systematic and cold. There was no such
science in Poland. Most charitable work was done by

the Church and a whole lot was done privately, without any science about it, without anyone knowing about it, either—the way Jesus prescribed.

Of course, the want and the suffering after the war were on an unprecedented scale. I understood that part of it ; we needed the huge organisation. Yet we refused so many, too, because they didn't fit in, or because they happened to be of a different nationality.

I used to ask a lot of questions about it all and received many replies : " It *is* a science, a social science," one of the workers would explain. " If we didn't investigate, we would contribute charity to people who didn't need it, and that creates parasites. The reason we prefer trained people is because they know so much better how to handle all the departments. Mr. X. gets $10,000 per year. You know why ? Because when we raise funds, when we start a campaign, he gets the biggest contributions ; he knows how to approach Felix Warburg or Straus and get fifty thousand, or a hundred thousand, from them—so he's worth ten thousand a year to us, isn't he ? " " Yes, yes, yes," I would reply to all this, amazed and vanquished. And still I didn't like it ; it was scientific, it was cold, and the very word " charity " was a mockery. I had the silly idea that charity should be given by charitable people, people who had a natural bent for it, for only thus would the people who got it profit—profit in spirit, not in the body only—and so crawl out of the condition in which they needed charity, because they would have courage. It was *very* important to give people faith and courage, and only kind people can give them to others. . . . But these were the sort of ideas one couldn't mention out loud and so I stopped asking useless questions.

But that time when some sort of row arose about our book-keeping—or was it something else ?—and a squad

of certified public accountants descended upon the
Mission—that time, I confess, I became convinced that
red tape, double book-keeping, and science, in the giving
of charity, can go too far.   They reared their heads, so
to say, and devoured their own masters. . . .

The whole thing was very mysterious, of course.
Nothing was mentioned about the coming visitation in
the letters I wrote, or in those I read, either.   One
caught one's superior officers talking in whispers, and
when one entered the room they changed the subject—
awkwardly.   What was an accountant, anyway?   I
asked someone.   From the answer I deduced that he
was a cross between a book-keeper, a detective, and a
tattletale.   Why did we have to have them?   No
reply. . . .

Well, they came.   They descended like an inquisi-
tion.   Very spick and span in their brand-new
uniforms, with huge typewriters that had carriages six
feet long, with adding machines and other red-tape
implements.   They were very important.   Kings of
the Earth, with the rest of us worms, crawling in the
dust.   They made a lot of extra work, of course.   I
used to stay up nights again, making out huge sheets—
statements, they were called—and aside from the old
staff doing all this extra work at extra pay, many more
typists were engaged, which also cost money.   The
accountants themselves were the most expensive.   I
gathered that each of them got $300 a month, plus all
expenses and the cost of the trip from New York to
Warsaw and back.   And their chief probably got more.
And all of it was from the charity funds. . . .

It was on account of these extra typists that we had
a strike.   And when the strike was settled, it cost the
Mission even more than all the cost of the accountants.
And thus it seemed that some of the questions I had
asked had replied themselves—they certainly had.

The typists received a very small salary, so small that they couldn't live on it. There were a lot of them, possibly sixty or eighty, in our remittance department, which was really a sort of bank, transmitting money from individuals in America to their relatives in Poland through the services of the J. D. C., and without, I believe, any charge. And there were almost as many in the new accountants' department, where the men sat all day over their long typewriters making out statements. The American workers, as I have said, received all their expenses and salaries which none of them could possibly spend unless they bought up all of Warsaw, which they sometimes almost did—they bought rugs and art objects and jewellery and they dashed about the city in cabs.

Now the typists grumbled and complained and one day they had a meeting and decided to join the Union of Office Workers. The members of this union were book-keepers, stenographers, typists, and other such white-collar fry.

Before they joined, however, they talked to us other, more privileged, workers, those of us who had rather higher jobs, knowing English, and who had better salaries. They asked us whether we wouldn't join too, just to give them more courage if it came to a showdown or a fight. Eventually we all did.

The showdown then came, very quickly. The next time salaries were paid, they asked for a rise, a modest rise, and were refused. The rest of us then joined the Union ; we had a meeting and went on strike.

I still remember the feeling of excitement at that last meeting, and I remember, particularly, the odd attitude of all the directors. They seemed to think that we had perpetrated something utterly low and deceitful ; they seemed hurt more than angered. And me, particularly, they regarded as a fool. Didn't I know on which side

my bread was buttered ? they seemed to ask.   After all,
I had had many rises and could expect more ; why,
then, did I align myself with the cheap local help ; why
did I join a union ?   That such a thing as class feeling
or solidarity exists didn't seem to enter their heads.   I,
on the other hand, was terribly surprised to find that in
America stenographers and book-keepers had no union ;
they were seemingly quite content to work for small
wages, all their lives, much smaller than the average
Ford worker got.   It seemed incredible.

But, explained one of the young accountants to me,
in America only such rabble as miners, iron workers,
and so on, belonged to unions.   People who sat in
offices and wore clean clothes never thought of such a
thing. . . .   People who sat in offices, I understood,
could pretend that they were on a par with the rich
because they wore cheap, ready-made, clean clothes
and did not have to go down into the bowels of the
earth to earn their meagre wages.   They earned their
money by sitting on hard stools, growing hemorrhoids
and upsetting their own bowels. . . .   Not that I
thought of it exactly in those terms, but that was my
feeling about it.

Well, anyway, there was the strike.   After we had
held some more meetings and decided on a fair wage for
a typist, we sent a delegation to the Mission to present
the claims.   But our delegation was never allowed to
enter.   One of our office boys stood outside the office
door holding a gun.   I am not so sure about the gun
now, for I was not in the delegation, but so I was told.
However, I knew then that it was a lock-out.

Of course, then we all stayed home.   We stayed
home ten days, I think, when the directors asked
whether we would drop all the foolishness and come to
work.   We did not drop one demand.   The directors
could, of course, fire all these hundred typists and

engage other ones, but the rub was that we, the dozen or so secretaries who held special jobs and who knew English, were also in the strike, and we were hard to replace; in fact, some of us couldn't be replaced at all. I, for one. An English stenographer who knew Russian, Polish, and German, who could listen to English dictation and could transcribe it directly on the typewriter into any of these languages, was not so easily replaced. And so I sat in my room, full of youthful arrogance and glee. I was going to stick by the typists and the union, and see the thing through.

On the eleventh day our delegation and the directors got together and decided to settle the matter by arbitration. Three men were to vote on the proposal—an American director, a member of the union, and a neutral outsider. This outsider, I think, was a Polish lawyer. His vote was for the typists' demand, and the battle was won. We all went to work and the typists got their rise. Also the American Mission recognised the union and its rules. One of its regulations was that an employee discharged for no fault of his, or because of illness, was to get six months' wages as compensation. That sounds like a great deal, but as a matter of fact, in the Polish marks at the current rate of exchange, it amounted to very little.

Soon after, the accountants got their fat checks, gathered up their curios, kilim rugs, wooden plates, and artistic postcards, and sailed to America. Something or other was found out, or confirmed, or disapproved; the Mission had paid the costs and everybody was satisfied.

As Dr. Bogen tried to explain it to me : " You know, one has to be careful in accounting for charity expenditures. It isn't really just the big checks from Straus and Rothschild that count so much. Most of the money is just ten- and fifteen-dollar contributions from poor, ordinary Jewish folks in America. Every month they give their little bit for their poor Jewish people in Poland ; just part of their salaries, think of it. . . ."

I did. I thought of it a lot. I thought it was funny to pay all this charity money to those smart, expensive accountants just because somebody stole something, or lost something, or what was it, anyway ?

10

LOVE AT FIRST SMILE

MY sister went to concerts far more often than I, and at night, when she got home, she would tell me all about it. One day she told me that she had heard a new violinist. She seemed full of enthusiasm. " He is a real artist. A lovely tone, and powerful, too. And he is so sweet. Just a young boy."

" Who is he ? "

" He is American, but he studied here, at the conservatory, under Barcewicz. He is going to play again next week. I am going."

The next time she heard the boy, her report was still more glowing.

" He saw me ! " she said with excitement. " I sat in the first row and just before he started to play he smiled at me. Right at me. He is so charming." . . . And then she added : " And I smiled back ! " She talked of nothing else for a while and all of her friends began to tease her about it.

Soon after that, Pani W., the wife of a wealthy physician and a great patroness of art, had a musical gathering at her home to which both my sister and I were invited. " Be sure to come," she told me on the phone. " I have a surprise in store for you."

Somehow I missed that event, but Rita went, and subsequently I heard the story of that evening from Pani W.

Rita had come rather early at the invitation of the hostess, and went to the piano to give some improvisations. As is usual with her when in the right mood, she forgot herself and just played, oblivious of everybody. When she stopped and raised her eyes, the boy violinist was standing near her. He was the " surprise." What followed Pani W. described in this way :

" They began to speak English. They talked at the piano ; then they went into a far corner and sat there and went on talking English. It was not very polite, for none of us could understand them, but they paid no attention, my dear. They ate but little supper, they just talked, as if they could never stop, and then, a little later, they just got up and walked out, hand in hand. Like babes in the wood."

The boy was Victor Young, now of radio fame, song writer, conductor, and composer. If anyone had told him in those days in Warsaw that some day he would compose " blues," extol negro music, and conduct a popular band, he would have had a fight on his hands, for the boy was steeped in classical music and had a typical serious education of the conservatoire type.

At the age of nine, with a little sister still younger, he was sent to Europe to study. He stopped with his maternal grandparents in Warsaw and entered the Warsaw Conservatory under a scholarship. When he graduated, with honours, he was presented with a genuine Guarnerius by a local Mæcenas. Because of the war and Germany's occupation of Poland, the boy and his sister were compelled to stay on in Warsaw, and

soon after his graduation Victor began making appearances. He had everything a young virtuoso needs—
a great talent, a fine technique, and a charming personality. Although he was about eighteen when we
first met him, he was so slim and small that one mistook
him for a mere child of fifteen. He played all the time :
in concerts, with the famous Warsaw Philharmonic, in a
quartet, a quintet, and in between he gave lessons. He
seemed to be always on the run, and the dates he made
with my sister were always in the queerest places : in
the rehearsal room of the Philharmonic, in the lobbies
of theatres, in the music room of a cinema. Seldom as
we had seen each other before—though we lived, or
rather slept, in the same room—now I hardly saw my
sister at all. She, too, seemed to be on the run.

And by and by I began to observe another strange
phenomenon—the pockets of Rita's skirt began to
bulge with odd, lumpy packages. She possessed only
two skirts—for this was still in the early days after the
war when decent clothes were quite a problem in our
lives—and it used to irritate me to see her ruin her one
good skirt. " Why don't you put it in your bag,
whatever it is ? " I once said, irritably. " I can't.
You don't know anything," she answered, with equal
irritation.

One pleasant Sunday at a dinner at our aunt's house,
I sat next to her and saw her put a slice of the delicious
roast into a small napkin, roll it up, and slip it into her
pocket. She did it amazingly fast. No one else saw it.

After dinner, as we got up, I whispered to her in
English : " What on earth are you doing ? "

" Sh-h," she whispered back. " This is for Victor.
He never eats properly. He is always hungry, but he
doesn't know it. Whenever I meet him I always have
to feed him a little. He will enjoy this."

" My God, doesn't he eat any regular meals ? "

VICTOR YOUNG

Warsaw *1920*

"He never has time," she whispered earnestly. "Before a concert he is too nervous and after a concert he is too tired."

Soon there was another worry—the *other women*. Other women, it appeared, also liked Victor. They watched the dark-eyed, spirited young boy on the concert stage and, when they heard the liquid tones of his violin, their hearts melted and they tried to get closer. . . . There was a morbid young girl who threatened to commit suicide, and a rich girl who pursued the boy with offers of marriage, promising him a life of ease, and then there was an old countess at whose house Victor had played a couple of times. One night it was very late when the guests finally dispersed after the musicale and the countess kindly invited the boy to stay overnight. There was plenty of room, it would be no trouble, she told the tired young fellow as she conducted him to a guest room. Victor consented readily, as he was very tired, but later that night the old countess came into his room and then he had to be rude—very, very rude indeed. After that he became a bit shy of aristocracy, of all society folks in general.

And then, to top it all, there were the Triplets.

"They are all alike and they are all in love with him—all three of them," Rita told me one day. She was laughing, but I felt a serious undertone.

"Well, that ought to make it safe—somehow," I said.

"They hate me. I can just feel it. They are jealous cats," she continued, smiling.

"But who are they? And why do you have to see them?" I asked, mystified.

"Oh, they are a trio. They play in a cinema. And Victor used to teach two of them, the 'cellist and the violinist. He is still coaching one—in the intermission. We had a date in the cinema because he was going to

L

his rehearsal later, so I saw them. I knew it at once. They are cute, too, and they adore him. All three of them ! "

I was so diverted that I wanted to see them, and one day I went to that particular cinema with Rita. The programme had not opened and we found the triplets and Victor in a small practice room. Three dark, pretty girls, not more than sixteen, and as like each other as peas. The atmosphere was a bit strained and we left after a few minutes of perfunctory small talk.

" How do you tell them apart ? " I wanted to know as we walked down the street.

" I never do. Not unless they are playing. I know which one plays the piano, which the violin, and which the 'cello."

" How about Vic ? "

" He claims he does, but I don't believe it." . . .

However, all these obstacles proved ephemeral. Their romance could weather any storm. When communication with America was established again, Victor and his sister went back to America. Some months later my sister followed, and at the end of that year she and Victor were married in California.

II

SECOND ESCAPE

I HAVE had many escapes in my life. In fact, all my sojourns in different countries were nothing but the aftermaths of various escapes, beginning with the one from Germany at the outbreak of the war, when my sister and I, mere children then, were part of a group of

Polish and Russian war refugees, peregrinating for three weeks via cattle-cars, boats, refugee trains, and such, through Sweden and Finland, in what seemed to me then the most thrilling, breath-taking adventure.

However, this second escape from the Bolsheviks in 1920 beat them all by the combination of comedy and thrill it involved. The whole thing seems inexplicable even now, in retrospect. It seems odd and shameful that I should have helped a deserter, knowing that he was one.

Always, when thinking of it, I like to go back step by step, trying to find that particular point, that tiny moment, when the scales must have swung to the other side, when I must have decided that it was better to save his neck than to give him up to the Polish military for court-martial. . . . But I cannot find that particular moment at all. It seems lost in the confusion of that strange night. It may have had something to do with the American Vice-Consul who was with the party, or it may have been the supercilious Polish captain, but I am not sure—I am not sure of anything now.

The vicious and fierce attack with which the Bolsheviks stormed Warsaw in July 1920 took the city by surprise. The war had been going badly for some weeks and the Polish forces had lost, in quick succession, Kiev, Podol, and the Ukraine, but no one, I think, imagined for a moment that they could actually come to the gates of Warsaw.

I was away on a vacation when the news of the Bolshevik attack reached me. I returned to Warsaw at once and found the city seething with tumult and fear. Everywhere were placards announcing a special mobilisation of all able men to the age of sixty. The trains at the station for points west were overflowing with wealthy people, fleeing. There was a tremendous tension, bustling and confusion everywhere. The cabman told me they were building trenches on the Praga side and even women and children were helping. I went straight to the Mission quarters.

The scene in front of the office was quite warlike. A string of cars stood there, piled with luggage ; the American boys were running in and out ; everything was in commotion and one couldn't make head nor tail of it. The Polish employees stood about in whispering groups. I forced myself into the director's office and found Lieutenant G. in charge. He was a young Polish Jew from New York, energetic, crude, arrogant, but quite efficient.

" Say, where have you been ? " he shouted at me the moment he saw me.

" On my vacation. I just returned," I said quite calmly.

" Vacation ! With this going on ? Why didn't you turn back ? "

" I didn't know ' this was going on.' . . . I didn't read any papers for a week and up at the village they didn't have any news."

" Well, we are leaving in half an hour," he announced.

" Who is leaving ? "

" Half of the staff, the Americans. We are going to Danzig."

" But why should *you* leave ? " I asked.

" Say, d'you think we want to be captured by the Bolsheviks ? "

" You are Americans ; they wouldn't do anything to you."

" They wouldn't ! Well, anyway, it's the orders from headquarters."

He began to give some orders to people and, seeing that he had no more time for me, I turned to go. As I was nearing the door, the lieutenant suddenly called me back.

" Say, you know German, don't you ? "

" I do."

" Real well ? Write letters—talk to people, and so forth ? "

" Real well—write letters and read and talk," I replied.

" Say, I think we'll take you along. You will be useful up in Danzig. I am in charge of the cars. Now you go home and pack—just one suitcase—and be back in twenty minutes."

I turned to go and then thought of something and turned right back again.

" I can't go unless you take my sister along too. I can't possibly leave her here."

He rose, confronting me. He was rather a fierce-looking, dark young man.

" Now, listen, we aren't conducting any family party. The reason I want you is because of your German, of all your languages; we will need you. See ? "

" I do, but I can't go unless you take Rita too," I said stoutly, though inwardly I was quaking, and I turned around and walked to the door. Five or six steps. On the sixth step the lieutenant shouted at my back :

" Oh, hell, take her along ! But don't tell anyone— none of the Polish help. I am not supposed to take any Poles out ! Twenty minutes ! I am not waiting for anyone ! "

He was shouting. This lieutenant was much given to shouting ; I suppose at the front he shouted at his soldiers, and now he shouted at us. . . .

I jumped into the cab, went home, and explained things to my sister while we packed ; then we both jumped into the cab, stopped on the way to say good-bye to our aunt and cousins, and went on to the Mission. We started almost at once.

In the car we occupied, the first of the touring cars,

there were six people : in the front seat sat the Polish
chauffeur and a young American whom I had never
seen before.   In the tonneau sat Lieutenant G. and a
pale young Jewish fellow, also a stranger ; then my
sister and I.   The other three cars were filled with
other members of the Mission, all Americans.   We were
taking the shortest, most direct route to Danzig,
although it was a little more dangerous, coming at
times close to the fighting line.   The distance between
Warsaw and Danzig is about five hundred miles, but
as we had started in the afternoon we knew we should
not reach the city until night-time.   We travelled at an
easy pace, for there were many nice little places along
the road where the man who sat next to the chauffeur
liked to stop.   He liked to get out and stretch his legs,
he said.   When we came to a neat little village, bearing
all the earmarks of the hundred and fifty years of
German rule, he would say to Lieutenant G., " Say,
Lieutenant, tell the fellow to stop here ; that looks like
a nice little place.   Right here . . . looks like a nice
little inn.   I'd like to get some beer . . ." and he would
get out and disappear, to return very shortly in the
most amiable of moods.   The first time he got out
Lieutenant G. said to me :

" This is the American Vice-Consul.   We are taking
him for the sake of safety, because of his diplomatic
passport."

He seemed very nice, this Vice-Consul ; he was very
young, well-dressed and well-mannered.   It did seem
a bit odd that he should enjoy so much stopping at
these little wayside inns, but then I had heard vague
stories of the prohibition which ruled America and
guessed that he must have been a victim ; perhaps he
was trying to make up for lost time ; at any rate, he
carried his refreshments admirably.   You couldn't tell
a thing, unless you watched very closely.

Thus we travelled and, except for these occasional stops, the trip was quite monotonous. No one spoke much, although the tension was definitely lessened now that we were actually running away from Warsaw. We had nothing much to say to each other and we were an ill-assorted group to say the least.

Then came a diversion. At one of the little towns, while the Vice-Consul went to refresh himself, I noticed that the chauffeurs of the four cars seemed to get into a closer huddle than heretofore. All the cars of our little squadron always stopped when the first car, carrying the diplomat and the lieutenant, who was nominally in charge, stopped ; and the chauffeurs, all sturdy Polish fellows, usually got together for a little talk. But the huddle this time seemed unusually long ; there they were, standing in a close group, gesticulating warmly, talking away. They did not separate even when they saw the Vice-Consul emerge from the inn ; they seemed oblivious. The lieutenant called out to them sharply to return to the cars and to proceed, but to my astonishment they didn't pay any attention. Then the Vice-Consul, as if waking from pleasant dreams, asked me : " What seems to be the matter ? "

I said : " Shall I go down and ask ? "

" No, you call them to me. Call them right here."

I called over to the group and they came closer. They looked up with a sort of sheepish defiance and one of them said : " The thing is, *panienka* (miss), we don't want to go any farther. It's dangerous for us because we are all of conscript age and if we cross the line to Danzig we might be called deserters." (I recalled the placards which were pasted all over Warsaw, proclaiming general conscription.)

" What nonsense that is," I said. " You are driving cars for Americans, for neutral people ; you are not sneaking away ; no one can hold you responsible for this."

" Well, they might, and you see we have just been talking and reasoning and we thought you better find some other chauffeurs and let us go."

At that point I saw the Vice-Consul get out of the car. He had put his hand in his pocket and was holding something in it. His bearing was very quiet. He came quite close and then said to me, quietly, while he looked at the men :

" Now you translate."

I told him what the men had told me. He listened to it, then took his hand out of his pocket ; it had a shining little gun in it. He held it sort of negligently. " Translate, word for word : ' You men are all in American employ. In my employ. I am taking these American citizens out of the country and no one can stop me, because I am a member of the American Government. Not even the Bolsheviks, if they catch us, can stop me, because of my passport. This is a diplomatic passport. . . .' " He then took out his passport and showed it to them, while I translated his speech. They looked at it sheepishly, and all agreed to take us on farther. They asked me to assure the American gentleman that they would take us wherever he wanted to, but I had a feeling that it was not the sight of the diplomatic passport that did it.

" You tell them," said the Vice-Consul quietly, " that if they pull any more monkey business, they will get this." He raised the gun a bit and then put it back in his pocket. I did not even bother to translate, for the men seemed to understand and we all separated and went on our way. From that moment the leadership shifted unobtrusively but definitely from the lieutenant to the Consul ; but what I liked most about him was the fact that he didn't raise his voice, and the way he expressed himself. "Monkey business," he had said. I had never heard such an expression ; it seemed amazing and very quaint.

We drove on in silence. Only the lieutenant talked a bit, in Yiddish, in an undertone, to the other strange young man. I don't recall that we stopped any longer at any of those "pleasant little places," though I may be mistaken.

We reached the border about midnight. It was pitch dark when the first sentry stopped us and, though we expected it of course, it came as a shock. There were three of them ; they blew a whistle and planted themselves firmly in front of the first car. One of them pointed a flashlight at us ; the Vice-Consul pulled out his diplomatic passport, opened it to his picture, and handed it to the first soldier, saying curtly :

"American, diplomatic passport. All Americans."

Then a funny thing happened : the soldier snapped the passport, shoved it back at the Consul, and said in terse Polish :

"What the hell do I know about passports ! I got orders not to let anyone through."

"What ! What's the fellow saying ?" asked the Vice-Consul.

"He is an ignorant soldier ; he doesn't know what a diplomatic passport means," I explained.

But the Vice-Consul caught the tone of the soldier's voice, though he didn't understand his words.

"Tell him he has got to let us through or there will be trouble. Tell him about my diplomatic passport. Tell him we are Americans."

I translated. The soldier didn't listen. "All of you get out and follow. Mr. Officer will decide who is American and who is not. I have my orders."

I took the Vice-Consul by the arm. "Please, let's go quietly," I said. "This fellow is a stupid soldier ;

the officer will understand. I will explain it to him."

" You bet he will or there will be plenty of trouble for his government," said the young American. He seemed suddenly very irate ; all his easy amiability had vanished. The occupants of the other cars got out, while from nowhere, in the dark, there appeared about a dozen soldiers, all with rifles on their shoulders, who quickly formed a cordon around us. We began to move in a compact, guarded group toward a building which loomed dimly on the side of the road. I held the Vice-Consul firmly by the arm ; my sister was on my other side. The rest of the people formed a tight group about us. We moved slowly and then I caught sight of Lieutenant G. and the pale young man who was in our car. The lieutenant looked very nervous and the strange man had a look of abject fear, and in a flash I knew what he was. He was a deserter.

For a moment I felt stunned ; I grabbed my sister's hand and then I knew she had guessed it too ; she had seen his face as I had seen it and she knew. " What are you going to do ? " she whispered.

" I don't know," I replied.

For a moment I felt nothing but pure hatred and disgust. If the fellow was caught and shot, it served him right. And the lieutenant too, for helping a deserter. I realised, too, why the silence in our car, in the tonneau, had been so unpleasant—it was this pale fellow's fear, the miasma of all his furtive thoughts, which had seemed to envelop us in a sickly mist. And now he was to be caught . . . and shot. . . .

We walked slowly across the dark road, pressed by the soldiers on all sides, and filed through a narrow door into the building. The single large room seemed very light after the darkness outside. There were a few soldiers, and clerks sitting at their tables behind a wooden barrier, and at the foremost table sat a Polish captain, the chief of this border patrol.

I knew, too, how they shot deserters in a Polish court-martial; they tied their hands and stood them up against the wall. . . . We moved slowly and, though the man was a few feet behind me, I seemed to feel his fear oozing out of him, out of that pale, colourless face with the furtive eyes. . . . I didn't know whether to denounce him or not; disgust and pity were inextricably mixed. I thought, too, of the American whom I held by the arm; an American consular officer, unwittingly trying to protect, with his diplomatic immunity, a deserter from the Polish army. . . . The scandal it would cause—the scandal for him, for the Mission . . . and all the time there was, too, that terrible tension, that awful, humiliating feeling of being surrounded by the armed soldiers . . . and the feeling of that poor wretch's fear, his furtive eyes and white face. And then, amidst all these confusing thoughts and emotions, I saw the Polish captain rise.

He was very young, very elegant, with tiny, twisted black moustaches and an air of supercilious arrogance. That Polish failing, didn't I know it well ? Suddenly I went to meet it with all the arrogance I, too, possessed —and in those young days I had a goodly fund of it. Dragging the Vice-Consul by the arm, I began to talk quickly, without letting the captain ask a single question. I was going to do the attacking and I was going to beat him with his own weapons; it was our only chance.

"This is the American Vice-Consul from Warsaw and I am his interpreter," I said loudly. "The rest of us are all members of an American Relief Mission. We were going to Danzig when your sentry stopped us, and when the Consul showed him his passport, the soldier insulted him. If you post sentries for passport duty you ought at least to pick people who can read ! The whole thing is outrageous ! "

" *Prosze Pani* . . . *Prosze Pani*, please explain to the Consul that the soldier was only trying to do his duty . . . carrying out my orders. . . . He meant no insult."

" But he almost threw that passport in the Consul's face. American diplomats aren't used to such treatment."

" But this is war, *prosze Pani*. The Bolsheviks are only two miles away from here. I assure you, he didn't mean anything. He has an order to inspect every car that passes the line, and bring any doubtful people in here to me. I assure you, *Pani* . . ."

" What is the fellow jabbering about ? " inquired the Vice-Consul at my side, glaring at the elegant captain. " Didn't you tell him who I am ? What's this all about ? " He seemed angrier every moment ; his face was getting red, too. I had a fleeting thought of all the stops and the beer he had taken. . . .

" He is trying to explain that the soldier didn't realise about your passport and was just trying to do his duty."

" Now you tell him to let us go and to apologise. You tell him that if I put in a complaint in Washington there will be hell to pay and he will be demoted. You tell him that."

I did. I translated faithfully. This nice American, getting sore, was playing right into my hands.

On hearing about Washington and his demotion, the captain got a little pale. He said :

" *Prosze Pani*, explain to the Consul. Why, you can proceed at once, and I am going to punish the sentry-men, *prosze Pani*. . . ." With a swift gesture and a command, he dismissed our guard. They filed out and we remained standing in the room, crowded but free. The Vice-Consul stood, glaring fiercely.

" Just one little formality," said the captain. " Your

passports." My heart almost fell into my bloomers.
He looked at the diplomatic passport; then at my
Polish passport. . . .

I took a jump. " The rest are all members of the
Mission," I said. " And then there are the four
chauffeurs. We are in a dreadful hurry, you know, all
this silly delay . . ."

" Yes, of course," he said, " I shan't trouble you all.
I will just detain the Polish chauffeurs. I have to
stamp theirs, so they can get back safely. You know
the law about deserters." He smiled.

" Well, can we go ? " said the Vice-Consul, still
glaring

" Yes, we can go," I replied.

I called the chauffeurs to come forward. The rest of
us began to file slowly out of the small room. The pale
young man who had stood unobtrusively at the back of
the room was the first to go. Lieutenant G. went out
silently. The Polish captain was still standing and
apologising : " Please, you can all return to your cars . . .
my apologies to the Consul . . ."

We got out. The amiable young American still
grumbled a little as we entered the car. Perhaps he
was one of those people who get angry very slowly, by
degrees, or perhaps he did not like the Polish captain
with his elegant moustaches and his supercilious air ; or
perhaps it was the fumes of all those little refreshments
he had taken during the day, rising belatedly in protest. . . . Heaven alone knows. All I knew was that
his timely anger had helped me with my bluff and we
had saved a damned coward's life. . . .

A feeling of relief, a feeling of disgust, and then an
immense fatigue enveloped me as I sat in the car leaning
against my sister. We were now in the territory of the
Free City of Danzig . . . I should see D. every day . . .
I fell asleep.

12

THEY PRAYED FOR ME

THE two boys who came to my window that morning
were so small that I had to get up and lean out to get a
look at them.

The window was small and square, without any pane
—in fact, nothing more than a hole in the wall of one of
the wooden barracks in the emigration camp of the
Port of Danzig. I sat on the inside, my table and
typewriter flush with the hole, and I constituted the
Personal Service Department of the J.D.C. Mission.
For, on getting to Danzig, some of our more enterprising social workers looked up the camp, reported dreadful conditions to the headquarters, and suggested a
branch, which was immediately approved.

The camp, which had been fitted out for five hundred
people, was now filled with about four thousand. Most
of these were Jewish refugees from the Bolshevik front,
with a tiny sprinkling of Polish and Lithuanian peasants. Most of the emigrants were women, whose
husbands had gone to America before the war to make
their fortune. Four years of war and the aftermath
had created a wall between them. The men did not
always send for their women ; some of them had
acquired other women in God's Own Country ; others
had died or gone wrong ; some had volunteered in the
army and had been killed or wounded. And now these
women and children, driven by the Bolshevik offensive,
came on to Danzig to pick up old threads. . . .

It was my job to tie those threads, and every morning when I got down to the camp I found a long line of
applicants waiting for me at the window. The line

formed as early as four in the morning and waited patiently for my appearance.

Most of the people had come to the camp in just the clothes they had on, without money or passports, their most prized possessions being old grimy letters from America, mostly of pre-war vintage, and a hope that they could get across the water to an American heaven on earth. They also brought lice, typhus, scabies, and unspeakable dirt. My wish of the year before to join in some field-work and see the misery at first hand was suddenly and amply fulfilled. I did not have to go out to Kovno and Grodno and Suwalki ; Kovno, Grodno, and Suwalki came to me, right to my very window. . . .

The two boys' turn came and I got up and leaned out to take a good look. Although the window was fairly low from the ground, the older boy's eyes and forehead just came up to the window-sill ; the smaller chap couldn't reach at all. He stood calmly, holding on to the bigger fellow's trousers. Both had brown hair, nice faces, and large, grey, very trusting eyes. They had an ordinary Jewish name which I have long since forgotten, but their faces I shall not forget as long as I live.

The bigger boy couldn't manage to speak at once. So many of the people in the line couldn't speak at once ; the tension of waiting for long weary hours would snap suddenly and find them unprepared. His lips trembled just a little, then he controlled himself quickly and said :

" We are going to England, to an uncle, my brother and I. I take care of him because he is so little. I want you to write to our uncle and tell him we need money for the ship."

" Have you got a passport ? " I asked the first routine question.

" Sure. Here it is," and he handed me the grimy

little book. "My brother is on it," he added. "I take care of him."

I took the passport but didn't inspect it at once, for these children interested me. The older boy seemed such a grown-up little chap, though he looked no more than nine or ten.

"Where are your parents?" I asked, and wished the next moment that I hadn't.

"Both dead. In the pogrom. The Russian soldiers killed them because they were in the house. My brother and I, we hid in the haystack. We were not in the house. We hid well." He said it in the tone of one who had told the story so many times that the import of it had ceased to matter.

"And how did you get to Warsaw?"

"We walked, and sometimes we hid on trains and other people helped us. And in Warsaw I went to the British Consul and got a visa. The passport is both for him and me because he is too little to have one of his own. Will you write our uncle for the money for the ship?"

"Sure. You have your uncle's address?"

"Here it is," and he produced a soiled letter with a London address on it. "You see, we have nobody in our village and this uncle, he wants us to come. He said he would adopt us and send us to school. So you write him, will you, that we are safe here in Danzig; we are safe and waiting for the money for the ship." He stopped for breath, and then added: "You think he could wire the money? Perhaps he could send us a little more, because . . ." he stopped, smiling shame-facedly, "someone stole all my money the other day. From under my pillow."

"I am sure he will if I ask him. Now you give me your uncle's letter," I said. I then looked at the passport and found that the older boy was eleven and the

younger nine, but I found no visa ; a little puzzled, I
thumbed it over again, thinking I might have missed it.

" The English visa is right at the very end," the boy
said, "on the last page, I think.   The Englishman gave
it to us free.   I didn't have to pay for it."

" He did ? " I said, and felt queer.   I paged through
the passport and on the last page but one saw something that made me feel worse : there was the stamp of
the " British Passport Control " office in Warsaw and
underneath it a tiny " V.R." in ink.

The V.R. meant " visa refused," and it also meant
that no other Control was to give the bearer a visa to
England.   It was, in fact, a definitive bar to entry into
the United Kingdom, and the holder of such a passport
was usually put on the British Black List which is
mailed to all consuls.

" Did you find the visa ? " the boy asked hopefully
from behind the window.   " It's right at the end."

" Yes, I found it all right," I said, and then added :
" But you may have to get another one—one from
Danzig, you see . . . "   I lied, for I did not have the
heart to tell him the truth.

" Will you tell me where to get it ? " he said at once,
eagerly.

" Yes," I said, because I didn't know what else to say
for the moment.   " Now let's see your uncle's letter."

And I pretended I was interested in it, thinking all
the while how I ought to explain to the boys that they
couldn't go to England, after all, but would have to
return to Poland and be put in an orphanage.   Even
that would be a lie, for no Warsaw orphanage would
take in two boys from another province.   Their own
village was a heap of ruins behind the front.   *The
truth was they had no place to go to.*

I looked at the boy and he looked back at me ; he had
a nice child's face, clever, but not precocious, and fine

M

grey eyes that looked straight at you.   I decided that I would tell the lie about the orphanage, so as to make the blow a little easier, after all.   And then, to gain time, and because I felt I couldn't kill them right out there, in that line of waiting people, I told them to come into the barracks.   I leaned out and said to them : " You go round to the side and I will open the door " ; and to the line I said : " These boys are so small I am going to take them inside ; I can't talk to them through the window."   I had to say that, for it looked as if I were making an exception, and these patient people who had all been waiting from four or five in the morning were jealous of any special favours.   The line murmured, shifted their feet, and consented.   I went to the door, unfastened a hook, and let the boys in.   They were smiling happily now, sure that all their troubles were over.

" I am going to wire your uncle in London for some money," I said.

" Don't forget the ship," said the bigger boy.   " We need the money for the ship."

" Yes, of course," said I, thinking that I would not tell them yet that they couldn't go to England at all . . . not for a few days yet . . . and I sat down at the typewriter and typed the usual wire : " Your nephews stranded, penniless.   Wire some money immediately care Personal Service Department.   Letter follows." And it was then that I thought of D. !

Lord, if anyone could help, it was he.   I wrote a note, telling him the boys' story and making a dinner date. I marked it " personal," and gave it to the boys.   I gave them also the money for the telegram to England, some money for food, and two passes to leave the camp and to return, a regulation the port authorities required. Then, feeling a little relieved, I began to attend to the rest of the line. . . .

"A plucky little chap," D. commented on the older boy that night at the restaurant where we were having dinner. "The porter, you know, didn't want to let them in, but he simply refused to be turned out; he clutched your note in his fist and said he was going to see me and he wouldn't leave till he saw me, and finally the porter had to give in and brought the boys to me. 'There are some funny little beggars want to see you, sir,' he said; 'they do look 'orribly ragged.'"

"But what will you do?" I asked excitedly. "Is there anything you can do at all; is there any way by which you can change the 'V.R.' and give them a visa to England?"

"I can't get them a visa over Marshall's head," D. said. "Marshall is the head of the Passport Control Office in Warsaw. . . . I know him fairly well, but not intimately."

"Well, then, couldn't you write to him? Explain things to him; tell him they have a chance of getting into a good home in England, and if they stayed in Poland they would probably turn into little beggars. All their people are killed and they seem such decent children."

D. gave a sardonic little laugh. It wasn't as simple as that. He couldn't tell that to Marshall; Marshall wouldn't care whether two little Jewish boys turned beggars or not. Marshall would probably wonder why the devil he, D., interfered with his office and why he was at all interested in a case like this.

"Oh, but you are going to ask him?" I begged. "Please do!"

"Yes, of course. But I don't want to be refused. Leave it to me—I'll figure it out. . . . Now, let's eat."

We began to eat, and in the course of that dinner, bit

by bit, I learned something about English psychology : it seems Marshall hated all " sentimental lard " and one couldn't appeal to him that way—it would be the surest way of turning Marshall against the boys ; nor could D. tell Marshall that he was wrong in refusing the visa, for Marshall had a higher post officially, and this wouldn't do at all. The thing was to put him in such a position that in all decency he would have to say yes.

I listened, fascinated. Dinner proceeded and from time to time D. scribbled something with a pencil on the menu. By the time we got to the coffee, he seemed to have it all pat. " I've got it," he said, with a chuckle. I leaned over the menu card, rather excited. Like most English public-school men, D. prided himself on composition. A letter or telegram to the F.O., or to anyone else, for that matter, was not merely a message. It was often a piece of diplomacy and invariably a bit of literature. On the menu card was just one simple line, something like : " Have looked into the X case. Chaps seem to be all right. Do you mind if I let them through ? " (I don't remember the exact wording, of course.)

" Is that all ? " I asked, surprised.

" It's enough," said D. with a smile. " And it's just right. He will do it purely as a favour to me and I think it's the only way we can work it. He would never refute his decision if I made it look too important. You see, it mustn't look as if I criticised his judgment in any way ; it must not be important ; it must be absolutely casual. . . . He might just think it a bit odd my taking interest in two little Jewish beggars and he will feel : ' Oh, well, let him have his way ; what do I care ? ' I will send the wire off to-morrow morning and we will know his reply the same night."

It worked. Marshall's wire came that night, telling

D. to go ahead and let them through, and the next day the boys got the money from their uncle in London. A few days later they left for England. To my surprise, D. saw them off personally, and then, at dinner, mentioned very casually that he had taken them down to a department store and got " the little beggars new suits." It seems he fitted them out from top to toe, for he " couldn't let them go ' home ' the way they looked."

" Oh, how nice ! " I exclaimed and felt sorry that I hadn't seen them off too. I had seen them the day before, though, when everything was ready for their trip. They came to the window and the older boy grinned and said :

" We came to thank you, *Pani*, my brother and I."

" Never mind," I said, smiling too. " I told you everything would turn out all right."

" Oh, I knew it," he said. " I knew it the first time I had seen you. I am . . ." he stopped for a tiny moment, then suddenly continued very firmly : " I am going to pray for you. Always, every night."

" Thank you," I said. And then he put his little brown paw through the window and we shook hands. And the smaller fellow put out his hand too and we shook solemnly. " We are both going to pray for you," the older said, " because you were so kind." They turned and left.

I turned to my table, feeling terribly silly. For two cents I could have burst into tears. Their little childish forms were receding in the distance ; as always they walked side by side, the smaller one holding on to the bigger one's trousers. . . . They were going to pray for me, little knowing that it was Lady Luck who had helped them ; for how else can you explain the chain of circumstances : their coming to me ; my knowing D. well enough to ask a favour ; D. knowing Marshall well

enough to know how to make him go back on his own
decision—all of this a combination of sufficient power to
erase a " V.R.," than to do which there is nothing
harder in all the red tape of English bureaucracy.

13

A HARD DAY

THAT day was probably the hardest of all the hard days
I spent working at the camp. When I got to my
window in the morning it started to drizzle. The line
was there, waiting as usual, about two hundred of them,
stretched in a long irregular queue. It was on the
advice of the Port Inspector that I discharged all my
duties through the window. The people were not
clean, he said ; they had diseases, and it was safer.

An elderly woman, her face lined and seamed with
myriads of wrinkles, her skull-cap with the tawdry lace
a bit askew, was standing at the window transacting
her little business. She had been there twice before.
She was an old-timer. There were people like that in
the camp, people who never seemed to be able to get
away, for whom things always went wrong. Their particular ill luck seemed to follow them wherever they
went. She had brothers in " Amerikay," as she called
it, but the letters she first brought to me were almost
ten years old and our headquarters in New York
couldn't find the brothers. I had told her at the time
to see if she couldn't find some more recent letters ;
surely if the brothers wanted her to join them, they
would have written more recently. She went away

murmuring complaints. Now she came again to my window, looking rather brighter than usual.

" I have a letter for you, *Fräulein*," she said, " a different letter," and, putting her hand into the recesses of her blouse, she got out a greasy envelope and handed it to me through the window. Two fat lice dropped off it on my table as I took it from her. They had dropped on a telegraph blank and I rolled it into a tiny ball and threw it on the floor. Lice didn't affect me so much by that time, for I had been working in the camp for more than six weeks. This letter was comparatively new ; it was only six years old, dated 1914, and I made out a new telegram to New York. I gave it to her to take to the local telegraph office and took the next applicant.

The drizzle was getting worse. By ten it became a rain. The line shivered in their pitiful clothes and on a sudden impulse I shouted to the crowd to come into the barracks. They rushed to the door and within ten minutes they filled the room completely, hemming me in on all sides, jabbering and gesticulating. Within five minutes I regretted the impulse, yet cursed myself inwardly for my fastidiousness. The air in the room was so foul that I thought I couldn't breathe. I knew smells, various smells ; I thought the worst smell I had ever encountered was that of gangrene, rotting human flesh. I had smelled it in the first year of the war when I used to help a bit in a Russian hospital of which my stepmother was in charge, and when trains from the front brought soldiers whose wounds had not been dressed properly for days, even weeks. But this smell was worse.

I worked very quickly, trying to think of lunch-time. Only two more hours—only an hour and a half—perhaps by that time the rain would cease—no, it rained harder than ever—well, only one more hour now—my God, how long could I stand it !—half an hour—it was eleven-thirty—my head swam, I felt a sudden hot wave of giddiness just one breath of fresh air and rain, I thought, and I would come right back. I got up, rushed blindly to the door, pushing these people with my hands, ran down the three wooden steps and retched. . . .

It was funny to find oneself on the table of the dispensary. I tried to get up, but the doctor in a white smock pushed me back, gently but firmly.

"*Ruhig, ruhig, kleines Fräulein.*" (Quiet, quiet, little miss.)

Then the nurse appeared. A nice, blonde, efficient German girl. I knew her by sight and liked her. I had often seen her crossing the yard, though I had never spoken to her. She helped me to a couch and made me lie down. I had fainted, she said, right in front of my barracks, and had a few bruises. What was it that made me feel so ill ? she asked. I had no fever. . . .

"It was the smell," I said. She laughed, and I laughed too.

Such was the beginning of that day. Having rested in the dispensary, I returned to my barracks. The rain had stopped and I asked the people to line up outside. I went on with my routine. The line that day seemed an endless procession of Jewish women, women of thirty or forty, who were old, with lined, seamed faces, discouraged and mournful. Soon it seemed as if the line had but *one face*, one mournful Jewish face—the individuals had disappeared. It was that way until a new kind of face appeared, a face that was so different that I remembered it for ever. . . .

This social work was strange, that way. One became hardened, perhaps in sheer self-defence, and the people were "cases." Case so and so. Case so and so. Case so and so. And then suddenly, one day, for some little reason, a case became an individual, a human being like oneself. One felt touched, profoundly sorry, and, underneath it all, ashamed that such things could exist at all in this day and age. . . .

The face in my window which made me forget about cases and think of human beings belonged to a young Polish peasant woman. She was tall, blue-eyed, with honey-coloured hair, parted in the middle. She was clean and very frightened. She came close to the window and looked at me dumbly, unable to speak.

" What can I do for you ? "

I thought to encourage her, but to my surprise she began to sob.

" Jesus Maria, the *panienka* speaks Polish ! "

" Yes, I am Polish.   Why does this astonish you ? "

" My golden *panienka* !   Why, the people in the line, they were saying that you are American and speak nothing but American, and others they claimed you spoke German to the Jews here, and others they said you spoke Russian to the folks from Lithuania, and so I thought to myself, how will *I* ever speak to the *panienka*—I who know nothing but the Polish ! "

" Well, now you know I can, tell me your trouble."

" I can't find my husband, *panienka*.   We have been here for six weeks, I and my children, and we have the tickets, but we haven't enough money.   I sold two of my pillows and most of my sheets and I don't know what we will do. . . ."   And she began to sob.

It was the usual story of lost addresses and old letters and no letters during the war, and I went through the usual routine of finding the latest address and wiring to headquarters to start a search.   All was as it always was, except at the end.   The woman bent her head toward me and asked in a fearful whisper :

" *Panienka*, how is this America ?   Have you been there yourself ? "

" Oh, yes, I have been there.   What do you want to know ? "

" Are there any Christian people there ?   Or are they all Jews and Americans ? "

I kept a straight face.   I knew what she meant—she meant Catholics, Catholic Poles.

" Why, you are going to Detroit, aren't you ?   Yes, there are lots of Christians there.   You won't feel lonely.   Don't worry."

" Oh, thanks be to God, *panienka*.   Good day."

Toward evening it began to rain again and I let the people come inside the barracks.   But there were fewer of them now and the air was not so stifling.   I hurried through the rest of the cases and was covering my typewriter when an old patriarchal Jewish man approached me timidly.

" *Fräuleinchen* . . .''

" *Was wünschen Sie ?* "   For a moment my German disconcerted him.   Then he continued, still very timidly :

" *Fräuleinchen*, I heard you were so good, so kind . . . you helped people.   I want to ask you something, *Fräulein* . . ."

" Go ahead."

He stood before me, with his long white beard, his large sad eyes begging humbly.   It made me feel queer. I was so young and he was so aged, and he had a certain dignity.   Why should he humble himself ?   He seemed to hesitate, so I said :

" Is there something I can do ? "

" *Fräuleinchen*—I have been here for two months— two long months—with my two daughters.   Last week my younger daughter went into the water . . ."

I turned, startled.   So it was his daughter who had committed suicide.   I had heard the tale from the Port

Inspector, the story of a young Jewess who had jumped into the canal.

" And now my other daughter is very sad, too."

" I am very sorry," I said.

" My other daughter is very sad. All day long she sits in one spot and broods," the old patriarch said. " Oi, *Fräuleinchen*, it is a sad world."

" Well, soon you may be going to America," I said.

" Oh, I don't know when we will go," he sighed. " We have been here two months and there is no end to this waiting. First we had no passports and that was the trouble ; then when we had passports there wasn't enough money for the ship. We would have had enough money if we hadn't had to wait, but was it our fault we had to stay here for so long ? And you have to pay for everything and everything costs so much in this camp. And then my daughter goes into the water."

" I am sorry," I said, and prepared to go. But the patriarch wouldn't let me. He came quite close to me and barred my way, bent his head toward me so that his hand touched my coat, and said confidentially :

" *Fräuleinchen*—couldn't you find a husband for my other daughter ? "

" What ! " I said.

" Oh, *Fräuleinchen* —it is the only thing that would save her reason. I know it. All day long she sits and broods and thinks of her sister. You know everyone here, you are so good and kind, I heard tell. Couldn't you find a nice young Jew who would be willing ? I thought and thought and I know it's the only thing that would make my daughter happy again ; it would take her mind off the water."

But that I couldn't do, even at the risk of losing all that lovely reputation for kindness. I couldn't take the time to find a nice young husband for this Jewish girl. I couldn't take the time and the trouble in my few spare hours.   I was trying to get a husband of my own, and was bungling the job because I loved so much and so badly.   No, I couldn't help him.   And I told the old patriarchal Jew that he would have to engineer this himself ; he had the time and he knew just what kind of young Jew might make a good husband.   And then I left the camp and, because it was very late, I went straight to D.'s place without stopping at my rooms to change.

" How is the camp and how are all your Jews ? " he said jocularly.

" Oh, they are all right.   I vomited all over the camp this morning and fainted on top of it.   And I am awfully tired.   Help me off with my coat."

D. did, and then, suddenly, his beautiful brown eyes were full of horror and his face was convulsed with disgust.

" Great Scott," he said, " is that a louse ?   Look here—on the sleeve.   And another ! "   He seemed quite beside himself and I laughed.   I took them off carefully and said :

" They are honourable lice.   They are the emblem of my work.   I ought to embalm them and carry them with me as a testimonial."   But I took them into the kitchen and threw them into the garbage can.

14

SABIRA

SHE was a Kalmuk woman, small, thin, extremely pale, with the Mongol eyes and high cheekbones of Asia.   She dressed in dark, inconspicuous clothes and moved about

with tiny, furtive movements, as if perpetually hiding
from someone, shrinking away. . . . Later, when I
knew her better, she explained to me that she *did* shrink
from people, from contacts. She was so sensitive that
the impact of other people, just passing strangers on
the streets, made her actually ill. . . . Sabira was a
fortune-teller.

I met her through some friends, casually, and at first
she simply aroused my curiosity as an odd human being.
There was something uncanny about her. Only her
voice appealed to me : it was soft, low, and calm. It
seemed at variance, somehow, with the rest of her. For
a long time, however, when my friends urged me to go
to see her " professionally," I used to refuse, laughing.
. . . Fortune-telling seemed such nonsense—a racket.
How could any intelligent person believe in it ? " But
she is different from the ordinary run," they insisted,
" she is marvellous." I laughed. And then, one day,
I just went.

I felt at loose ends, rather despondent. Perhaps
that's why I went. I don't recall now.

I rang the bell of her flat. The door opened and
there was pitch darkness. I couldn't see a thing.
Sabira's low voice said :

" Follow me. This way." And then, in a soothing
murmur : " You are very sad ; you mustn't give in to
your moods so easily."

I followed her, startled, for I knew that she could not
see my face. We walked through the dark hall, into a
tiny room, barely furnished with a bed, a couple of
chairs, and a small table. I asked :

" How did you know what I feel ? You could not
see me."

" I do not have to see you," Sabira replied. Then
we sat down at the table and she said simply :

" What do you want to know ? "

" I hardly know myself—everything—whatever you do tell people."

" Do you want to know about your character ? "

" *Pozhaluista*," I said politely, smiling inwardly (we talked in Russian) and feeling a bit more reassured, and thinking something like this : " There goes the game." And, of course, I thought that I knew myself well.

The little woman took my hands, both of them, and examined the palms, first by plain sight, then with a magnifying glass. And as she examined them, she spoke, in small, abrupt sentences, as children do when they read not too well :

" You are ambitious. You can work hard when you have to, but you would rather not do anything. You like small comforts. You are generous, but you don't forget yourself, either."

By that time I had stopped smiling inwardly. I sat intent, listening. It was all true ! And until that moment I had never really known it ! Sabira's voice went on :

" You are versatile—too versatile for your own good. You have a good mind. But it works in odd ways. You live for yourself and in yourself—not for others. You are very impatient. You are inconsiderate. You are jealous."

I felt a sudden resentment.

" Of course I am," I said. " Everybody who is in love is jealous." I thought of D. and how all the women looked at him, on the street, in the restaurant, how my girl friends looked at his picture when they came to my rooms.

" You don't know what love is," Sabira replied calmly ; " real love is neither selfish nor possessive."

" All physical love is selfish ; it can't be otherwise," I repeated stubbornly.

Sabira smiled. She had a rare smile. She repeated again :

" You don't know much about love yet. You are very young and you imagine you do. Some day you will. Some day you will remember all that I have said."

I had an impulse. I opened my bag and took out a letter I had just received from D. in England. He was " home " on one of his annual visits. It was in English, a language Sabira did not know. Nor did she know of D., or anything about him. I had heard about her " mysterious powers " ; now I was going to test her.

" Sabira, can you tell me something about this person ? "

" I can try," she said. She took the letter, spread it in front of her on the table, and put her hands on it. . . . I watched curiously. For some moments she was very still, her hands on the letter, her eyes with a curious inward look. . . . Then her hands began to tremble, at first ever so slightly, then more and more. . . . Her eyes began to take on a glazed look. . . . I watched fascinated, with something akin to horror. . . . I had never seen a person in a trance ; I had never even seen an ordinary hypnotic performance. (I had always classed all such phenomena somewhat summarily as " fakes.") I could not move. For one long moment Sabira sat thus ; then her eyes assumed a normal expression. She looked tired. She said in her odd low voice :

" He is very handsome," and described him rather correctly. " He is not well. He looks very pale. It's his liver. You should tell him he mustn't drink."

I nearly jumped off my chair. In that letter D. had written that he had had quite an attack of " liver " and that the doctor told him to cut out all alcohol for a while. Now I was thoroughly frightened.

" My God, Sabira, how can you tell all this ? Do you see him ? "

" I saw him. Not very clearly. Sometimes things are blurred. I just say what I see."

" My God ! " Shivers ran down my back.

Sabira smiled : " Don't ask me how this happens. It's a gift. There are many things about it I don't know myself."[1]

" Sabira, tell me some more about him. Can you tell his character, too ? "

" From his handwriting, perhaps," she replied, and began to study the letter again. As I said before, she did not know English and we spoke in Russian, for her Polish was very limited.

" He is a man who has many powers which he doesn't use," she said, and then added : " It's a pity. He is a strong man."

" What powers ? " I asked, tremendously interested. I had always admired D.'s brain, which was better than mine. He had more will-power, too, yet he lacked all ambition. He actually could not understand ambitious people. The qualities he most disliked, however, were vanity and conceit.

Sabira pored some more over D.'s characteristic handwriting, which was forceful, yet somehow rigid, neither free nor flowing.

---

[1] In those days I did not know anything about what is called commonly psychic power. Although it occurs more often in the East than in the West, I had not witnessed it until I met Sabira. The gipsies who used to roam about the countryside in Poland and Russia possessed it. But they were often thieves and there was always the rumour of their stealing children for ransom. Our mother had forbidden us children ever to talk to them, and if I encountered them when alone, I used to run for dear life. Later, in America, I read with the intensest interest Mary Austin's descriptions of Indians who also possessed similar powers. In her book, *Everyman's Genius*, she has a remarkable chapter on supernormal faculties which instantly brought back to my mind the little Kalmuk fortune-teller.

" His mental powers and emotional both ; it is a pity, for he is a fine man. He seems frustrated."

I recalled in a flash D.'s curious vein of cynicism, very real, though expressed in that charming, impersonal, slightly deprecating and mocking manner in which sensitive Englishmen seem always to discuss the important things, the things that really matter. Unlike the Russians or Poles, they seem never to let themselves go : always the unwritten credo is : form, control, avoidance of emotion. . . .

We talked some more after that, all about character, and the little Kalmuk woman seemed to me full of wisdom. Toward the end I asked her, rather humbly now, what she thought were my worst traits.

She smiled and said :

" Impatience and the habit of living inwardly, for yourself. You must live with the world, look around you. Then you will learn to be happy."

Egocentricity ! . . . But Sabira did not use this word. I doubt whether it existed then or, if it did, whether she knew it. She was not very well educated. As for myself, I did not understand all this then. I rather resented it. I understood it all only years later, when I embarked on life with a small daughter, and, feeling my responsibility to her, began to read some books on behaviour, child psychology and training, and discovered to my amazement that children learn mostly by emulation and that, in order to train her, I had first to train myself. . . .

At the time, as I said, I dimly resented it. The little woman seemed to have queer notions, queer recipes for being happy. . . .

As if divining my mood, Sabira said kindly :

" Don't worry, anyway. You have lots of time to grow and to change."

N

" What do you mean ? "

She took my hand again.

" You will live to be eighty-four.   You will be a nice
old lady, surrounded by friends.   You will be stronger,
too, than you are now ; after forty your health will
improve, and you will have learned many things."

" How   can   one   change ? "   I   asked   obstinately.
" One's character is formed by the time one is twenty."
I had just read William James's little book called *Habit*
and was unduly impressed by it.   But Sabira did not
need William James.   She had her own queer wisdom.
She said something that later, as I went through life,
came to me rather often, and that I still consider an
excellent piece of advice.   She said, rather gravely :

" You can change—if you want to.   You can do a
lot if you really want to.   It takes time, but you have
a lot of time.   Just don't waste it."

She rose and on that cheerful note of my growing to
be eighty-four the queer consultation was ended.   I
said my good-byes, and went home.

There was a very amusing sequel to my first visit
with Sabira.   As always when my imagination is
caught, I talked of her for days to all and sundry, and
one day a couple of Polish officers, young, sophisticated,
clever, and cynical—they had been through the war—
heard me orate and said they were going to " expose
her " and prove to me that she was a fake like all the
rest of them.   I dared them to do it and they made
their appointment with the Kalmuk and promised to
give an honest report of what had taken place to the
same   group   of   friends   who   had   witnessed   our
dispute.

When they came with their report one of them
started a long, jocular tale of how Sabira was " caught."
He did not proceed very far ; the other young man
interrupted him rather suddenly and said :

"I am going to be honest about it. She did not admit us."

"What!" we all said, astonished.

"We rang the bell and the door opened into a dark hall. We wanted to walk in, and suddenly she blocked the way and said: 'Young men, you came here to laugh at me. You can go home.' And she closed the door on us. . . . What puzzles me," he added, "is how she knew. It was too dark to see us and we did not say anything; we had no time."

15

A NEW FRIENDSHIP

I DIDN'T know Pan and Pani M. very well. Just well enough to drop in on them without a telephone call. But, that afternoon when I called and found Pan M. drunk, our friendship was cemented securely.

It was a Sunday afternoon, I remember, and I had nothing to do. I felt out of sorts and moody and thought of the M.'s house, where one didn't have to speak about the weather, or speak at all, for that matter, unless one was so minded, and where one was likely to find Pani M. ensconced in an arm-chair, reading, and her husband sitting at the piano. So I took a tram-car and went there. I got out at their street and walked the half block toward their house. It was late in the afternoon, the hour when the prostitutes of Warsaw come out on to the streets looking for customers. There must have been several who lived near, for one always saw them at that hour walking back and forth on that block. They were a depressing lot, young women, most of them, with pale and sad faces, dressed plainly in skirts and blouses, and with the inevitable dark shawl around their shoulders. As usual, I hurried past them, wondering vaguely what sort of men could ever want one of these for a gay night's enterprise—for in those days I still thought of these things as being gay and not in the light of an urgent necessity. So I hurried past them and ran up the two flights of stairs and rang the bell, hoping that M. would be at home and would play some of the new delicious *valses* which were just the rage then.

His wife opened the door, looked at me, then said with relief : " Oh, it's you, Lola. Come in, dear."

M. was home too. But he was not at the piano. He was lying on the floor in the dining-room ; his face was pale and he was breathing hard.

" That's how his lovely friends bring him back to me," said Pani M., indicating her husband's bulky form on the floor, " his lovely Bohemian pals. They know he can't stand drink and I begged them not to give him anything, but they enjoy making him drunk in order to hear his nonsense. They only just brought him in a few minutes ago, carried him in from the cab, put him down here, and left without a word. And here I am. And it's the maid's Sunday out."

" Can't I help you ? Can't we put him to bed ? " I said in genuine distress.

" No. He is too heavy. Just fetch me some cold water from the bathroom tap."

She put some cold compresses on his head, I brought a pillow, and after a while he came to and, with our help, was able to walk to his bedroom and get into bed. He sank into sleep and for an hour or so his wife and I kept a quiet vigil in his room, sipping tea and feeling that we had known each other for years—all our lives, in fact, for that is how just one hour of companionship in the presence of reality affects one. I recalled, too, all the stray gossip I had heard about them, how amusing the artist was when he got tight, because he spoke exactly what was on his mind, and how " strict and dreadful " his wife was, keeping him always on the straight path, away from his friends and fun. . . .

When M. woke up, a little later, he felt very much better. Some colour had returned to his face, that odd, fleshy face, with a boldly curved nose and a strong chin, the huge, bulging forehead of the creative man, yet so childish, too, with big blue eyes and a full, sensitive mouth—a head that was both fine and gross, strong and weak.

He recognised both his wife and me and he asked us to come closer, to sit down on the bed by him. " My head aches," he said, " but oh, what a party ! The food and the wine and the women—the little women. . . . Ah ! " And he smacked his lips.

" Don't talk so much, dear," said his wife, casting an anxious glance at him. " Stay quietly and I will get you a glass of tea." She left the room and M. went on talking disjointedly. . . .

Pani M. returned with the tea. He drank it and lay back contentedly and said again that he was feeling very fine, very fine indeed, and there was only one thing he needed, just one thing, and, giving me a confidential wink, he said quietly : " Go get me a little whore."

Casting another anxious glance, Pani M. said : " Now, darling, be quiet, please. You should rest and not talk."

It was at this point that I realised that he was not yet completely sober.

" I am fine," he said, raising himself impatiently. " I am rested. I tell you, all I need is a little . . ."

" Darling," she said rather sternly, as one talks to a child, " will you please stop talking nonsense and try to sleep ? " And she forced him down on the pillow and added under her breath : " Lola is here, please . . . "

He said peevishly : " I *know* she is here. I just talked to her." Then, giving in quite suddenly, he lay back, looked at us with his large eyes, and said quietly, with a kind of profound and childish bitterness :

" Oh, what good is it to have a wife and a friend if they can't do one a little favour like this ! " And then he closed his eyes, turned on his side, and went instantly to sleep.

16

CONSOLATION

The setting was identical : Pan M. was in bed with a hang-over ; the maid was out for the day ; Pani M. was getting some tea, and I had dropped in for a casual call. Everything was identical, except my own state of mind. My own state of mind was the kind that drives some young people to suicide and others to drink. But I had not thought of these panaceas, I had been walking aimlessly around the streets. I had walked for hours without the least idea of what I was doing and then, from sheer habit, my feet took me to the familiar street, up the two familiar flights of steps, and there was the familiar scene. . . .

" Why do you walk up and down like that ? " said Pan M. peevishly. " Can't you sit quietly ? I have a headache."

" I am sorry," I said, and sat down. And got up. And walked again, just as before. . . .

" Say ! . . . What *is* it ? "

" Oh ? . . . Oh, nothing."

But he wasn't quite as sunk as I had thought. He called me to his bed.

"What the devil's the matter? Did you lose a lover?" And he laughed at his own joke.

I said "Yes," and he stopped laughing. His fat face looked suddenly very kind.

"Is it the English boy who lives in Danzig?"

"Yes, I sent him a wire this morning. I told him I was through, but I lost him long before that. He never loved me; he only thought he did."

"Well, don't fret about it," he said after a pause, "you will have lots more. How old are you?"

"Twenty-two."

"Well, there you are. You will have many more before you die. In a few years you will laugh about it."

"I don't think I shall ever laugh about it. Nor will I ever know another boy like this one."

"We all think that way about it at first. . . . Don't fret. . . ." His fat, childish face was so kind that, for his sake, I tried to compose myself. I even forced a smile.

"There now— I bet I could make you laugh. I bet I could tell you stories which would make you laugh."

"Please don't. . . . I shall be all right."

"Well, I bet I could," he said obstinately. "I can make you roar."

And he began telling stories while I walked up and down wondering how I could ever live again with that awful emptiness in my heart.

It was the first time in my life that I had heard really dirty stories. I did not hear anything at all at first; I walked up and down the room, up and down, in sheer misery which was worse than any physical pain. I heard all the words, but I did not get the sense. He went on talking, telling one dirty story after another,

It was the third or fourth story that I heard, and suddenly, in the midst of my misery, I began to laugh. And the moment I could laugh, I could cry too. I flung myself into a chair and sobbed and laughed all at once, and, after a while, felt very much better.

I remember only two of these stories now. They are very good and quite unprintable. When, occasionally, I tell them in sophisticated American circles where stories like that are now quite *comme il faut*, they provoke roars of laughter. And I laugh too. I laugh a little, but inside I always feel funny, and some day, if I have had one cocktail too many, I shall probably forget myself and burst into sobs.

Part III

AUSTRIA AND GERMANY

I

ANOTHER ESCAPE

THIS escape was different from any other. I was running away from my room, or rather from the thoughts with which the room was permeated. I had been unhappy in it and it seemed to me that if only I could get away from it, from the sight of the four walls and all the familiar things, I could be happy again. I was too young to know that I was trying to run away from myself.

I wouldn't say so much about the whole thing—for the situation is commonplace enough in itself—if there had not been a funny side to it. The funny part of it all was that it was practically impossible in those days in Warsaw to move. For this was in 1921, in the Days of Supreme Congestion, when it was far easier to get a job than a room and when the graft connected with the renting had grown to such huge proportions that there was a special commission created to combat it. I knew of a case where a couple were going to divorce, had secured a special dispensation from the Pope, a perfectly good decree from the civil court, yet had to stay in the same room because they could not rent another, and after waiting for months and months finally became reconciled and lived happily ever after.

I knew all this, but I felt that I could no longer go on living in the same place, and one day I had a happy

thought. I went to Dr. H., the director in charge of
the Mission at the time, and said :

"I am tired of Warsaw and I wonder whether you
could give me a transfer to any of your other branches.
Berlin or Vienna or Paris. I don't care which, just so
long as I can get away."

"Why, what's the matter with Warsaw ? " said Dr.
H., looking at me shrewdly. " I think it's a lovely
town. Isn't it your home town anyway ? "

"Oh, no. I have always lived in Russia—until the
Bolsheviks, that is. I just used to come here to visit.
But anyway, I want to get away and I should
appreciate it if you could send me somewhere else."

"Well, well, we'll see what we can do," he said. " I
am going to write to the different branches and perhaps
we can arrange something."

A week had passed. Two weeks. Three. . . . I
went to Dr. H. again.

"How about my transfer ? " I asked. " Have you
heard anything yet ? "

But the director was very vague. He was so vague
that I grew suspicious. I wanted to see the carbon
copies of his letters. He refused to show them to me
and said in the jovial, placating tone one uses to
recalcitrant children :

"You don't really want to leave us, Miss Kinel.
We have treated you well and you know all about this
work. Come, be a good girl."

I was a good girl all right, I felt, but I lost my temper.
In those days I had more temper than control. Words
came tumbling through my lips, a quick and dreadful
jumble. All I recall saying was :

"You have deceived me ! I quit ! I am through !"
I remember also Dr. H.'s face, with its look of grieved
surprise, as I ran out of the office. . . .

Back in my own room, I cooled off and thought things

over and saw that I had made a fool of myself.   Now I
had lost a job and the only chance I had of getting away.

The following day I rang up the Consulate and all the
stray Americans I knew, announcing that I was going to
work by the hour or by the day.   I had to go on earning
a living, but I felt that I could not be tied down to a
steady job.   Before two days had passed I had more
calls than I could fill.   Even some of our own men at
the Mission had work for me, and there were several
American business men in Warsaw who were struggling
along with their correspondence and who welcomed my
call.   Most of them lived in the Hotel Bristol, and I
used to go there every day with my portable typewriter
and work all day and occasionally after dinner.   I was
doing the work of a public stenographer, though in
those days I had never heard of such a profession, or
the name for it, either.

After a few weeks of this I had a call from Dr. H.   I
went, thinking that he would ask me to join the Mission
again and intending to refuse, for I liked the free-
lancing work ; besides, I earned much more in this
fashion, being paid by the hour.

" Come here.   I want to show you something," the
director said without any preliminaries, and, picking up
a paper from his desk, he handed it to me.   " Now
does that satisfy you ? "

It was a telegram announcing that the Vienna branch
of the J. D. C. was willing to exchange one of their men
stenographers for Miss K.   It also specified that I was
to be paid in dollars.   I was to have seventy-five dollars
a month and my travelling expenses.   I was to leave
at once.

For a moment I was speechless.   It was a tremendous
break : I could get away and travel again, and for the
first time in years I should be paid in real money, for
our own Polish marks were coming down in an inflation

which was only slightly less severe than Germany's. Best of all, I should get away from the room, the old streets, all the familiar scenes which constantly served to remind me of D. I thought in this way I could forget the whole affair quicker.

That night, as I lay in my berth in the Vienna express, I had the rosiest dreams for the future. I knew I should love Vienna. I was making various plans. I decided to refuse all night-work and do some studying ; perhaps take up music again and practise or write. And Sundays I would devote to sports ; I would not neglect my health as I had been doing hitherto. And with the salary I was getting, I could save some money each month. If I stuck it out for a year, I could save enough to go for a real trip some-where—perhaps to Italy. . . .

The futility of planning was never better demon-strated to me than on that trip. I stayed in Vienna only three days. And six months later I was in Italy, though not as a free tourist, but as a personal secretary to Isadora Duncan.

2

VIENNA

THE most cherished dream of an English girl steno-grapher is a fur coat. Other clothes, like dresses, silk undies, shoes, and hats, matter too. But a genuine fur coat is the greatest dream wish. I found that out on my very first day in Vienna, during the lunch period. It was the winter of 1921. . . .

Most of the stenographers in the Vienna branch were English. They had been taken on in Paris and in

London, then shipped to Vienna, this being cheaper
than importing American girls from New York. These
girls were the first English women I had ever met. I
had known all sorts of English men, both in Russia and
in Poland, but never a female. They interested me. I
divided them evenly into the pretty ones and the ugly
ones. The pretty ones had marvellous complexions,
lovely hair and eyes, and looked as if they could step
right into a chorus of a musical show. The ugly ones
were predestined old maids. They were old maids at
twenty ; they were dry, juiceless, skinny, and had bitter
tongues. Never before had I really beheld an old maid,
I thought. England bred the super type. Both the
pretty and the ugly ones aspired to fur coats. In fact,
most of them had one already and the others were on
the verge of buying one ; they just couldn't make up
their minds whether it was to be a three-quarter seal-
skin or a full-length astrakhan or, perhaps, a leopard
sports coat. . . .

All this luxury was possible because of the exchange
and the inflation. The Austrian krone, like the
German mark, was falling daily, and the salaries of
these girls, paid in dollars, were equivalent to the
salaries of Austrian cabinet ministers.

They all lived in good hotels, used taxis, and spent
their week-ends in the famous Semmering. In fact,
one of them was asking me whether I wouldn't join
them on their next week-end trip when word came
that we were to pack at once to leave for Paris.

This news was a dreadful shock. It came as a shock
to those girls who had not yet bought their furs and
would now probably not be able to acquire them, for in
Paris a fur coat was still beyond a stenographer's
pocket-book. It was a shock to me ; not because of the
furs, to which I did not aspire, but because, after having
for weeks—no, months—tried so hard to get to Vienna,

I was now to leave it on the third day. It was exactly the third day since I had got out at the station and been whisked away to an hotel by one of our officers.

I remember we were all in one big room, having just returned from lunch, when one of the officers came and gave us the order. I had never been able to take orders quietly and so I asked why.

He replied : " We have orders from headquarters in Paris to send all the girls back at once. We don't want to be responsible for the girls. The men will stay on. You know about the general strike, of course. . . . Well, there are rumours of revolution ! You had all better go back to your hotels and pack. We will try to charter a special train for to-night. You will go via Berlin. One of the men will accompany you."

" There isn't going to be a revolution in Austria ! " I said, but the officer, giving me a startled look, ran back to the director's rooms. After a moment's hesitation I went after him.

There wasn't going to be any revolution, I thought. It was stark nonsense. These Americans didn't know, they were so easily frightened. I determined to talk to the director. . . . I walked along the hall to the other end of the building where his room was, thinking back over the three days of my stay in Vienna. On my arrival, at night, I was whisked away rather mysteriously by one of the J. D. C. officers to an hotel. I was deposited in a bedroom occupied by one of the English girls, as they couldn't find a separate room for me. On the way, in jerky sentences, he explained to me that there was a lot of trouble in the city ; there had been a big workers' demonstration. And on the Prater, the main street, they stopped at each large hotel and res-taurant and broke the windows, and in some cases molested the people. In one of the hotels, it seems, they had insulted two of our American girls, had torn

their fur coats off them, had shouted : " Down with the
bourgeoisie . . . we are hungry," and had made threats.

I did not respond with any exclamations of horror or
disapproval, as he probably expected. The Viennese
were hungry ; I was terribly sorry for the workers.
The Viennese were by nature a kindly, cheerful people ;
if they got up a demonstration, they must have felt
desperate. I sat mutely with conflicting emotions.

The next day I found a room. I talked to the woman
who boarded me, to the old porter, and to the waiters in
the restaurants where I had lunch and dinner. I liked
these people, their gentle ways, their soft accent, their
küss die Hand, and I had the average Pole's gratitude to
the Austrians, who alone, of all the nations that had
oppressed Poland, did not persecute us. They had
allowed the Poles the use of their language, the study of
their history and literature, and they had allowed them
some self-government.

I thought of all this as I waited for a chance to speak
to our director. He was " busy," or " in conference."
I was being put off and off by his various, flustered
secretaries. As I waited in the other room, the
absurdity struck me of a newly arrived stenographer
like me talking to the man in charge ; but I did not care
in those days. I didn't much care what other people
thought of me. Finally I simply walked into the room
without ceremony.

The director was a young man by the name of
Rosen-something. He looked very nervous and *distrait*.

" I beg your pardon for interrupting," I said boldly.
" We were given orders to pack and told we would have
to leave Vienna because of these troubles. . . ."

" Who are you ? " he interrupted me.

" I have just been transferred from the Warsaw
branch two days ago ; my name is Miss Kinel. . . ."

" Oh, yes, I remember now," he said. " What can I

o

do for you, Miss Kinel ? " His tone was formal and frigid. " I am very busy right now."

" Look here," I said informally, " I don't believe Austria will have a revolution. The people are just miserable and hungry here, but they haven't the spirit for a revolution. I have been through several. I know all the signs. There aren't any here. It isn't like that at all. I don't think you should send us away."

" I am sorry, Miss Kinel," said the young director pompously. " Really, I have no time to discuss this with you. . . ."

" Well, you ought to," I said impertinently. " I know what I am talking about. I have spoken to people—to waiters, and my landlady and the porter and others. I tell you, it isn't a real revolution—just a few anarchists trying to make trouble. All that the people want is food."

" Well, Miss Kinel, we have orders from Paris. We may withdraw the entire branch. In case of trouble I don't want to be responsible for the girls we brought down here. I am sorry I have no more time for you."

But I wasn't giving in yet. " Can't *I* stay on ? " I said. " I wish you would let me. I am not afraid of trouble, and you don't have to feel responsible."

" I am afraid not," he said. " You will have to go with the others to Berlin to-night and there we will decide what to do next."

I left, but not without a parting shot :

" Well, there isn't going to be a revolution in Austria," I said, " and if there were, we should stick here all the more. There will be lots of calls for relief now, and, after all, we are a relief mission."

That night I left for Berlin with the rest of the girls. They carried their lovely furs on their arms. They wondered about Berlin ; whether clothes there would be as dirt cheap as they were in Vienna.

I mention this little incident because, although I was a rather impudent young girl in those days, sometimes I judged conditions correctly. There was no revolution in Austria and subsequently the J. D. C. had to enlarge their activities there.

3

I FIND A JOB

THE Berlin Mission did not need an extra stenographer, I found out when we got there from Vienna. The English girls were sent home to England and I was offered the choice of returning to Warsaw, where the J. D. C. would be glad to have me back, or leaving.

I had run away from Warsaw. I could not think of going back, and I decided to leave the Mission and find some other work in Berlin. I didn't know a soul in this city and, thanks to the hurry with which the Vienna director expedited our departure from Austria, I was without a German visa. Legally I had no right to stay in Berlin more than twenty-four hours. However, when the porter of the small hotel where I had put up came to ask for my passport in order to take it to the police, I put him off, telling him that I was " in transit " and was leaving in a couple of days.

I remember how I thought to myself that morning : " Well, to-day I have to get a job or they will deport me to Poland." Once I had a job, I knew they would let me stay on. And then, having decided on that, I cast about trying to figure where I could best get a job. And the funniest part about it all is that I had, at that moment, early in the morning, not the least doubt that I would find that job. . . .

I ordered my breakfast and I thought. . . . I thought back : Berlin. . . . Surely it was in Berlin that Pani M. had told me of having met a journalist who wrote for a big American monthly. A man like that would need a good secretary, a girl who knew a few languages and had a little gift for writing. . . . But I didn't know the man's name, or the magazine's. . . . It had something to do with music—music. I took the telephone directory and began to look for the word " music." Soon I found two magazines : *Musical American* and *Musical Courier*. The magazine *Musical Courier* had the representative's name right below : Mr. X. . . . The name seemed slightly familiar. I was not sure, but I thought I would take a chance. I called up the number and got Mr. X. . . . on the line. I told him boldly that I had come from Warsaw, that Mrs. M. was sending him her kindest regards, and that she had asked me to look him up. He replied that he was hardly ever in his office, for he was always running around, and if I wanted to see him I could run down to the Beethoven Saal at noon, where Eleanor Spencer, the American pianist, was rehearsing for her Berlin début. " I shall be sitting in the third or fourth row. You will find me easily," he said, and then described himself as small and dark.

I went there. Mr. X. . . . was small and dark, reminding one slightly of King Alexander of Jugoslavia. I recognised him easily and sat down beside him very quietly, as Miss Spencer was playing. We listened to the first movement of a MacDowell concerto ; then went out into the passage. Mr. X. . . . had shrewd brown eyes ; he looked sharp and smart, but he had an amiable smile. I plunged.

" I have heard a lot about you from Mrs. M.," I said, lying boldly, " and she always used to say that I would make an invaluable secretary to you. I happened to be passing through Berlin and thought I would look you up about it."

Mr. X. . . . then asked me what I could do.

" Oh, nearly everything," I replied. " I am a good secretary—I know shorthand, typing, and all that sort of thing. I am very musical and have a good education, and I like to write. I have never had a job where writing was necessary, except once on a little paper, but I know I can do it. Also, I know languages. I could do your German correspondence as well as the English, and if you need any translating, I could do that too— from Russian, Polish, German, and French."

Mr. X. . . . smiled: " This is grand ; it all sounds very nice. But, you see, I have a secretary."

I do not know how I looked then, but I remember that for a long moment I did not say anything. Then, without a word, I turned and moved to go away. Mr. X. . . . stopped me :

" Look, you come around to my office to-morrow morning and we shall have a talk."

" What for ? " said I. " If you have a secretary."

" You come, anyway," he said. " I'd like to talk to you. Maybe we can arrange something."

I went—and stayed. I worked half a day. The other secretary, it developed, worked only in the afternoons and was often ill. He could use me in the mornings. I worked like this for a week and then Mr. X. . . . told me he was willing to engage me steadily and that I would work a whole day.

" But how about your other secretary ? " I said, feeling very uncomfortable.

" Oh, it's all right ; she isn't well and she never did give me her entire time. I really need someone for the whole day. It's all right. Don't worry."

I did worry, though. It was fine to get a job so quickly, but it wasn't pleasant to think that someone

else was out because of it. I felt funny. I confronted
her awkwardly.

"Oh, you are the new girl," she said. "Mr. X. . . .
spoke of you." She then showed me around and we
talked a little about the work.

She told me briefly that it was interesting and Mr.
X. . . . was nice to work with but that the salary was
not large. . . . Then she said good-bye and left.

4

TOO MUCH MUSIC

PERHAPS it was because I like music too much. Or
perhaps, because, trying to criticise, to judge the performance, while enjoying it emotionally, I felt like a
house divided against itself. At any rate, after the six
months I spent in Berlin as an editorial assistant on
a musical paper, I discovered that I should never
again envy a music critic or a theatrical or movie
critic.

Berlin has twenty-five concert halls. In the full
season there are, on the average, twenty-five concerts
each night. Of these Mr. X. . . . had to cover the most
important ones : any great virtuoso, or the *première* of
some important new composition, or an important
guest conductor, or a new *Wunderkind*. I covered the
next in importance.

That is to say, every evening we jumped about from
one end of Berlin to another in a frantic rush, getting
about half an hour of each performance. Mr. X. . . .
jumped about in taxis, but I had to take the under-

ground or street-cars or buses. When I finally got home at night, somewhere after midnight, I used to be so tired that I went straight to bed. It was the only period in all my life when I didn't even have time to read. I read no books ; I merely glanced through the *Berliner Tageblatt* during the dinner hour at noon.

I did not have to do all this. I was busy at the office till six every day. But there were all the free tickets. Berlin in the evening was full of music, and you could have your choice from Haydn, Bach, and Beethoven to Schönberg, Respighi, and Goossens. "Why don't you hear so and so ? " Mr. X. . . . would say. " And then try to write it up to-morrow. If it's good, I will add it to my Berlin letter." That's how it started. . . .

To see myself in print, to think that my English was good enough to be printed in the biggest musical paper in the world, was the temptation. And once in a while I would get regular assignments—the lesser stars, of course. While Mr. X. . . . listened to Furtwängler and Kreisler and Flesch and Schnabel, I would " cover " some young pianist who was promising.

I remember one particularly. I went without any preliminary warning. The concert was in one of the smaller halls, holding some four or five hundred people. I was on time and sat waiting in that characteristic, tense, slightly expectant hush.

The man who came and seated himself at the piano was a tall clumsy German in his early thirties, already slightly bald, with a big head and huge back. He sat down at the piano, very much humped over because of his height, bending close to the keyboard. For a moment he remained motionless, bent over that keyboard with his huge hands poised loosely on the edge in an attitude that reminded one, somehow, of a loving mother bending over a child. Then he began to play. And the moment he began to play I ceased to think. . . .

To hell with criticism ! This was poetry and painting and the essence of dreams woven from a keyboard ; it was pianistic magic, no less, and only in the short intervals between the pieces did one wonder in a flash about the unheard-of, the consummate technique of this man which made such dreams possible—the marvellous *pianissimos*, the depth and caressing lightness of his touch, that perfect, miraculous ease with which he conjured up all the beauty of Chopin and Debussy and Ravel. . . . This man's name was Walter Gieseking. And in those days in Berlin he was just another young pianist with but a couple of tours behind him.

" How was it ? " Mr. X. . . . asked me.

" Marvellous, marvellous—the Debussy and Ravel and all the moderns—but Chopin too, and Mozart—all of it beautiful ! "

It was Mr. X. . . . who wrote the criticism. I had no words for it.

As a contrast to this I remember another assignment.

" I want you to hear this man to-night," my boss said. " I can't cover him myself. And make a little write-up—just a few lines."

" I was going to hear Furtwängler to-night," I said in dreadful disappointment. " Do I have to hear the entire programme ? "

" No, no. Just drop in sometime to-night. Fifteen minutes will do. Just so one of us will be there and hear him personally."

I managed to hear half a programme conducted by Furtwängler, then rushed to the other end of Berlin to hear this unknown pianist. I didn't stay fifteen minutes. I stayed five or six.

Next morning Mr. X. . . . asked for the write-up.

" I haven't got any," I said simply. " I think, in

kindness to the man, it is better not to say anything
than to have to tell how he plays."

"Write it anyway," Mr. X. . . . said, rather sharply
as it seemed to me. "Just a few lines. He's worked
pretty hard for this début and I promised him a write-
up."

"I can't write it," I said obstinately. "I would
have to say that Mr. Y. has made a mistake in his
vocation ; he should have devoted himself to the
grocery business, or perhaps to meat packing."

"Was it that bad ? " Mr. X. . . . asked, and
smiled.

"It was really terrible. Butchery. Not even
technique, not one clean passage. It was awful."

"Well, never mind," said Mr. X. . . . dismissing the
subject.

To my utter surprise the next issue of the *Courier*,
which we read very avidly, contained, in the Berlin
music letter, a small paragraph in which the said
pianist got a pat on the shoulder for having worked
out an ambitious programme and achieved a Berlin
début.

I couldn't understand it. I wondered. I finally
asked a young American pianist, with whom I had
become quite friendly, about it. He laughed.

"Conscientious critics have to be pretty long-
suffering," he said, and went on to explain that the
work of preparing a full concert programme is so
tremendous that to condemn a pianist out of hand
would be pretty cruel. He confirmed my impression
that X. . . . was quite disinterested and told me that
he was particularly nice to young artists. In Paris
students had to enclose a specified fee when sending
complimentary tickets to a critic, to ensure his coming.

Thus I learned about the music game. I learned
more, too; I learned how complicated was the career

of a musical star; how much it costs to launch it; how much appearance and personality count; and what arduous preparation goes to making the first concert début.

I am glad I had a glimpse of it, but I am glad I got out of it in time. When I go to a good concert now, I just sit in bliss, drinking in the music. I try not to think of all the work that went to make it and I am glad I don't have to criticise it.

5

COPENHAGEN IS FROZEN

I WAS quite flattered by the letter Pani M. sent me and the fact that she entrusted her husband to my care for a few days. I was at that tender age when responsibility is what one craves for and gloats over, and the responsibility of looking after the morals of a great artist doesn't often come into a young girl's life. . . . By the time the affair came to an end, I wasn't proud. I didn't even write to Pani M. I just let the thing slide into the limbo of forgetfulness, as we all do at one time or another.

Not that the letter said anything directly. M. brought it himself. He walked into the *Musical Courier* office one winter afternoon, fat, pudgy, and happy, his own precious self.

" How are you ? When did you get in ? Where is Pani M. ? "

" She is home. Oh, here is a letter for you." He handed it to me and continued : " I am going to stay

here just for a couple of days, then I am going on to
Copenhagen. I have been there before, you know.
It's a lovely town. And the way these Danes feed you!
I tell you, it's miraculous." He elaborated on this.
Life was nothing but a huge party for this fat, blue-
eyed pagan, and his jolliness was so infectious that after
five minutes of it I felt like going to Copenhagen
myself.

" But why isn't Pani M. going this time ? " I asked.
I knew she usually accompanied him everywhere.

" She will join me later. She couldn't get away.
You read her letter "—and he gave me one of his sly
winks. " Female worries. . . . I believe she wants you
to look after me. Ha, ha, ha. . . ."

" Oh, nonsense ! " I said promptly, and knew as
promptly that he was right. Pani M. was terribly
afraid he might get into a drunken debauch or fall into
the clutches of a prostitute. She looked after him like
a hen after a special duckling. . . . Great Scott, thought
I, what did she want me to do ?

M. left after we had made a date for the evening, and
when the door had closed on his fat back, I read his
wife's note. It was nice and conventional—open, of
course. She asked me to look after M., see that he
enjoyed his evenings in Berlin and spent them *well*.
(The italics are mine.) I read between the lines. I
read all her customary anxieties and worries. I felt
flattered and began to map out a campaign at once ;
after all, I had all these tickets to the opera and the
concerts and theatres, and after that we could go to a
Bierhalle and drink a lot of lager. Lager made one
sleepy—not excited, like wine—and by one or two M.
would be ready for his bed in the hotel. . . . Everything
would work out all right, I thought—what is two or
three nights, anyway ? Pani M. had to look after him
all her life. I thought of her with profound respect,

almost awe.   To be the wife of a great artist who is both an absolute heathen and a greedy child is no joke.

First Night

"Well, what shall we do to-night?   Ballet, opera, concert, drama?   I have tickets for everything." Thus I greeted M. when he turned up at the office that night.

"Ballet?   What ballet?"

"The Swedish ballet.   Supposed to be something entirely new and original."

"Swedish ballet?   But how can the Swedes dance? They haven't any temperament."

"Well, let's find out.   I haven't seen them yet. They have a roller-skate number which is supposed to be clever."

M. consented reluctantly.   We had dinner somewhere and repaired to the ballet.

The ballet was bad.   The comely Swedish girls had no fire.   The *maître de ballet* was fat and looked like a eunuch.   The music was worse.   The puny conductor, who had composed most of it, exerted himself strenuously, trying to produce something out of nothing. . . .

M. was bunched up over the balustrade of our loge, his eyes half closed, looking at the girls. . . .   For a long while, for twenty minutes perhaps, he sat like that, immobile, silent. . . .   I began to feel afraid.   My God, what did he think! . . .   If he would only say something, swear. . . .   Then he snorted, leaned back, heaved a deep sigh, and said :

"God, what lousy stuff!   Look at those girls. There isn't a woman among them.   And the music! What does that fellow suppose he's doing?   This isn't art, creation.   No line, no climax—he's no good, impotent!"

We rose. And we left.

We walked down the street and for an hour or so M. discoursed on art, on composition, on the creative line and kindred subjects. And although he explained it all in terms of physiology—these being the most natural to him—it was the best explanation of its kind I ever heard. I applied it thereafter many times in sizing up artistic compositions, whether of dance or music, and found it superb.

We wound up in a beer garden where we talked some more and M. drank a lot of beer. Everything then happened just as I had planned : he got drowsy and heavy, we took a cab, and I accompanied him to his hotel and saw the porter conduct him safely to his room. The first night was disposed of.

Second Night

We went to see a comedy ; it was excellent and we left in good spirits. Said M. :

" You know it's too early to turn in. Let's go somewhere."

" Very well, but where ? I don't like cabarets."

" No cabaret. I have an idea. I have a friend, a pianist. Let's look him up ; I haven't seen him in years."

We did. The pianist was a tall, slim man, grey, with a spirited but strained face. He was a formal but polite host, quite typically Polish. He made some splendid coffee and served it with various liqueurs and lovely cakes. His salon was beautifully appointed with a good Blüthner grand, lovely pictures, rugs, and such. M. waddled around, sizing it all up appreciatively ; then asked to see the whole flat. The host escorted us.

The hall was bare except for some prints and woodcuts ; the dining-room was in excellent taste but very austere ; the bedroom was a surprise : it was a small,

narrow room, all done in white, absolutely bare except
for a high, narrow white bed, a tiny table and chair. It
was exactly like a hospital room of the old order. I
thought to myself : " This is funny, I wonder if the host
is a misogynist or something." . . .

The host then seemed to think we had seen enough,
but M. insisted on seeing the rest. " Everything, my
dear fellow, show us everything," he said. We saw the
bathroom, toilet, and then went into the kitchen. All
the four walls, every bit of wall space available, were
covered with pictures of nudes—French girls in various
stages of undress and other cards of this kind.

" But why in the kitchen . . . why in the kitchen ? "
I asked, aghast. M. winked at me and nudged the
host with his elbow.

" He doesn't like to be lonesome when he cooks his
meals. He is smart."

The host remained bland and formal. He vouch-
safed no explanations. The evening trailed on. About
2 a.m. we took a cab ; I deposited M. at his hotel and
went to my rooms.

Third Night

I forget what it was. Concert or theatre. It was
out early and M. suggested a walk. It was very cold
but beautiful, a real winter evening, with the snow
crunching under one's shoes, the dark sky very high
above us, the stars twinkling, the air snappy. We
walked on the Tauentzienstrasse, a sort of main street
of a certain part of Berlin. There were many couples,
young, spooning couples, walking arm in arm. But
there were also quite a few single girls, girls in long,
clinging dresses and cheap fur jackets, girls who were
made up very brightly—in fact, ladies for sale. M.
followed them with his eyes a little way as they passed
and muttered guttural criticisms. We were approach-

ing a small square. A bunch of people were gathering
quickly into a crowd. Something was afoot.

"Let's see what it is," M. said excitedly, and pulled
me by the arm. We hurried towards the crowd.

A girl in a clinging dress and cheap fur jacket was
having an argument with a small, dry-looking, middle-
aged man. She spoke loudly and gesticulated. The
middle-aged man seemed to be defending himself in a
squeaky, aggrieved voice. A tall, trim policeman was
standing by ; the little crowd stood listening and commenting mildly. It was all quite orderly, not too noisy,
very German—like a family party. The girl said :
" I told him I wasn't going with him unless he pays
with *valuta*.[1] What can I do with cheap marks ?
They won't even pay for my cup of coffee." She
addressed herself to the crowd.

" It isn't like that at all," said the middle-aged man.
" She accosted me and I said yes, then when we were
about to go, all of a sudden, she wants to be paid in
valuta. I have no *valuta*. I would pay her in marks
what she is worth, but I am not a damned foreigner
who can sport *valuta*. I am a book-keeper and I get
paid in marks. And who is she to ask for foreign
money, anyway ? It isn't patriotic. It isn't at all
patriotic," he kept on repeating in grievous, squeaky
tones.

Someone in the crowd snickered and the girl turned
on him and said angrily :

" I am not going unless I get paid in real money,
dollars or francs. I don't accept worthless German
marks ; I am not that cheap."

The policeman listened attentively ; then, suddenly,
thought of his authority and said : " *Ruhig, ruhig,
Fräulein*. Don't scream or I'll have to arrest you.

[1] *Valuta* was the designation of all foreign money. It was the period
of inflation when German marks were falling daily and had practically
no value.

Now you decide quietly whether you are going with this gentleman or not. Not so much noise." Then, turning to the little crowd : " Please, please, disperse ; this is no laughing matter."

The girl in the fur jacket continued talking loudly and vindictively ; I saw the book-keeper shrug his shoulders and go away, muttering some imprecations ; the crowd began to melt away. We turned away, laughing.

This was the third night. To-morrow, according to M.'s plans, he would be on his way to Copenhagen. I would write Pani M. a nice letter, tell her how I had tried to entertain him, what shows we had seen, and so on. Everything was fine. We went to a *Bierhalle* and had beer, then M. returned to his hotel and I went home. Everything was fine.

Fourth Night

Everything was not fine. Everything was wrong. M. came the next morning and said he had just been to the station and he could not leave that day because Copenhagen was frozen.

" What do you mean Copenhagen is ' frozen ' ? I don't understand."

" It's frozen. I am telling you. The water around it is frozen. You know it's on an island and the train is usually transferred on a ferry, and now the water is frozen and one can't cross. One cannot go to Copenhagen, I was told. It's this exceptional frost. A thing like that has not happened in fifty years, they tell me."

" But what do the other travellers do ? Isn't there some other way of reaching it ? "

" Sure, if you want to ski your way across the frozen ice, or hire a sled. . . . Not for me, thank you. There are thin spots and you can vanish in the flicker

of an eye . . . not for me such sport. I am going to stay
in Berlin and wait till the ice melts and the ferry can
cross again."

No, not for him. He didn't like risky adventures,
I thought. And a thing like that had not happened
in fifty years. It had to happen just now, just when
I was supposed to look after him, I thought bitterly. . . .

That night we went to hear something or someone ;
then had a walk, dropped in somewhere for some beer,
and M. returned to his hotel and I returned home.

Fifth Night

Copenhagen was frozen. We went somewhere or
other, heard someone, drank beer, walked, and went to
sleep in our respective places. I was very tired.

Sixth Night

Copenhagen was frozen. I don't know what we did.
I don't remember, either, whether it was that night or
the following that M. phoned that he had met some old
friends and would spend the evening with them. I
remember I was very glad. I was tired of getting to
bed so late, and also we had begun to exhaust each
other's company ; I had heard all the Warsaw scandals
and gossip and he had heard all my news. And after
all, I thought, I can't stick to him like a leech or a
chaperon ; he is almost forty ; he can take care of
himself . . . no wife can expect that. . . . Thus I tried to
appease my conscience.

After that I saw M. only occasionally. Sometimes
he would drop in at the office or phone. He seemed
very jolly and happy. " Is Copenhagen still frozen ? "
I would ask. " Still frozen. Can you imagine it ? "
he would reply. " I am marooned. Can't get
away."

P

Copenhagen was frozen for two weeks. On the day
before he left, he came to say good-bye.

"Well, I am going to-morrow. The ferry goes
across, among a lot of ice-floes, they say. . . . Can you
imagine it ? It's almost three weeks since I came.
But I've had a nice time, a swell time."

"I am so glad," I said.

"Yes. You know that friend of mine you met ?"
He winked his inexpressibly naïve yet sly wink and said
in a low voice : "He has a little mistress—it isn't all just
pictures in the kitchen, you know—and she brought
along a little friend of hers, the cutest thing . . . the
cutest thing. Now don't you mention anything when
you write to Warsaw, will you ?"

"No, of course not," I promised. And I never did.
For I felt that I was a little responsible. I and the
weather.

6

JUST ANOTHER WAR STORY

THE last time I had seen Cousin Julek was in Petrograd
in 1918. He was an officer in the artillery, a clever
young man and rather handsome : tall, with a nice,
narrow, sleek head, an aristocratic long nose—altogether a dashing figure. I remember still the shock of
that meeting. It was on the Nevski Prospect, Petrograd's most famous avenue. We ran into each other
and I almost screamed. For there he was, in his beautiful officer's uniform, with his epaulettes—walking
flauntingly, unconcernedly, in *June 1918*, when half the
Russian officers had been killed by their soldiers and the
other half had mysteriously disappeared, when there

was not one epaulette to be seen on the streets, when
one saw only khaki soldiers' coats without any insignia
or the red badge of the Soviet army. . . .

" Julek ! " I said quickly in Polish. " Take it off—
they will murder you."

" I'm not afraid of the bastards," he answered in
Russian—not too low, either. " Besides," he added,
seeing that I was really nervous, " they wouldn't
attack me here, in broad daylight, on the Nevski. . . .
Don't be foolish. It would take some nerve, for I'd
put up a fight. . . ." And so we walked on and talked,
a little disjointedly, a bit nervously, as we all did in
those days. . . . And then, at parting, he shook my
hand a little more warmly than usual and said :

" Good-bye. You know, I am going south—any
day."

They all did in those days, all those officers who
thought that they might still fight the Bolsheviks with
Denikin or some other general. . . . " South " in those
days was still a magical word. It contained all the
hopes of the Whites and those peasants who wanted to
fight the Communists.

The South swallowed Julek as it had swallowed
thousands of others. We never heard of him after that.

And now, in Berlin, in 1922, I was to see Julek again.
Father had written that Julek had returned to Poland,
that he had just left for Berlin to have some special
medical treatment he needed and asking me to look
him up at his *pension*.

As I walked to the *pension* where Julek was stopping,
I recalled a previous letter from father in which he told
the story of a postal card. A postal card from Turkey,
addressed to an old great-aunt and signed " Julek."
The old lady remembered that one of her nieces had a
son called Julek, so she handed the card to Julek's
mother. And the mother, seeing her son's handwriting

on a postcard, the son who " went south " in 1918 and
was never heard from again, promptly fainted, so it was
someone else who first read the postal and learned that
Julek was safe and alive in Turkey. . . .

My head alive with memories of Julek, dashing and
handsome on the Nevski Prospect, and the bits of news
I had had from Poland about his return, I sat waiting
in the lobby of the *pension*, when a tall, strange young
man approached me and said, " Hello, Lola " in Julek's
voice, and kissed my hand and my face. And I stood,
paralysed with shock and pity, and cursed myself for
not having a poker face, for showing always, instantly,
how I felt. For the strange young man was Julek all
right, but his face was a different face—he had no nose.
A small piece of flesh with two odd holes of nostrils
projected in the middle of it, and it was not Julek any
more, only a pitiful, odd-looking stranger with Julek's
voice. But he was as gallant as ever, for he never let
on what he saw on my face ; he just grinned and said :

" I am a sight, aren't I ? You see, the doctor in
Constantinople just fixed me up temporarily so I could
breathe. And it wasn't a good job, either, for I still
don't breathe right. This German plastic surgeon is
going to give me a proper good nose. I shall probably
be in Berlin for three or four weeks. . . ."

" That's dandy," I broke in. " I am going to show
you around ; I have got all sorts of tickets, you know—
opera, ballet, all the concerts. . . ." I spoke without
thought, like a fool. . . .

" I don't think I shall go out much at night," Julek
said. " You see, they will need me at the hospital
nearly every day ; and then I will be all bandaged and
taped up—a nuisance. . . ."

" Well, then I will see you here whenever I can. . . .
Shall we go for a walk ? "

" Yes, let's."

And we went to the Zoological Gardens and walked about, and I tried not to see the shocked glances of the passers-by whose eyes would rivet themselves for an instant on the young man's face, the face with hardly any nose. . . .

" Look, tell me what has happened since I saw you on the Nevski."

He gave an odd grin :

" Plenty. I went south the very next day after I saw you. . . . I fought in Denikin's army. . . . I got married there, too—to a nurse. Shortly afterwards we were in an attack and my nose was blown off. I had other wounds too, and lost my wife. I don't remember much after that. We moved south all the time and after the big defeat we fled to Turkey. I was sick all the time. In the Russian camp in Constantinople I got typhus . . . lost my hair . . . my nose wasn't healing well—rather, the spot where it had been . . . I was cut off from all of you. . . . One day I wandered about the camp. I was near the women's ward, and I heard my wife's voice. . . ."

" *O moj Boze* (Oh, my God), Julek ! "

" She also had had the typhus and had no hair. . . ." He continued his account, with the little dry smile with which all these brave young men used to recount their war experiences. " But after that things went better. When I got some strength back—you know typhus drains you terrifically—I went to the International Red Cross and they gave me a job on their staff. My good French came in handy. A Russian camp surgeon made this nose, just a makeshift, you know, so I shouldn't frighten people ; then I saved, we tried to leave the camp and settle down in the city, but they wouldn't let us, for we had no passports, no documents of any kind. We were just White Russian refugees to them. After a while they moved us all to an island. The camp there

was nicer—we had a place to ourselves, my wife and I.
We had a baby and we engaged a Russian *niana*—she
is still with us—we brought her along to Poland. . . ."

" But, Julek, how did you get out, after all ? "

" I wrote to Poland, to our Great-aunt Emma, asking
whether she knew anything about our family. I
thought they were all in Petrograd, starving . . . the
accounts in the Press in Turkey were awful . . . I had
no idea you had all escaped."

" Yes. Your mother and all your family came in
1921, just about a year ago."

" Well, as soon as I knew they were all there, I pulled
all the strings and finally we got out. . . ."

After that I saw Julek every other day or so. He was
always bandaged up and taped up, and every time I
saw him the lump beneath the white gauze seemed a bit
bigger and longer. . . . His nose grew. It grew by bits,
for it was piecework, and Julek, who insisted on watching the surgeon's work in a mirror, told me how
cleverly it was all contrived : how the German surgeon
took bits of cartilage from the lobes of his ears and
later from between his ribs—for cartilage, it seems, is the
only kind of flesh to grow a nose from, having the
property of not growing together, so that it can be used
to form good nostrils for breathing ; and how he finally
took a piece of skin from Julek's forehead and another
from somewhere else—a nice, big piece of skin with
which to cover the new nose—and how he finally
finished the job. . . .

And then one day Julek took off the bandages and
there he was, a presentable young man, though still
different from the old Julek, for the new nose was not
so long, nor did it have the aristocratic, imperious swing
to it. It was plain and short, but it was decent enough,
with proper nostrils and all. And a few days later
Julek bid me good-bye and returned to Poland.

7

BERLIN ART LIFE

As a child, in Russia, I once saw a Moscow Art Theatre production of the *Cherry Orchard*. I was only nine or ten, but was deeply impressed by the beauty of the play and the memory of it became one of those haunting lovely things that are more like a poem than a mere memory. I never forgot the mood of it, the clear sadness, the little touches of comedy and the absolutely magnificent simplicity of it all. It was not " like a play." It was more like peeping into a real house, with real people, through some magical window . . . it was not theatre at all. . . .

In Berlin, in 1921, there came on a tour one of the Studios of the Moscow Art Theatre, and it became the sensation of the season. Again I went to witness their magic. It was one of the big Studios, including some of their greatest actors: Stanislavsky himself, Kachalov, Olga Knipper-Chekhova, Germanova and many others. The plays they brought this time were their best, tried-out masterpieces, and so the magic was truly wonderful. I was lucky too. I had to interpret between my employer, Mr. X. . . . and the manager of the Russian group as Mr. X. . . . thought they ought to go to America (eventually they went under the management of Morris Guest), and as a representative of our office I was invited to come free to all the performances.

I didn't miss any of it. I went again and again and saw it all: Tsar Fiodor with all the byzantine and barbaric magnificence; Gorky's *Lower Depths* and Chekhov's *Three Sisters* and all the rest. And each evening I had again the overwhelming sensation that this was not " acting," not something artificially and skilfully *created*, but a genuine piece of life or history, living organically right in front of me and which by some trick I was able to witness. I have no doubt that the entire audience, eighty per cent of which was German and couldn't understand a word, felt the same. Since then acting technique has been perfected everywhere; *mise-en-scènes* have become more accurate and imaginative and the ensemble technique in the films has reached as high a degree of perfection as that of the Moscow Art Theatre. Yet when one considers that a scene in the films is often taken thirty or forty times—as many times as is necessary for a perfect shot—one has to marvel at the flawless performances, the unity of mood and effect that was achieved day in day out by this group of Russians.

Russian art in those days was far more alive in Berlin than in Soviet Russia, which was in the grip of famine, exhausted by two years of civil war. Luckily for the artists, the Commissar of Art and Education at the time was the liberal and enlightened Lunacharski, who gave the arts a benevolent and understanding supervision. Writers, musicians, painters and other artists were free to leave and come and go as they pleased. There was not yet the complete strangling of the arts with Marxist ideology, towing the party line and all the other Communist nonsense which later hampered all art in the Soviets. And so, in Berlin, outside of the *bourgeois emigrés* who numbered thousands, there were groups of Soviet artists of all kinds. There was an art club, two cabarets and many so-called " circles ": groups of poets, critics, painters, etc. There was also a good half-dozen publishers and their writers, Soviet and anti-Soviet alike.

Later in the spring there arrived from Petrograd Alexander Glazounov, the famous composer and conductor and head of the Petrograd Conservatory. I had to see him on business and I still have a clear memory of that talk.

Mr. Glazounov was standing at the window of his room in a very modest *pension*. His back was turned to the room. He was tapping the pane thoughtfully and spoke now and then a few gruff words. He was considering a contract for an American tour. In the absence of my employer, who was empowered to make the offer and who was in England at the time, I was handling the matter—or rather, trying my youthful best to do it.

Alexander Konstantinovich was deep in thought. He was a huge, heavy man with a typical Russian face: broad, shapeless, bulbous, yet somehow full of character and kindliness. I recalled the many stories I had heard about him in Petrograd. He had one great failing: he was too kind and this was so well known that occasionally pupils took advantage of it. It was common knowledge that anyone who knew how to put on a little convincing crying act, could get a scholarship, for he couldn't stand tears. He simply beamed upon the poor, unfortunate pupil and arranged for free tuition. However, as he accepted only greatly talented children, this kindness was not misplaced.

Mr. Glazounov, after a long pause, turned around heavily, gave me the contract which he had been holding in his pudgy hand, and said: " I am afraid not. I cannot go to America. America is not for me."

" Alexander Konstantinovich," I said, " won't you please reconsider? Don't give me the answer now. I shall come around in a couple of days."

" No, no. I am quite sure now. I can't go," he repeated.

I did not want to give in so easily. It was not only the fact that I had instructions from Mr. X. . . . to try my best to get Glazounov sign the contract. I simply

felt that Glazounov was passing up a good deal. He
needed it terribly. He had just come from Petrograd,
where he had gone through incredible hardships during
the years of civil war and famine. He looked ill, his
suit was shabby. I could not understand his refusal.

" Alexander Konstantinovich, won't you tell me
why? " I asked. " Is there anything in the contract
you don't like? Perhaps we can change some clause
to please you? "

He looked at me with his small, deeply buried eyes.
" No, my dear *baryshnia*, it seems a nice contract.
I am just too old, too ill. I hate to make the long
trip across the ocean and I don't know the language.
What shall I do in America without English? I shall
be lost. I think I had better return home."

" Oh, but that is not a real reason," I protested,
" the trip is nice. You will go on a good liner in a
first-class cabin and you won't need to know English.
There are plenty of Russians in New York and,
perhaps, the management will assign you a secretary,
a Russian, to accompany you on the tour." The contract, as I seem to recall it, was for fifteen appearances
for the sum of $10,000. To a Russian from the
destitute Soviets this was a huge amount, I knew.

" I know . . . all that money," Glazounov said sadly,
" and I need it, too. And the children at the conservatory—all so hungry, no clothes. . . . You know,
we haven't even any paper. No paper to write music
on," he went on feelingly.

" Well, then, why not sign? " I said excitedly.
" We shall try our best to make you comfortable . . .
why don't you go? "

" *Niet, nie mogu* (no, I can't)," he repeated; " that
trip across the ocean . . . and without the language . . .
I cannot do it."

This time I did not protest. We shook hands and

I left. I felt terribly sorry for this kindly, pudgy Russian, as great and true an artist as ever lived. A few days later I read in the paper that Glazounov returned to Russia: to poverty, hunger and cold.

8

WIESBADEN

I HAD been working in the critic's office for six months when I caught a very severe cold. The doctor had ordered immediate rest in the country. However, when I asked Mr. X. . . . for a short vacation, he simply let me go, saying that the musical season was over, anyway, and adding that I could have my job back in the fall.

I went home to my room in a turmoil of real and mental fever. I had been working pretty hard, particularly during a few weeks when my boss was away on a trip and I had complete charge of the office. He had praised my work and although my salary, paid in German marks, was small, I hung on because I liked the work and hoped, eventually, to receive a better salary in dollars.

Now all these hopes were dashed. I had drawn on the small reserve I had from my previous job and I had only a few dollars left. The worst of it was the funny sickness I had. The German doctor never really diagnosed the trouble and so I didn't know what it was. I had a low but persistent fever and terrible headaches which, at times, made it impossible to think. What I actually had was a good attack of sinus. But I did not know it then. I did not discover it until a few years later in America. In those days European doctors did not seem to know or bother about sinuses. Some people just had frequent colds and suffered from headaches, that was all, and I happened to be one of them. And I was anæmic, they kept on saying; I needed sunshine, food, and rest. . . .

Next morning I got up late and with the usual headache. My landlady brought me my coffee and my mail. In the mail there was an invitation from an aunt and cousin from Wiesbaden. I recalled that they had written before, asking me to run down to see them and stay for a week-end, and I had not even acknowledged it in the press of my work. . . . I thought of grandmother's God, who seemed really to be looking after me a bit ; I hastily packed a small bag, wrote a note to my sister in America, stored my trunks, and left for Wiesbaden.

My aunt made quite a fuss and had her own doctor see me. The fat, old, pompous German professor didn't know why I had fever either, but ordered bed for a week. I stayed just one day, then got up and escaped outside into the sunshine. It was spring and it was lovely. I walked up and down the crooked, hilly little streets, drinking in the dry, spicy air of the mountains. Within a week I was completely well.

Wiesbaden was in those days an international beehive, in some respects more important than Berlin. For here sat the famous Reparations Commission with its staff of economic experts, bankers, book-keepers, and clerks, trying to reckon how to squeeze things out of Germany. My cousin was in charge of one of the Polish departments. He was paid in French francs, which, converted into German marks, made him quite a millionaire. The lowest clerk in that commission was rolling in German marks and could buy out the town. At night all these foreigners congregated in various little cafés and cabarets. Dancing was universal from five o'clock on, and it was all very gay with the characteristic post-war gaiety. My aunt, a very

beautiful and charming woman, had a large circle of
friends, mostly Frenchmen and Poles, and my sudden
sick leave turned into a real holiday. In the morning
I loafed about, at night we went out, and the week-ends
were spent in little trips in the Rhineland.

At the end of the third week I got a wire from my
sister and fifty dollars. Much as I loathed leaving the
place, for I had not had as gay a time in years, I packed
and left for Berlin. I put an advertisement in the
English newspaper and then left for Berg Dievenow, a
tiny fishing village on the Baltic, where my fifty dollars
would last me for a long, long time. A week later I
had a wire in response to my advertisement. It was
signed " Isadora Duncan." . . .

9

ISADORA AND ESSENINE

IT wasn't Isadora at all who was awaiting me at the
Berlin address mentioned in the telegram. It was a
young American boy, an art student, I believe, by the
name of Miltoun. He introduced himself as Isadora's
friend and we went out to a café to discuss the business.
He had seen my advertisement, he explained, and,
knowing Isadora's predicament in not being able to
talk to her Russian husband, he thought I might do
for a secretary. And now he was to decide whether or
not I should do. . . .

We talked and we drank coffee, bad, weak coffee of
the sort the Germans call *Blümchenkaffee*, meaning
" coffee of the little flowers "—the flowers which you
detect on the bottom of Saxon china cups because the

damned coffee is so weak—while this young man was
sizing me up for the job of being Isadora's and Essenine's secretary. . . . After half an hour's conversation
which covered a great deal of territory, from Bolshevism to art, he exclaimed :

" You will do ! You are just what she needs . . . and
all those languages . . . splendid ! Now let's go and
send the wire. Can you leave to-night ? She is in
Wicsbaden, you know."

" Wiesbaden ! How funny ! I just came from
there."

" Well, you will have to go back then. Is to-night
all right ? "

" Yes, quite all right."

" And let me tell you something," he added confidentially, " don't take too much luggage. Isadora is
always on the go. She may tell you she wants to stay
a week in some town and a couple of hours later you will
find you are leaving. . . ." Prophetic words !

We stopped at the nearest telegraph station and he
asked me to spell a German word for him. I leaned
over the telegraph blank and saw the following :

DEAR ISADORA MISS KINEL IS A PEACH LEAVING TO-NIGHT

This, I remember, puzzled me not a little. I guessed
that it was slang and hoped that it was complimentary,
for the expression was new to me and I could not understand why I was called a fruit and why, particularly, a
peach. Why not a pear, or a plum ? If he had written
that I was a lemon I should have been equally puzzled
and hopeful. But I refrained from asking. We parted
with a handshake, I rushed to my hotel, packed, and
took the next train for Wiesbaden.

Next morning, rather breathlessly, I knocked at the

ISADORA DUNCAN

Enlarged from a Passport Photograph
Dusseldorf 1922

door of Isadora's suite at the Hotel Rose. A pleasant voice said " Come in " and I entered.

A fat, middle-aged woman in a salmon-coloured negligée was reclining gracefully on the couch. She had a small head with Titian curls, a beautiful but cruel mouth, and sentimental eyes ; she spoke with a sort of clipped accent. When she rose, after a while, and began to move about the room, I saw that she was not fat or middle-aged : she was beautiful, she had an innate, a marvellous grace. . . . This was Isadora. . . .

After a while a young man in white silk pyjamas came out of the adjoining bedroom. He looked like a Russian dancer from an American vaudeville show : pale golden, curly hair ; naïve eyes of cornflower blue, and the grace of a very strong, muscular body. . . . This was Essenine. Later I discovered that he was not always naïve. He was sly, too, and suspicious, and instinctively clever. And he was very sensitive, just like a child, and full of twists and complexes—a peasant and a poet, both.

10

WHEN ISADORA DANCED

When she danced it was divinity speaking, no less. She tells us again and again that the dance must come from within, from the soul, " from some melody of another world," but when she danced it was a thing beyond explanations, beyond analysis, above words.—SHELDON CHENEY.[1]

I had been with Isadora and Essenine fully a month before I saw her dance. It was in Brussels, where she

[1] From the Introduction to *The Art of the Dance*, by Isadora Duncan. Theatre Arts, Inc., New York. Copyright 1928 by Helen Hadicott. Privately printed.

had a three-day engagement. I must confess that
when the day drew near my curiosity and excitement
were tinged with an odd feeling of fear : Isadora was
middle-aged and almost corpulent, and, although the
inimitable grace which imbued her every movement had
already captured my imagination, I was actually
frightened that when I saw her dance I might be disappointed. This, I felt, would be nothing short of a
calamity. Also, she had had only a few short days of
actual preparation or exercise. Throughout the weeks
that I had been with her, I had never seen her take the
least precautions in her diet or practise or do any of the
things that dancers are said to do. . . .

When I got to the theatre, it was crowded and the
atmosphere was charged with that anticipatory tense-
ness which is present when an audience expects a big
thrill. The curtains parted and revealed an empty
stage, save for an upright in the corner, with the pianist
seated at it. Around the stage were draped Isadora's
famous blue curtains. . . .

When the inevitable murmurs and noises had subsided, the pianist started to play. From the opposite
corner the blue curtains parted ever so lightly and
Isadora appeared. . . .

And now I am coming to the hardest part in this
book, for how can anyone ever describe the magic that
was her dance ? All I remember now is that I sat in
that box in a rapture that one can compare only to a
sort of religious exaltation. All my absurd fears
vanished as if they had never been. I was filled with
joy and a profound humility before this miracle of
beauty.

If someone asked me to describe the individual
dances I should also be hard put to it. Each dance
was like a little, rounded-out composition or poem,
charged with emotion and meaning. There never

seemed a single unnecessary gesture or movement : like all geniuses, she seemed to achieve a maximum effect with a minimum of means. There was not anything, of course, that could be called " pretty " or " frilly " ; every line was of divine simplicity and beauty. In the final analysis, I should even hesitate to call it dancing, for although the range of the various movements varied from the very slowest motions to some really high jumps, there never was such a thing as a " step." One movement flowed out of another as inevitably and naturally as the leaves grow on a tree, and each dance was one beautiful, undulating line, a magic fluidity of motions of which each single one, arrested, would have revealed a composition worthy of the greatest sculptor.

Withal, though hardly any of the dances could be definitely labelled, they were full of profound meaning. They seemed to reveal all the different emotions through which a human being, or humanity itself, passes in a lifetime. They were universal. There was one Chopin prelude, for instance, in which Isadora merely walked from one end of the stage to the other. How to describe these dozen steps that were yet one continuous line ? It might have been called " Despair, Death, and Resurrection." Or " Sorrow and Joy." It started at medium strength, ebbed to a point of complete stillness, gained vigour and, slowly, reached a climax. . . . There was the famous Schubert " Moment Musical " where all the beautiful emotions of mother-hood seemed consecrated in a few simple, unforgettable motions. Who can ever forget the inimitable grace of her lovely arms with which she seemed to rock a baby, those poor arms which had been empty so long ? And then the Brahms *valtzes*, one in particular, where Isadora was like a Goddess of Joy strewing flowers around her. . . . I could have sworn I saw children on

Q

the stage . . . there, where I knew was nothing but the empty rug . . . where Isadora smiled and danced, bending joyously right and left. . . . It was pure magic. . . .

II

WHEN ESSENINE RECITED

IT was in Brussels, too, that I first heard Essenine recite in public. Until then I had heard him read some of his poems, often merely a line or two, while we were both proof-reading the first big volume of his lyrical poems, which was being published in Berlin. I think he read them to me for " reactions." He looked at me sharply, watching my face. He seldom believed what people told him and had a peculiar way of " finding out things " for himself. His eyes would narrow, become mere blue slits, and he would watch warily while putting naïve questions and pretending that he was stupid. . . . Sometimes he would shoot a question suddenly, giving a sort of third degree. He would ask questions about my tastes in literature, then, in the midst of the conversation, he would pick up a sheet of paper and read, watching me all the while. I have a telltale face, and if he saw genuine pleasure he was terribly pleased, like a child. He read well, varying his voice, his intonation, often his accent, to an amazing degree. . . .

But it was in Brussels that I got the full flavour of a recitation. It was after Isadora's last appearance ; we had an informal party at the hotel. There were present Isadora's sister Elizabeth, who had come with a friend from Berlin expressly to see Isadora dance ;

Mr. Isaye, the manager ; the pianist ; several other friends ; Essenine and myself.

Isadora, dressed in one of her Greek tunics, supped reclining on a couch. She looked very young and beautiful. It was a lovely gay meal with everybody in a sparkling mood. Even Essenine, who could not join in the general conversation, was cheerful, gracious, and smiling.

After the supper, at Isadora's request, he agreed to give a recitation. He went to the farthest end of the room, turned, facing us, and began to speak. He chose excerpts from his dramatic poem, *Pougachiov*, the story of the great Cossack rebel who rose against Catherine the Great, led the peasants against her soldiers, and was Russia's first great revolutionary. It is considered Essenine's most important work and is really a complete drama in eight scenes.

I was instantly spellbound ; Essenine's voice of the Southern Russian peasant, soft and slightly drawling, ran an amazing gamut of expressions, from the very gentlest crooning, which was like a caress, to some utterly wild, hoarse shrieks. He *was* Pougachiov, the tortured peasant . . . at first long-suffering, patient, bewildered, and then wild, cunning, wrathful, terrible in his anger and desire for freedom and revenge . . . and then, at the end, when he was betrayed, humble and forlorn. . . . In turn Essenine-Pougachiov complained in a singsong murmur, recounted, spoke ; he shouted, spat, and blasphemed, his body swaying in rhythm with his words until the entire room seemed to vibrate with his emotions ; and then, at the end, in defeat, he crumpled up . . . he sobbed. . . .

We all sat in silence. . . . For a long moment none of us could lift hands for applause ; then it broke out in a wild tumult. . . . I alone in the group knew Russian

and could feel the music of his words, but they all felt
the power of his emotions and were shaken to their
depths. . . .

12

A TRUNK

ISADORA had a trunk—one of the eleven with which she
travelled in those days. There is no anecdote connected with it and I mention it only because to me it
symbolised a sort of truth. I don't even know whether
the story is worth telling to strangers. But anyway,
just for my own sake, for the sake of that something in
us that demands that life be explainable in terms of
growth, I am going to put it down. I shall try to
recapture that odd emotion I felt when I first
" realised " this trunk. . . .

It held all of Isadora's love letters, the books she
most cherished, innumerable photographs, and the
programmes of her recitals and clippings about them
from newspapers. It was, in short, a sort of résumé, a
printed résumé, of Isadora's life, her life as an artist and
her life as a woman—or shall I say courtesan ? For,
I think, she was the greatest courtesan of our times, in
the rich grand old sense of this word.

Well, there was that trunk. And there was I—in
charge of it, so to speak. And I didn't do much about
it. Isadora would say : " Oh, I wish you would get at
this trunk some day and straighten it all out. It's a
dreadful mess." And I, thinking of it as a job, just a
job of sorting out a lot of old, musty stuff, would say :
" I will. Just as soon as I can get a whole free day to
do it. I have to go to the bank this morning and see

the French Consul in the afternoon." And thus I kept putting it off, putting off *the job* !

Then, one day in Düsseldorf, I tackled the thing. I spread myself generously on the floor of Isadora's salon and began to put the stuff in separate little piles : books, magazines, letters, old contracts, and funny, odd scraps of writing in Isadora's characteristic, almost illegible hand. They were precious scraps—her thoughts on the dance, on art, on the education of children. Some of them are probably now embodied in that lovely book of hers, *The Art of the Dance*, which Sheldon Cheney edited after her death, gathering in it all of her expressions and convictions about her art. It is a beautiful book, holding in its grand pages the very essence and spirit of Isadora's thought, and those who think that she was merely an eccentric dancer and a courtesan should read it and discover the great artist. . . .

There were programmes innumerable in all the languages of the world ; there were thousands of press clippings—bunches of them in rubber bands and stray ones which fluttered about the trunk and the room. There were packets of letters and many single ones, letters beginning with " Dearest " and " Darling " and " My very own," which I sorted according to their handwriting and which I didn't read. And then there were the photographs—of many men : clever men, old men, middle-aged men, and young men. Beautiful young men. Never have I seen so many beautiful photographs in my life, so many fascinating faces. There was one which still haunts me to this day. It was the face of a young man and there was in it that ultimate refinement of features, a blending of masculine strength and sheer, tender beauty, which happens once in a million times. I looked at it for a long time and finally put it down on its pile —face downwards. I put

them face downwards for once during that long afternoon Essenine came in and, seeing all the photos of the
handsome men, he grew pale and his eyelids grew pink,
which was a sign that he was vexed.

It was late in the afternoon when I got through.
Everything was sorted in neat, separate piles, and
among these I sat on . . . dreaming. . . . Isadora had
had such a rich life, so many affairs. Some of them
must have been real and she must have been hurt. . . .
And she had had two lovely children and had lost
them, but still she went on, still she enjoyed life. . . .
She had Essenine, I thought. . . . She is forty-eight
and she is young. She is younger than I, for she is
alive and I am dead—I have been dead since I left that
room in Warsaw where I once had prayed : " Dear God,
don't let me ever love any more ; please, God, don't let
me feel. . . ." I am not going to be dead any more, I
am going to try to be alive. . . . And so I sat there,
dreaming. . . .

" Heavens, what a mess ! " said Isadora when she
returned. " How are you getting along ? "

" Beautifully, just beautifully," I said. " I have
just figured out how I can put some order into this
stuff." But I didn't tell Isadora that her trunk had
also helped me to put a little order into my own soul.
It wasn't exactly a thing one could talk about. . . .

13

AN EDUCATION

ALTHOUGH I was twenty-three when I joined Isadora
and Essenine, I was still rather naïve. About some

things.   As I went on travelling with them, I began to
learn about the world—a bit here and a bit there.
Some of these bits came with a funny shock, a sort of
tiny mental jolt.   I remember the first one very well.

It was in Düsseldorf, on the third day after I had
joined them.   It was three o'clock at night, in a big
hotel.   I was asleep in my room, adjoining Isadora's
suite, when someone knocked at my door.   I woke up
and asked :

" Who is there ? "

" It's me, Isadora.   Let me in."

I got up and unlocked the door.   Isadora swept in ;
looked at me ; looked at my bed ; then said :

" Essenine has disappeared."

I said : " Are you sure ? "

She said : " He's gone.   I can't find him anywhere."

" Perhaps he is in the toilet ? "

" No," said Isadora with infinite scorn.   " I've
looked."   And she walked out as swiftly as she had
walked in.   Grabbing my kimono, I followed her, for
I began to be infected by her anxiety.

With rapid strides she walked up the hall to the end,
where was Jeanne's little bedroom.   Jeanne was
Isadora's personal maid.   Isadora knocked, and when
Jeanne opened the door she walked right in, looked at
Jeanne's bed, and said in French :

" *Monsieur est disparu.*"

" *Mais non, madame !* " said Jeanne, and looked
frightened.   Whereupon Isadora turned around on her
heel and walked right out, Jeanne and I following.   We
went to Isadora's big salon and had a hurried consultation.   Isadora was all for calling the concierge and
instituting a search.   She was quite wrought up.   I
was against it—for no plausible reason at all.   Then,
acting on a sudden hunch, I went to the middle of the
big room, raised my voice, and called in Russian :

" Sergei Alexandrovitch !   Where are you ? "

" Here I am," his voice replied instantly.

We rushed towards it.   Hidden by a heavy *portière*, Essenine was standing outside on a tiny balcony, in his pyjamas, taking in the fresh air.

Peace and happiness were restored and we all returned to our respective bedrooms, and it was only when I was tucking myself in once more that I reflected wonderingly . . .   " Now why did Isadora look in my bed when she came in . . . and why did she look at Jeanne's bed too ? . . .   Funny. . . ."   And then, in a flash : " Oh, good Lord ! "   But, of course, I had been with them only three short days . . . and Isadora didn't know me . . . and I didn't know Essenine.

And then there was another bit.   Very illuminating. Isadora was preparing for an appearance in one of Europe's capitals.   Every morning the pianist would come and they would practise together.   An upright was brought to her room and they would lock the door so as not to be disturbed.

Essenine did not like the locked door.   Sometimes he would forget about it, come up in a hurry, turn the handle, and find that it didn't open.   Then he grumbled. . . .

" Why should they lock themselves up ? " he said to me one day, after having bumped into the door.   I met him in the hall, outside.

" Sh . . . sh . . . don't talk so loud.   Isadora is practising," I said.

" To hell with practising.   All I want is a book. They needn't lock themselves up for practising."

" Please, Sergei Alexandrovitch . . . don't talk so loud."

At this moment Isadora opened the door and came out, followed by the pianist.   Seeing Essenine's angry

face, she guessed at once the reason and, pointing with
a charming gesture to the pianist, she said in her broken
pidgin Russian :

" Please, that's nothing. Please not worry. He is
a pederast."

. . . Eight bells and all is well, as they say on boats.
All was well, except that the word " pederast " is the
same in all languages. I don't know how the pianist
looked. . . . I walked away down the hall as fast as I
could.

They were young and amiable and they admired
Isadora intensely—two young American boys of the
kind that used to be called expatriates. They would
bob up unexpectedly, always together, always jolly,
admiring, and helpful. We met them first on a train in
Germany and there was a lot of rejoicing. Then they
bobbed up in Ostend. They bobbed up in Brussels
too, and stopped at the same hotel.

It was then that Essenine began to be suspicious.
He glared at them with an unmistakably hostile stare
when they happened to drop in, and one day he tackled
me point-blank :

" Who are they ? "

" Friends of Isadora's—admirers, you know. She
has so many."

" Why do they follow us about ? "

" Follow us ? Oh, I don't think so. They just
came to see her dance. You know, they are Americans,
probably have a little income and travel about. There
are lots of them in Paris and everywhere ; they study
art or something."

" Is that all you know ? "

" That's all. . . . Look. . . ."

" How long has Isadora known them ? "

" I don't know. What do you want to know for ? "

"*Nichevo.* That's all."

He turned abruptly and left. He was jealous Jealous and suspicious. And it seemed so silly : they were such harmless young fellows, so utterly devoted to the great Isadora, simply content to be about, to bask in her glory. . . .

And then—it was but a few days later—Essenine's attitude suddenly changed. It was unmistakable. He actually smiled at them. They couldn't talk together at all, of course, for the boys knew no Russian. They contemplated Essenine, the blond, husky Russian poet, with a sort of polite curiosity—not too obviously, of course, for they were well-bred—and as for him, he now actually grinned at them in a friendly fashion. Approvingly. And later that day—the boys had spent the whole day with us—he met me in the hall and beckoned to me mysteriously.

"It's all right," he said in a whisper, and I knew at once to what he referred.

"Why, of course they are all right," I replied.

"I just found out to-day. Come, I want to show you." He walked on ahead, and, glancing around him quickly to see that no one was in the hall, he stopped at a door. I knew the door—it was the boys' room.

Essenine tried the handle gingerly. It gave. He opened it slowly a crack, looked in, then told me to look. Full of sudden curiosity, all excited, I looked : I saw a small hotel bedroom, a single bed, a wash-stand, a table and chair. I turned to Essenine, mystified.

"One bed," he said, pointing. "See ? "

"Perhaps the fellows are poor," I said, full of sympathy.

"Poor like hell. They always take a room with one bed. Jeanne told me."

"But why—why should they ? " I asked naïvely.

Essenine grinned and I said, " Oh-h." . . . And Essenine was jealous no more.

Thus I learned about life. Little bits here and there. And now, once in a while, when I talk of Isadora and my adventurous youth, and some of my friends—the older generation—ask : " It must have been an education, travelling with a great woman like that. Wasn't it ? "—I reply very solemnly : " It was. It was very educational."

14

TWO ASPECTS

IT was in Venice. . . . The gondola was large, with an elaborate baldachin in the centre ; the gondolier was tall and lanky, with something proud in his carriage, in the way he dipped his heavy oar and then straightened himself out again. . . . The night was beautiful, with a sky full of stars ; and the water of the lagoon was like a huge, shiny black sheet.

Under the velvet baldachin Isadora sat alone, very still—with that enchanting grace which made one think of her as a beautiful sculpture that had become alive. In the dim light one could see the curve of her full white throat and one beautiful arm resting on the edge of the boat. The rest of her form was obscured by the shadows.

In the bow Essenine was telling me about his life—in a manner simple and detached, as if he were talking of someone else. The silence of that Venetian night was so full that the distant sound of a gondolier's song and the tiny splash of the oar, as it dipped at long, regular intervals, seemed but to intensify it, and Essenine's voice was hardly more than a murmur, a soft murmur telling tales which seemed incredible and fantastic.

He talked of his early childhood as a poor, barelegged peasant boy; of the day when he wrote his first poem, at the age of nine; of the many poems he had written from then on, in secret, so no one should know; of how, at seventeen, he chose but a few and burned all the rest; of how his people were trying to make a *pop*[1] out of him—because he was so clever and so precocious—and how often he had been flogged because he ran away from school; of his uncle, the " ruthless " man who administered the beatings; of beautiful faces and of the most beautiful face he had ever seen, that of a young nun in a Russian convent—a face that was absolutely guileless and pure; of his rise to fame and his life in Petrograd; of his running away from the army; of women; of convents; of words, of words that were alive and others that were dead; of the language of plain people, peasants, pilgrims, and thieves, which was always alive; of many other things. . . .

His voice was soft and his eyes dreamy, and there was that about him which made one think that his soul was like a child's, mysteriously wise yet utterly tender. . . .

There was a slight thud, a little splash; the boat landed somewhere, the murky water licking the bottom step of a dark Venetian quay; there was Isadora's voice, speaking Italian to the gondolier; the hands of small beggar boys, outstretched for pennies. . . . The magic spell was broken. We were back in Italy.

On the way home Essenine and I sang Russian folk

[1] A *pop* is a priest of the Greek Orthodox Church.

songs and the gondolier, a little surprised at this com-
petition in his own game, nevertheless applauded
heartily. After a while, Essenine, still in a talkative
mood, started talking of Russia again. But it was a
different Essenine now. The other, the poet, who
seemed simple and naïve and, somehow, wise, whom I
had known only for a short hour or two, had vanished.
This was the ordinary Essenine I knew : bland, non-
committal, pretending to be somewhat of a fool, but
rather secretive, with eyes which had such sly corners
to them. He talked of Bolshevism and I asked whether
he knew Lenin.

" Lenin is dead ! " he whispered back.

I nearly jumped. This was in 1922 and Lenin was
very ill.[1] He was surrounded by famous German
physicians ; every now and then one read in the papers
their official bulletins.

" Why are you joking like this, Sergei Alexandrovitch ? "

We both whispered, as if we were afraid that someone
might overhear.

" I am not joking. He has been dead for almost a
year," came the whispered reply, " but we cannot let
this be known, for Bolshevism would collapse in one
hour. There is no leader strong enough to take his
place. Can't you see ? "

" But, Sergei Alexandrovitch, one cannot conceal
such news ! It's impossible. One might succeed for
a few days, perhaps a week, but no longer."

" We have succeeded. We had to. No one knows.
Only a few trusted people." His voice was that of a
conspirator. It was at this moment that I began to
guess his hoax, but, instead of protesting, I now pretended to be convinced. I wanted to hear more. It
seemed so very exciting.

[1] Lenin died in 1924.

"You see," the quiet voice continued, "once in a great while, if someone insists, the physicians let him in just for a minute and show the visitor that Lenin is asleep. He is not asleep. He is embalmed! Dead! Marvellously embalmed. These Germans did it; it took them weeks to do it. They are putting off the announcement from week to week, until we can find a strong leader. Bolshevism cannot exist without a strong man. In the meantime they keep on issuing bulletins of his 'gradual decline.' Haven't you noticed it? Haven't you noticed how few people are admitted? That there are no interviews?"

I sat completely entranced. What a story! Even if this was just a hoax, what a magnificent plot! It fired my imagination. The quiet voice continued:

"But if you squeal one word, you won't live! There are ways and means. We have spies everywhere!"

I said not a word. My back was full of shivers; I was divided between admiration and a desire to laugh. Essenine sat with a satisfied, secretive smile. He looked a little insane. . . .

"What are you two muttering about?"

Isadora's voice. . . . Isadora, who had been so silent all night and had sat alone, lost in Heaven knows what dreams, now joined us, and another spell was broken. But that night I could hardly sleep, for the story he had told me, so fantastic and yet so plausible, had got hold of my imagination. It still seemed probable. What a plot, if it were true!

15

TRANSLATING POETRY

I wasn't flattered when Essenine asked me to try to translate some of his poetry. I was a bit frightened and a bit shocked, for, young as I was, I knew that it was a sacrilege and an impossibility both. Essenine's poetry is almost purely lyrical : it is music expressed in terms of Russian words, of Russian phonetics, and so could never be rendered into any other language. Even in Russian it was the sort of poetry that is a hundred times more beautiful when read aloud than when read in silence, and here I was asked to mutilate it. . . . However, he seemed so anxious that Isadora asked me to have a try at it anyway, just to humour him, and also offered to help, and so I went at it with a sort of dogged despair.

This was when we were in Italy, on the Lido. I had a room on the very top floor, under the mansard, of a small new hotel next to the Excelsior, where Isadora and Essenine had a suite. Parts of the hotel weren't even quite finished and were being painted. It was in August, the hottest month in Italy ; it was stuffy and humid and there was *a smell*. The smell was a combination : part fresh paint, part Italian food from a restaurant below, part ocean. It hung about my room in a hot, sickening pall while I sweated and laboured over tender lyrics, trying to fit gorgeous Russian into English—a language which, at the time, I had barely begun to feel. . . .

I had nothing to help me, either, except a Roget's *Thesaurus* which I had picked up in an English bookstore in Brussels. And the worst of it was that I did not even have the choice of the poems. Essenine simply asked me to do " this one . . . and that one . . . and try that one too." Some of his best, the most famous and most beautiful poems. At times I rebelled. How well I recall the useless harangues we had when again and again I tried to explain to him that poetry could not be translated. He, who knew only one language, could never quite understand.

" Sergei Alexandrovitch," I would say, " take your ' Song about the Dog.' You have the first line :

Utrom v rjanom zakutie . . .

Now even in Russian you have chosen the particular word *zakuta*—though you might have chosen a number of other synonyms—because, presumably, this word fits best into the cadence, into the image you were trying to create, and because it has an assonance with the word *suka*. Isn't it so ? "

He would listen intently, with puckered brow, his blue eyes very serious, like a child's.

" Yes," he would reply.

" Now then, if I translate literally into English,

Of a morning in a kennel of straw,

I can possibly evoke a similar picture, but *the music, the thing that makes it poetry in Russian, won't be there,* because in English perhaps quite a different set of words would serve to make a beautiful sentence and give your cadence, since the law of phonetic beauty is different. And thus if I changed each or nearly each word, I should naturally change the entire poem too."

" But if you leave out rhyming or assonances," he would insist, " you could preserve the sentences in almost their entirety, couldn't you ? "

" I might leave out rhyme and use blank verse, but I should still have to have the cadence. And to preserve my cadence, I should have to combine words of certain lengths and syllables, and the literal translation would not always call for such words."

" Well, then, leave out both rhyme and cadence," he would say desperately. " Just translate the literal words. After all," he would add wistfully, " I draw beautiful pictures. I give visions. And I have ideas. These are worth something. . . ."

And off I would go, returning to my stuffy room—I wrote usually at night, for in the daytime Isadora liked to have me about in case I had to interpret—poring over my *Thesaurus*, trying to find equivalents that would somehow fit. . . .

The following morning I would bring the poem over to Isadora's room and read the translation to her aloud. Craftily, hungrily, Essenine would watch Isadora's face, and she, with the kindness and delicacy of which she was so capable, would smile and show that she was pleased. Sometimes she tried to help me, for her English was better and more fluent than mine and she had read lots more poetry. I would tell the poem in simple prose sentences and she would try to put these into some rhythm. And always she tried to conceal her real disappointment. Essenine was very sensitive where his poetry was concerned, and to have hurt him would have been like hurting a child. . . .

One day I asked him why he so much wanted an English translation of his poems.

" But don't you see," he replied, surprised that I should put such a question, " how many millions of people will know me if my poems appear in English ? How many people will read me in Russian ? Twenty million, perhaps thirty. . . . All our peasants are illiterate. . . . But in English ! " He spread his arms

R

and his eyes shone. . . . "How big is England's population ? "

We began to count on our fingers. England, 40,000,000 ; the United States, 125,000,000 ; Canada, 10,000,000 perhaps—I wasn't sure. . . . Australia ! New Zealand ! India !

Essenine's face was lighted up, his eyes glowed !

"Sergei Alexandrovitch—" I spoke very gravely, for it was a serious matter. Worlds, veritable worlds, were at stake. "I would rather only a small fraction of the world read you in the original than all the world in translation. A translation could never be you and could never be beautiful. Even a beautiful translation would not be you. It would be a new thing entirely— part you, part translator."

His face fell. It became grey. His eyes became grey. I felt like a murderess. . . .

16

A CONVERSATION

ONE doesn't need a language to make love ; one doesn't even need many words for ordinary daily intercourse. A few words and some pantomime can accomplish a lot. But in an argument we all like to prove our point and we all like to drive it home.

While in Russia Isadora had picked up a sort of Russian, a quaint language of her own, twisted, naïve, and broken, but very charming, which quite sufficed for everyday use with Essenine. As a matter of fact he liked it enormously, as I did also, and sometimes when

we talked together, we used some of Isadora's quaint
expressions for the fun of it. However, in a serious
discussion of any kind this pidgin Russian was wholly
inadequate. That is where I came in, translating for
both of them. . . .

Isadora and Essenine were talking of art. Said
Essenine :

" A dancer can never become very great because
her fame doesn't last. It is gone the moment
she dies."

" No," said Isadora, " for a dancer, if she is great,
can give to the people something that they will
carry with them for ever. They can never forget
it, and it has changed them, though they may not
know it."

" But when they are gone, Isadora ? These people
who have seen her ? Dancers are like actors : one
generation remembers them ; the next reads about
them ; and the third knows nothing."

I was translating and Isadora listened, with that
perfect attention and sympathy she always had for
Essenine. He got up slowly, leaned against the wall,
and, folding his arms—a habit he had when talking—
looked at her tenderly and said :

" You are just a dancer. People may come and
admire you—even cry. But after you are dead, no
one will remember. Within a few years all your great
fame will be gone. . . . No Isadora ! "

All this he said in Russian, for me to translate, but
the last two words he said in the English intonation,
straight into Isadora's face, with a very expressive,
mocking motion of his hands, as if he had waved the
remnants of the mortal Isadora to the four winds. . . .
" But poets live," he continued, still smiling. " I,
Essenine, shall leave my poems behind me. And
poems live. Poems like mine live for ever."

Beneath the obvious mockery and teasing tone there was something extraordinarily cruel. A shadow passed over Isadora's face as I translated what he said. Suddenly she turned to me, her voice very serious :

" Tell him he is wrong, tell him he is wrong. I have given people beauty. I have given them my very soul when I danced. And this beauty did not die. It exists somewhere. . . ." Suddenly she had tears in her eyes and she added in her pitiful, childish Russian : " Krasota nie umiray." (Beauty not dies.)

But Essenine, already completely satisfied with the effect of his words—for there seemed in him often a morbid desire to hurt Isadora or to belittle her— became all gentleness. With a characteristic gesture, he pulled Isadora's curly head towards him and patted her on the back, saying mockingly : " Ekh, Duncan." . . . Isadora smiled. All was forgiven.

Thinking it might be time for me to retire, I strolled to the window and, waiting for a minute or so, said casually, as if the scene I saw out there had just suggested it to my mind, that I would go down to the beach.

" Oh, don't go yet," said Isadora, and with a dry little smile, but with complete good humour, she added : " Sergei might want to say more sweet things to me and you will have to translate, you know."

I stayed. Isadora went out to sit on the balcony and Essenine picked up a book. Presently he lifted his face, his eyes shiny and bright, and said :

" There is no one like Pushkin after all. What beauty ! Listen." And he read a little poem. Four lines. I remembered it, for I had had it in school. But I had never realised how beautiful it was until I heard Essenine say it. He read another, then a third, and went into raptures over these simple, beautiful lines of Russia's most famous classic poet. . . .

Then there came a poem with the word " God " in it
and, remembering something funny, Essenine grinned
and said :

" The Bolsheviks have forbidden the use of ' God ' in
print, you know.   They even got out a decree to this
effect.   Once when I sent in some poems the editor returned them to me requesting that all the ' Gods ' be
replaced by other words. . . .   Other words ! "

I laughed and asked him what he did.

" Oh, I just took my gun and went to the fellow and
told him he would have to print the stuff as it was,
decree or no decree.   He refused, so I asked him
whether he had ever had his mug beaten, and then I
went into the composing room and reset the type
myself.   That's all."

Hearing the murmur of our voices and our laughter,
Isadora returned from the balcony and wanted to know
what it was all about.   I told her briefly.   For a
moment she said nothing, and then, to my surprise,
she said in Russian :

" But Bolsheviki right.   No God.   Old.   Silly."

Essenine grinned and said with mock irony, as if
talking to a child that was trying to be clever and
grown-up :

" *Ekh*, Isadora !   *Viedz vsio ot Boga.   Poezya i dazhe
Tvoyee tantsy.*" (Oh, Isadora !   Why, everything comes
from God.   All poetry and even your dances.)

" No, no," replied Isadora with great intensity, in
English.   " Tell him that my gods are Beauty and Love.
There are no others.   How do you know there is God ?
The Greeks knew this a long time ago.   People invent
gods to please themselves.   There are no others.   There
is nothing beyond what we know, what we invent or
imagine.   All the hell is right here on earth.   And all
paradise."   She was standing upright, like a caryatid,
beautiful, magnificent, and fearful.   And suddenly she

stretched out her arms and, pointing to the bed, she said in Russian, with tremendous force :

" *Vot Bog !* "   (This is God !)

Slowly her arm came down. She turned and went back to the balcony. Essenine sat in his chair, pale, silent, and completely annihilated. I ran out on the beach and lay down on the sand and cried, though, for the life of me, I could not have told why. . . .

17

TOO MANY WOMEN

AFTER Essenine had joined Isadora he was practically never alone. In fact, never, I believe, save when he was in the bathroom. After their marriage in Moscow they flew to Berlin. There he was fêted by the Russian art colony in a series of real Russian libations which finally affected his health. It even began to affect Isadora, who could stand more than he and who, in the days when I knew her, was actually the better for a few drinks—more mellow and charming. However, I believe she was a little jealous of all these numerous noisy Russians and their boisterous adoration. So she took Essenine to Wiesbaden for a rest and a cure. It was here that the doctor who examined Essenine told her that his condition was serious ; that he must stop drinking for at least two or three months, or she would have a maniac on her hands. Essenine, who had just had a sort of nervous breakdown and suffered from neuritis, promised to comply with the doctor's orders.

All this I learned from Isadora a few days after I
joined them in Wiesbaden. I understood then, too,
why Essenine's face was so grey and his lips blue, and
why he was often so terribly tense. He had been
drinking for several years, drinking heavily, as most
Russians do, and this sudden complete stop must have
been a bad strain on his nerves. And Isadora's love,
very tender and kind, was also a bit too smothering and
devouring. It must have been but another shackle or
strain to the savage and sensitive poet. And so, I believe, I understood exactly what he felt that day on the
Lido when he wanted to go out for a walk. . . . I
understood, but Isadora, unfortunately, didn't, and the
complications which thereupon arose were manifold. . . .

It was after dinner of a hot day in July. The hotel
room was warm and very stuffy. Essenine announced
that he was going out for a walk. Isadora asked
whether he would please wait until she changed her
costume.

" But I am going alone," said Essenine.

Isadora looked at him queerly and I was surprised
to hear her say quite firmly :

" No. *Vosmi* Jeanne or Miss Kinel." (No. Take
along Jeanne or Miss Kinel.)

Essenine's eyes became very angry :

" I am going alone. I want to be alone. I just want
to walk alone." All this in Russian, of course. I translated while Essenine sat on the bed and started to put
on his shoes. His desire to go for that walk seemed so
genuine and his hurt pride at being dictated to like a
naughty child so evident that, forgetting the role of
secretary, I turned to Isadora and, interpreting his
wish, I added :

" Oh, do let him go out, Isadora. It must be terrible
to be cooped up with us three women so constantly.
Everyone wants to be alone sometimes."

Isadora turned to me a face overwrought with anxiety :

" I won't let him go alone. You don't understand. You don't know him. He may run away. He did that in Moscow. And there are women."

" Oh, but Isadora ! I think he has had enough of women. He just wants to be alone, just to wander about. Look, how can he run away ? He has no money, he is in his pyjamas, and he can't speak Italian."

Instead of replying, Isadora went to the door and stood in front of it with the air of one saying : " Only over my dead body."

Essenine watched all this English harangue with angry, bloodshot eyes and tightly compressed lips. He needed no interpretation. After a long moment of un-endurable tension he suddenly sat down in a chair and said very quietly :

" Tell her I am not going."

Isadora left the door and went on to the balcony. She was crying : she cried like a child, the tears rolling down her cheeks, her face woebegone and helpless. I put my arm about her and stroked her head and begged her not to cry, although I felt that she was utterly wrong and the boy was right. She began to sob, a little hysterically, muttering something about her love in be-tween little gulps. Essenine got up from his chair and threw himself on the bed, face downwards. He had not yet put on his shoes and socks and the pink heels of his bare feet, peeping from under the white silk pyjamas, looked round and childish. Isadora pushed me away and, kneeling on the floor near the bed, she began to kiss those round, pink heels. I thought this a proper cue for an exit and left. . . .

18

HOW ESSENINE WENT FOR A WALK

WHEN I came the next morning to the little beach house in front of the hotel where Isadora and Essenine usually spent their days, and Isadora ran out to meet me and whispered that Essenine was drunk, I was not much surprised. . . .

" We must get him away from here," Isadora whispered, " he gets so wild. Talk to him in Russian . . . tell him something to make him come up to our room."

We approached the beach house. Essenine was sitting in a deck chair. In front of him, on the table, was a bottle of champagne, almost empty. I said :

" *Zdravstwuitie*, Sergei Alexandrovitch."

He lifted his heavy eyes slowly and waved his hand. His face was grey and puffy and I had the funny sensation that at any moment he might go berserk. Isadora stood by me, squeezing my arm, urging me to say something, but with the sudden instinct which comes to one sometimes in an emergency I simply sat down in another deck chair as if nothing were wrong and waited for a cue. Isadora remained standing by my side, her eyes on Essenine's face.

" That Italian riff-raff," he said—his voice was hoarse —and waved an eloquent hand. " They ought to be thrown into the ocean. These dukes and counts and marquises . . . scum of the earth. . . . Want a drink ? "

" No, thanks, maybe later."

" *Sytye bourzhoye ! Chevo ikh ! V vodu !* " (Bloated bourgeois ! To hell with them. Into the water !)

His eyes, whose blue had turned into grey, framed

with reddened eyelids, looked around slowly, just as a
fighting bull might before charging. He leaned forward ; his neck seemed swollen. . . .

I had a sudden inspiration :

" You are right.   But we don't have to look at them.
Let's go up to your room where we can drink in peace."
He considered this, staring at me heavily ; then his blue
lips curved into a semblance of a grin.   He liked the
idea.   He stood up unsteadily and Isadora, who had
been hanging on our lips, was immediately at his other
side.

Thus, supporting him between us, we led him slowly
from the beach, past the other little canvas cottages,
past the flower beds and the splendid tennis courts
where the cosmopolitan *jeunesse dorée* was amusing
itself, up the neat gravel walk to the big lobby of the
Excelsior.   We walked very slowly, Essenine a bit
wobbly, muttering incoherent imprecations, but I don't
think that anyone noticed us particularly, the aristocratic " riff-raff " and the rich Americans continuing
with their gay, lazy life, oblivious of the blond young
Russian peasant who wanted to throw them into the
ocean. . . .

We got him safely upstairs and Isadora ordered immediately two more bottles of champagne.   Then,
calling me into the dressing-room, she said :

" Run quickly to the hotel doctor and get a strong
sleeping potion.   Sergei will be wild if we don't put him
to sleep.   The doctor will understand.   And have the
waiter put it into one of the bottles before he brings it in
here and let him mark the bottle.   We will do the
rest."

I ran as if on wings.   Within fifteen minutes the
waiter brought the two bottles and showed me dis-
creetly which one contained the medicine.   Essenine
was sitting on the bed in a dejected attitude, except that

his eyes roved restlessly. I took the marked bottle and, pouring out two glasses, raised mine gaily and said :

" *A nu*, Sergei Alexandrovitch, let's drink ! " I took a sip out of mine. It was decidedly bitter.

Essenine took one big swallow and, making a wry face, he dashed the glass to the floor and said cunningly :

" So that's your little game, eh ? You think I can't taste the stuff ! Put me to sleep ? Poison me ? "

He got up heavily, his face distorted with malice, and lurched toward me. I stood paralysed with fear, but he lounged past me and staggered out into the hall. Isadora and Jeanne stood petrified. For a moment none of us seemed able to move ; then I rushed out after Essenine. He was ambling drunkenly, but very fast, toward the stairway. He disappeared around the bend just as I gained on him, and as I saw the elevator stop and someone get out on our floor, I dashed in, hoping to meet Essenine on the main floor. However, when I got there he was nowhere to be seen. I ran to the stairway, thinking I might still find him, but he wasn't there either. I ran back to Isadora's room :

" Essenine is gone, Isadora. I couldn't catch him ! "

" I can't depend on anyone," she cried in reply. " He mustn't be left alone when he is in this state. He might kill himself or someone else." She was quite unnerved.

" I shall ask the *portier* to send some bell-boys to hunt for him," I said. " He can't have gone far ; anyway, he can't leave the island." And I ran downstairs again to find the *portier*.

He didn't bat an eye when I gave my request and seemed to take in the situation immediately, sending out several bell-hops to look for " *le poète russe, habillé en pyjama blanc*." I returned to the room.

Isadora was lying on the bed, her face buried in the pillow. I sat down on the edge and said :

"Please don't worry, Isadora ; I am sure we will find him soon. He can't have gone far and he didn't have any money to hire a boat. And he can't talk, and anyway I am sure he is just sleeping it off somewhere under a bush. That's what all Russian peasants do when they get drunk—it's in his blood."

Isadora sat up with surprising swiftness, turned to me, and said gaily :

"Oh, we could look for him ourselves. Let's hire a car and look under all the bushes. I would never have thought of that. How clever. . . . Jeanne ! *Vite ! Je veux faire ma toilette !* "

I must have looked stupid—I was so stunned. Not so much by the idea of hunting for Essenine among the bushes as by the change in Isadora. A moment ago, it seemed, I had left a middle-aged woman on the verge of hysterics. Now there was a gay Isadora out for some kind of adventure or fun. I stood up and my eyes came in line with the table.

Half of the other bottle of champagne was gone. Isadora caught my eye and smiled mischievously :

"Come on, have a drink too. As long as Essenine is drunk, we might as well be a little drunk too."

I shook my head and said with youthful soberness :

"You finish it, Isadora. If you two are drunk, perhaps Jeanne and I had better remain sober."

And so Isadora finished it and then we went in search of Essenine. It was noon of a day in August—the hottest month in Italy. The road was dusty and the sun, reflected by the hot sand and the white walls of the houses, was glaring pitilessly. We drove very slowly, stopping at every bush, clump of brush, or bit of hedge that looked as if it might conceal a man. Often we got

out and searched. I don't know what the chauffeur
thought. I did not ask.

One hour passed, another. . . . Isadora talked at
intervals. The wine had made her dreamy and she
rambled on in a half-reminiscent way. She talked with
a humour and irony peculiar to her, which were delicious. She spoke of her lovers, of the strange fate
which seemed to give her only eccentric men for lovers ;
she discussed the nicest way to commit suicide—for
that is what she had decided to do if we found Essenine
dead. She ate salted almonds, which she liked so much,
having purchased a whole bagful from a little street
vendor. She offered me some and then said, half
seriously :

" But I oughtn't to die without writing my biography. It's amazing, you know. You could help me
write it—you like to write."

" No one could do it better than yourself,
Isadora."

" Oh, but I am too lazy . . . I hate to hold the
pen." . . .

The afternoon ebbed away ; we had looked at all the
bushes on the island and we returned to the hotel. I
was very tired, and even Isadora looked drooping. She
thought she would rest on the sand for a while and we
went to the little beach house. The half-empty bottle
of champagne from the morning was still there. The
place looked strangely empty. Isadora turned away
from it and went to the adjoining beach house of the
Baron and Baroness de M. The last thing I heard her
say, as she stretched luxuriously on the sand, was :
" No, I don't think I shall commit suicide yet ; my legs
are still very beautiful."

On the way up to Isadora's room I asked the porter if
they had found the poet. They hadn't. The bell-boys
were still searching for him. Wearily I went upstairs

sitting on a chair in front of Isadora's dressing-table was Essenine !

When he saw me enter, he turned around and grinned. He seemed quite sober.

" Sergei Alexandrovitch, where have you been ? We have been looking for you everywhere ! " I exclaimed.

" Oh, I had a good nap."

" Where, in heaven's name ? "

" Right here in the hotel garden ; under a bush."

" Oh ! Oh ! " I could have cried with vexation, but Essenine roared when I told him how we had searched for him. Why didn't we look closer, he asked. And then he explained how, when he saw me follow him in the hall, he did not continue running down the main stairway, but, reaching the next floor, doubled back and ran to the end of the hall, where there was another stairway used by the servants ; how he ran down those steps and straight through the hotel kitchen into the backyard, from which he made his way into the garden and hid in a bush. By some accident none of the servants noticed him. . . . He seemed immensely pleased.

Ringing the bell for Jeanne, I told her to notify Isadora and the porter that the poet was safe and sound. Essenine, though considerably sobered by his nap, was very restless. He walked around the room for a while, then announced suddenly that he was going for a walk. . . . My God, that walk ! It was still on his mind. I knew for sure now that it was that argument about the walk that had got him off the water wagon after he had stuck to it faithfully for more than two months. But how could one let him go out alone now, when he wasn't yet quite rational ? I was considering what to do next when Jeanne returned with Isadora's admonition that we should not leave him alone—" *pas un instant.*" She said that Isadora would soon come up.

Essenine, unaware of what Jeanne and I were saying

in French, was trying to dress, or, rather, take off his pyjamas. He could not do it. His hands trembled and he fumbled helplessly with a knot in the cord. " Let Jeanne help you," I suggested. " No. No, I will do it alone," he said like an obstinate child. He was going to dress alone and then go out alone, he repeated over and over, like a child—all alone and " no damned women."

" Yes, yes," I said. Jeanne and I merely wanted to help him dress. Which of the suits did he want ? Finally, with joint effort, Jeanne and I got him into one of his beautiful suits. He sat down near the dresser and combed his hair. He was very vain and proud of his blond hair and he used to give one particular curl over his forehead a little twist. Then he helped himself generously to Isadora's perfume, powdered his face, and sat contemplating the visage which looked at him from the mirror.

It was a strange and ghastly countenance. When, years later, I read of his suicide in the Petrograd hotel, his face as it looked that day in the mirror in Venice bobbed up before me with all its force : large, roughly-hewn features ; deep-set eyes whose blue had turned to a bleary grey ; heavy, dark eyebrows, like wings ; pale dry skin, and flaxen-blond curls which seemed so youthful and innocent and out of place. The powder, which, in his drunken clumsiness, he had applied rather heavily, gave him the weird and masklike air of a tragic *pajazzo*. Moved by a sudden impulse, I took some of Isadora's lipstick and applied a little to his blue, dry lips. It completed the picture. He looked half gigolo, half clown. He seemed pleased, stood up, and said :

" Well, I am going."

" I am going with you, Sergei Alexandrovitch," said I very quietly.

" No, you are not ! " His eyes narrowed.

For an instant I was at a loss.   One can't tell a man
who's half tipsy that he needs care or help ; nothing is
more certain to make him mad.

" Can Jeanne go with you ? " I asked.

" Jeanne ? *Khorosho. Idiom*, Jeanne." (Come on,
Jeanne.)

Jeanne was sitting on a chair in the corner with the
resigned air of one who thinks : " I am ready and
patient. Do what you want. Come what may."
She jumped up when I told her she was to accompany
Essenine on his walk.

" *Mais il faut que je change mes souliers et prenne un
chapeau*," she begged.

But there was no time for *souliers* and *chapeau*, for
Essenine was already out in the hall, and so she hurried
after him in her bedroom slippers, the kind that flop. . . .

Late that night when the two finally returned, Jeanne
looking quite exhausted, Essenine sober, silent, and
morose, Isadora wanted to know where they had been
and what *monsieur* had done.

" *Mais partout, madame*," Jeanne replied. All over
the island they had tramped.   First they walked down
towards the other end of the Lido, to the Grand Canal,
where the little steam launches arrive which take the
people back and forth, to and from Venice. . . . *Monsieur* had stood and watched those for a long time.
Then he walked back again, the length of the island.
He walked so fast and took such big steps she could
hardly keep up with him ; often she had to run.   Once
he had stopped at a fruit seller's and wanted to buy
some grapes, and had talked Russian to the Italian and
got very angry when the man didn't understand.   She
had tried to help him then and he was " *tellement étonné* "
when he saw her.   He had forgotten she was with him
as she had kept steadily behind him, letting him walk

on ahead as if he were actually "walking alone," the way "*monsieur* had wished." And then, finally, he went straight back to the hotel. "*Et c'est tout, madame.*" Jeanne reported all this almost in one breath and now waited for further orders, but Isadora, seeing how tired she was, dismissed her for the night and Jeanne left with a last polite "*Oui, madame; merci, madame.*" . . . And thus, finally, Essenine had a walk. . . .

19

A BAD TRANSLATION

THE conversation in which I had to assist on the following morning was the most ghastly of all my interpreting jobs and I made a sorry business of it. I saw, the moment I entered the room, that some sort of serious discussion was going on and Isadora and Essenine weren't getting anywhere, for he turned to me at once with a little cry of relief :

"*A, vot Miss Kinel. Perevoditie !*" (Ah, there is Miss Kinel ! Please translate.)

Then he settled back in his chair with an air of being ready for business :

"When we get to Paris I want my own key. I want to come and go as I please and *walk alone if I feel like it.*"

"What is it ?" demanded Isadora.

I translated, avoiding Isadora's face and looking straight ahead of me.

"No damned ordering me about. I am not sick and I am not a child. Tell her that."

I did. With a slight modification.

s

Isadora was silent.

Essenine paused slightly   Then :

" I am not going to beat about the bush—or cheat. . . . I want absolute freedom—other women if I like. If she wants my company, I shall stay in her house, but I don't want any interference."

It was at this point that I broke down on my job. I cried :

" I can't tell her that, Sergei Alexandrovitch. Please ! "

" You have to ! It's your job ! "

" I won't ! "

From Isadora, anxiously :

" What does he want now ? "

" Oh, he is just restless . . . he doesn't mean half of it . . . he wants to . . . do as he pleases when you go to Paris. . . ." I knew I looked guilty and confused and that Isadora guessed I wasn't telling all of it. This time she did not insist. She merely watched Essenine's face. He was working himself up a little more :

" I am not going to be kept cooped up in a hotel like a slave. If I can't do what I want, I shall leave. I can take a boat from here and go to Odessa. I want to go back to Russia."

Isadora caught the word " Odessa " and her eyes were full of fear. Essenine saw this and he leaned back in his chair with a satisfied look. He had scored a point. It was obvious : he could get anything if he threatened to leave. For some moments he looked abstracted, his forehead all creased, his whole face puckered up. . . . Then he smiled slowly and said musingly :

" It will be interesting . . . these Frenchwomen. . . . I have heard so much about them."

He said this exactly with the air of a small boy who is

ESSENINE

Enlarged from a Passport Photograph
Dusseldorf 1922

С Есенин
1922
Греcе~
ин~
15

terribly eager to taste some kind of new pastry he has heard talked about.

I studied him for a moment and then said, calmly and with conviction :

"*A viedz Vy poriadochnaya svolotch.*" (You know, you are really quite a dirty skunk.) And then I stopped—amazed at what I had said. But Essenine merely looked up, as if interrupted in his pleasant dream, and smiled. There was an awkward pause. I got up to go. Seeing me leave, Essenine said suddenly :

"What about my last night's telegrams ? Has there been any reply ? "

"I haven't sent them. . . . You see . . . you were still a little drunk and I thought . . ."

His face went white as it always did when he got angry. He said with a sort of quiet menace :

"You know, you ought to do what you are told. Not what you think." He got up also. Isadora, too, got up.

I was filled with anger and humiliation and tried to explain why I thought he couldn't possibly want those telegrams to be sent if he were sober. They were addressed to two of his literary friends, one in Moscow, another in Berlin, and he asked them to come at once. I knew that Isadora and he were going to America very soon to fulfil her contract, and I knew that one friend at least, the one in Moscow, would probably never even reach them before they left, what with visas, passport difficulties, and so on.

Essenine listened with a set face. His anger never broke out at once ; he would merely become pale and his eyelids turn pink, but one sensed the turmoil within him. Isadora, watching our faces, now demanded to know what it was all about, and I translated briefly. To my surprise, she took Essenine's part.

"You should have sent them. You should obey his

instructions, no matter how nonsensical they may seem.
We could always send another telegram later, refuting
the first," she said. " You mustn't contradict him.
You know how sick he is.   The doctor in Wiesbaden
said we should never make him angry."   She spoke
very kindly, as if trying not to hurt my feelings.

I said I was sorry not quite sincerely, and went to the
door. " Come and join us for lunch," cried Isadora.
But I made no reply.   I went down to the beach, had
a swim, and then lay on the sand, meditating on the
vicissitudes of being a secretary to people of genius and
temperament and wondering whether this was how
things would always be when Essenine went off the
water-wagon for good; also swearing to myself privately
that this was the last job of private secretary in my
career. . . .

My vow was fulfilled amazingly soon, for when I
returned to the Excelsior after luncheon, I found
Jeanne alone, packing, and with the news that *madame
et monsieur* were at the bank getting money and that
they were leaving for Paris to-night.   The familiar
" *Faites vos malles, mademoiselle*," was lacking.   There
was no message for me.   I might not have existed.   So
I returned to my own room and packed too.

When I went up to Isadora's room later in the
afternoon, she stretched out her hand and cried :
" I am terribly sorry.   It's Essenine.   He hates you
now."

She looked troubled and very gracious in her desire
not to hurt me.   I said :
" Never mind, Isadora.   It's just as well.   I was
really quite rude to him this morning."
" He says he can't trust you," Isadora said, " not
after that incident with the telegrams and yesterday

with the medicine in his wine. He can never trust you again."

"But, Isadora," I cried, "haven't you told him that it was your idea, not mine, to put the medicine in the wine?"

She smiled a little guiltily and said simply:

"No."

Great Scott, what was one to do? I saw her point at once: as long as I was being fired anyway because Essenine "didn't trust" me, I might as well be blamed for everything. . . . We talked of this and that and, while we talked, Essenine entered. . . . He was full of warm cordiality, the made-up kind at which he was quite adept, obviously with the desire to part on good terms although it was clear he was glad that the traitress was going. He asked me to see his literary friends in Berlin, gave me numerous addresses, describing his more intimate boon companions very minutely, even to the fact of their being good lovers or not. . . . "This one is very . . . and that one is not so good . . . and that one is no good altogether . . ." All this in the frank, coarse, Russian way which he liked to adopt when he teased anyone and which was humorous in spite of the coarseness. . . . But I was not in a humorous mood. I was stiff with resentment. . . . I said just "Yes" and "No" and "All right." . . .

Said Isadora, who hated friction and who always forgave things and forgot slights:

"Oh, do make up with him. Don't be angry . . ." And so we shook hands all around and said good-bye. . . .

I left the Lido on the same afternoon, feeling a little lost. Leaving Isadora and Essenine was like stepping off a brightly lit stage with the actors on it etched in sharp, clear outlines and with lots of high lights—and jumping into the dark, murky orchestra where the people, by comparison, were shadowy, unreal, and half dead. . . . After Isadora and Essenine, the ordinary world seemed a little grey.

20

RUSSIAN ART CLUB

I WALKED into the main room of the club with a little anticipatory thrill. Here I should meet some really big writers. The first person I spotted was Gorky. Surrounded by a few respectful satellites, he stood in the corner of the room : thin, angular, haggard, and dominating.

" Would you like to be introduced ? " asked my escort.

" No, no," I said quickly. The man gave me a curious glance. Gorky was *the* Figure in Berlin's Russian set in those days ; he had the peculiar position of being free politically, unlike any other writer. The Bolsheviks respected his proletarian origin (thus among Communists he was a born " aristocrat ") and he could denounce them or praise them as he saw fit. The old régime writers and the general Russian public respected him for his works.

" He doesn't come here often. He is sick, you know—t.b.," my escort said in a respectful whisper.

" Yes, yes, I know." We sat at a little table and I observed Gorky's group for a while. I was disappointed, for some of his early works were great and somehow I expected a fine personality, but about this

odd thin man there was something rigid, didactic, and
slightly theatrical. I had the desire to say : " For
years he has been sick. Very sick—t.b. Always we
read of it. But he never dies, the Great Martyr."
But of course I couldn't say anything so rude. Besides,
I was glad of this opportunity to see all these people at
close range.

It happened through one of those chances. On leaving Venice, I went to Berlin and stopped at the same
old *pension*. Among the boarders there were a few
Russians, one of them a well-known critic, Vassilevsky
by name. On hearing that I had travelled with Isadora
and Essenine, he took me under his wing and introduced me to several Russian writers. They were very
curious about Essenine, whom they regarded as a sort
of *enfant terrible* and genius combined. And so for a
while I basked in the reflected glory of the poet.

Among the people I met were Count Aleksey Tolstoy
(not related to the great Tolstoy, but from a different
branch), Ilya Ehrenburg, Kusikoff, Igor Severianin,
Vetlugin, and others. Of them all, the most impressive by far was Tolstoy : a tall, heavy, middle-aged,
handsome man, with a big Russian face and the
manners of an aristocrat. He had a soft, slow dignity,
yet was simple. I liked him at once. Although known
to the English public only through two or three books—
The Road to Calvary being the best known—he is a first-
rate and prolific writer, famous for his style, which is
both simple and charming, and full of a delicate
humour. Like Chekhov, however, he should never
have been translated. The humour is all between the
lines, like a faint aroma, so peculiarly Russian that
translation, even the best, kills it completely.

Of the poets, the most striking figure was Igor
Severianin. His resemblance to Oscar Wilde was quite
startling, except that Severianin had a less heavy chin

and, though inclined to be corpulent, was not as soft as
I imagine Wilde must have been at that age.   Though
in his forties, he was still very handsome, almost beautiful, tall, dark, with gorgeous eyes and beautiful white
hands.   He belonged to the decadents, to the past, the
old pre-revolutionary Russia when the most exquisite,
refined luxury existed side by side with, or in ignorance
of, poverty and filth.   He was peculiarly the poet of
Petrograd, where in the luxurious cafés, surrounded by
throngs of admiring women, he declaimed his melodic,
extravagant lyrics.   In Berlin I heard him once.   It
was an exhibition, the sort of thing the layman expects
of a poet : a long-stemmed Russian cigarette in his
beautiful hand, a flower in his smoking-jacket, his
beautiful eyes resting dreamily on a girl's face, he talked
poetry.   It was lovely.   It should have turned my
head, for I was still so young and susceptible.   But I
had come straight from my sojourn with Essenine—
whose simple lyrics made you humble with their perfect
and deep beauty, whose poems never aimed at effect,
never dealt with love or with women, but with the
earth and trees and humble peasants and robbers and
thieves and animals—and the spectacle seemed a bit
shoddy and the exquisite poems had a tinge of
vulgarity.

A far better poet, though neither handsome nor
striking, was Ilya Ehrenburg.   He had then just
finished his first big prose work, a satire entitled *Julio
Jurenito*, and gave a reading at the club.   Once a week
a member of the writer's club was asked to read por-
tions of his newest work.   The rest of us sat in the small
auditorium—the writer on the platform, at a table with
a pitcher of water and a glass—quite like a small lecture-
room.   After the reading there was criticism.   I have
never heard of any other writer's organisation practising this, and perhaps only Russians are simple, truthful

and strong enough to undergo this ordeal. For the things were discussed, criticised, and knocked up mercilessly.

When Ehrenburg came on the platform, he was obviously jittery. He was a tall, lanky young Jewish man with a shock of unruly hair. His voice was hoarse and he read too fast. But the stuff he read was good and he received loud applause. Years later, in the United States, I read the book as it was published. It is a remarkable work, a long rambling satire on the whole of contemporary life, covering everything from politicians, dictators, contraceptives—as distributed by an enterprising American missionary in Paris *bordels*, along with little earnest pamphlets about saving souls—to pipes, lunatics, the Jewish question, and what not. A fantastic book, clever, sometimes profound, always biting and written in a hilarious style. The hero, Jurenito, a sort of modern superman, is a Mexican expatriate with a flock of screwy disciples, the book being narrated by his Russian disciple.

A few years ago I ran across an English translation of the thing and nearly died of anger and chagrin. It was butchered beyond recognition. As always Russian humour could not be caught in another language.

An odd figure in this assembly was the poet Kusikoff. A boon companion of Essenine's in his Moscow period, he still had about him an aura of that wild time when the *Imaginisty* (Imagists), a group of the most daring young poets, with Essenine at their head, had launched their literary movement and generally run the town ragged. Kusikoff was a young Georgian : swarthy, slim with affected manners, he strutted about Berlin dressed in his native costume—long coat tight around the waist with a flowing skirt bottom, enormous silver belt, a long scabbard, dragging on the pavement, and a row of bright, shining cartridges on his chest. His

poetry was in far better taste than he, quite
" imagistic " and alive.

At this period, probably under the influence of all
the stimulating Russian contacts, I began to write
Russian again. I wrote a few sketches, entitled
" Dreams," and one day, adding some poems I had
written in Venice while I was with Isadora and
Essenine, I gathered some courage and showed the
stuff to Vassilevsky, the critic. He was a short, dark
man, with a florid face and eyes that were both kindly
and shrewd. To my discomfiture he began to look
through them right then and there, in his study.
While he read, I watched his face with the feeling of a
criminal called before a judge. I had not written anything original in years and I had lost most of my youthful self-confidence and arrogance. . . .

He took the poems first. I thought they were
pretty fair, but was doubtful of my sketches. Having
read them all, the critic began to take them to pieces—
slowly, mercilessly, while I felt as though being vivi-
sected. Then he said they were " nice " and put them
aside with the gesture of one who is not the least
interested. I could neither move nor speak. . . . He
began to read the " Dreams." They were short pieces
written in a flowing-cadenced prose that became at
times blank verse. He looked up almost at once, shot
a curious glance at me, and said :

" *A vot eto chorosho. S Iziumenkoy* "—an untrans-
latable phrase, meaning something like : " Pretty good.
With a bit of kernel in it."

" Do you mean these are better than my poems ? "
I asked, amazed.

" Of course. There is something in these that is
new, original. It is all strictly yours. The poems are
not original—most young people write like that. Besides, they are badly written." Then, to my dismay,

he took the loose sheets and went to the dining-room, where his wife and several friends sat—in true Russian fashion—around a samovar. Waving the manuscripts, he pointed to me and said : " Here is a new author ! " Although it was said half jestingly, they all looked at me with a fresh curiosity. Hitherto I had merely been a young Polish girl who spoke good Russian, good German, and, what seemed to impress them most, good English. Now I suddenly seemed to show another unsuspected facet. The critic began to ask me about my writing in detail and I confessed truthfully that I wrote sporadically, very seldom, and in small doses. He wagged his head. He gave various bits of good advice which I promptly forgot, for I was not ready for it yet. He said something about " work " and I paid no attention. I remember that I had in those days the fixed idea that all writing should come utterly spontaneously, joyfully and easily. If it didn't, one had no business to write. The only thing that seemed to have stuck in my memory from this conversation was the revelation that it is hard to judge your own work—in fact, that almost any Tom, Dick, or Harry is a better judge than yourself. To write a thing is one story ; to know the exact effect it will produce on other people's minds is a different matter entirely. . . .

21

A RETURN

ALL in all this was a nice period. I met many interesting people, made some pleasant friends, and would have given myself up entirely to loafing if my tiny reserve of

money had not begun to vanish. It was time to look
for a job. This proved much more difficult than it had
ever been heretofore. Finally, after some vain efforts,
I got a half-day job with a Russian by the name of
Rode. He was a swarthy, corpulent man with penetrating, shrewd eyes. In Petrograd, before Bolshevism,
he used to run the most famous roadhouse, the so-called
Villa Rode, where officers of the Guard and other young
bloods listened to gipsies, drank, and caroused. Now,
in Berlin, he was engaged in various vague and odd
enterprises. He had magnificent visiting cards on
which he was styled "*Kommerzienrath, Geheimrath,*"
and so on, without, I believe, the least foundation. I
distrusted him but needed the work. My job consisted
of translating his German correspondence into Russian
(he knew only Russian) and writing his letters. The
"*Kommerzienrath*" did not have an office and I worked
in his home, in his study. It was a dark, well-furnished,
but stuffy apartment, full of velvet curtains, rugs, and
knick-knacks. Rode's wife was a beautiful young
Russian woman, very pale, with huge sad eyes. I
recall that I often felt sorry for her, though I hardly
knew her at all. . . .

One Sunday I went sailing on the Wannsee with a
German boy. We used his *Faltbot* (folding boat)—an
affair of small bamboo sticks, forming the frame of a
canvas boat, all of it weighing about twenty-five pounds
and, when necessary, folding up to form a pack like a
rucksack. On that day we attached a tiny sail to it.
We wore sports clothes, with bathing suits underneath
in case of emergency. The day was lovely, sunny, with
a blue sky, the golden trees of the forest around us in
full autumnal glory. The lake was full of craft of all
kinds. Around five o'clock the breeze became rather
stiff. We flew about the lake, which rapidly became
choppy. Soon there were good-sized breakers. The

folding boat sat very low in the water, the canvas was tied around our waists, while we ourselves were sitting flat on the bottom of the boat. In less than twenty minutes we were drenched. We had only two tiny paddles along, so we kept the sail, trying to make the nearest clubhouse. The adventure ceased to be a pleasure. When we finally got to the shore, we were stiff with cold and very tired. At the club we drank a couple of *Eiercognacs* and returned to Berlin. The next day I was down with the flu.

The flu ran its course and I was up in a few days, but the cold settled in my sinuses and I continued to feel ill. A Russian physician at the *pension* diagnosed me as " anæmic " and gave me a series of arsenic injections, but failed to send me to an ear-and-throat man, and I felt no better. The job with the Russian *Kommerzien-rath* ceased automatically and I moved into a cheaper *pension*.

I remember days spent in my tiny room in a sort of dismal haze of headache, futile planning, scanning the advertisements of the papers, and counting my money.... " Enough left for four weeks . . . for three weeks . . . for two weeks. . . ." If I could not find work within a week, I should either have to borrow from someone or go home. Home meant Poland, grand-mother, father, friends and relatives. It also meant a return to old scenes and memories. Although a year had passed, the memory of D. had not dimmed in the least. It was simply glazed over with all the new impressions I had gathered in that erratic year. More-over, having been independent financially for five years now, having never asked father's help, I was terribly reluctant to return in the role of a jobless prodigal daughter. My foolish stubborn pride suffered. I could not bring myself to write the letter announcing my arrival *sans* money, *sans* job, in bad health.

In my extremity I recalled that an aunt and cousin had owed some money to our mother, a considerable sum, something like five or six thousand francs. This was from the days when we all lived in Zurich. After mother's death, the money was supposed to be paid, eventually, to my sister and myself. I wrote to my cousin asking for something on account and got a cheque for two hundred francs by return mail. This revived my spirits considerably. I laid aside a sufficient sum for a ticket to Poland and started job-hunting again. It was in vain. This was 1922. Germany was in the worst throes of her inflation. So one cold day in November, almost exactly a year after I had left Warsaw for Vienna, I boarded the train to Lodz.

It rained dismally when the train rolled into the station, and as I sat next to father in an old cab, the horse *plunk-plunking* over the wet cobblestones of one of the ugliest, dirtiest towns in the world, I felt a dreadful wave of depression come over me.

Lodz is the biggest industrial town in Poland ; it is habitually enveloped in smoke from the hundreds of factory chimneys. It has no river, no parks, practically no trees. I have detested the place, with a sort of physical, unreasoning hatred, ever since I first saw it as a child, on my first visit to Poland. In those days, I remember, there was no sewer system (in a town of 300,000 population) and the poisonous waste from the chemical factories and dye works and textile works used to flow in little iridescent rivulets near the sidewalks and fill the air with stench. . . . Each successive visit, after that, brought the feeling back with undiminished force.

" It is an ugly day for a homecoming," my father said presently, as if divining my mood, " but where we live it is not bad. I get a house from the Government, free. It is right on the edge of the town, near the Monopol. It is plain but comfortable and we have a nice garden and a fruit orchard." (My father, it must be explained, on his escape from Russia was offered by the new Polish Government a similar position to the one he held with the Russian old régime Government.)

"It must be nice in summer," I said, thinking drearily that summer was yet far away.

"It is and, oh, by the way, I have just installed a hot-and-cold-water system and you can have a bath ready in two minutes."

I laughed at this. It was just like Dad. Just like old times. He loved comfort and all the modern gadgets, especially after his first trip to America, and in Russia, in the old days, when we lived in backward, provincial towns, he always improved the houses we lived in. I recall in Orel, a town where everybody had their water brought from the river in barrels, we had water coming from faucets, to the amazement of our servants. It, too, came originally in barrels, but father had a cistern built on the roof, from which a system of pipes brought down the water to the house. . . .

"Let father not worry about these things," I said, addressing him in the customary Polish way, in the third person. "I don't care whether I wait for a bath two minutes or twenty."

"Oh, but these little comforts matter in the long run," father said, and continued : "At any rate you will have a nice room to yourself. I put in a good desk, too, so you can write."

"I hardly ever write now," I replied. . . .

Having made the rounds of calls on all sorts of aunts and cousins and friends, I settled down—for the first time in years—to the life of a sheltered daughter. I liked it better than I had anticipated. First and foremost there was grandmother. Her never-failing affection enveloped me like a warm, luxurious bath. In her presence all my outward bravado and all the defences which egocentric youth builds against the world and people crumbled to nothing. Grandma's love was so selfless, so unpossessive, so kind, that no one could resist it. When I was a child, she was the only person to whom I ever opened my heart. With my mother, whom I adored, I was affectionate but reserved. She had always been frail and died when my sister and I were fourteen, just when we needed her most. My father I treated with a sort of courteous but distant affection, rather like an uncle. I never confided in him. Grandmother's love was like some magic, a lovely spell, for there was no compulsion in it. In her presence I became instantly—and, what's more, very willingly— just one of her grandchildren, someone she could coddle, love, advise, and scold. The self-confident, much-travelled young lady who told engaging stories about her odd jobs and experiences vanished and became merely an adoring granddaughter.

In the morning, just as I used to do as a child, I would come into grandmother's room, cuddle down at the foot of the bed, on her feather bed, and beg for stories. Not fiction stories, but stories from her life. She was a marvellous story-teller, could imitate dialects, mimic people and voices, and had a lovely sense of humour.

Her health at that time was already bad and frequently she spent days at a time in bed. This bed, high with the soft feather beds, and with grandmother's sweet face, her grey hair parted in the middle, her blue eyes, so kind, yet so wise and penetrating, peeping from the pillows, will remain in my memory for ever. Grandma's bed was the centre of the house. My two step-

sisters, now eleven and thirteen, brought down from
Russia by my stepmother on one of her annual visits,
father, and I congregated around it at all times of the
day. There were many visitors, too. People came
with flowers, rare fruits, and delicacies which grandmother could no longer eat. They came with solicitous
and solemn faces and left laughing. I am sure they
always received more than they brought. The frail
little old lady in the huge feather bed was more alive
than all her visitors. I realised this, I recall, rather
suddenly one day after a particularly stuffy crowd had
left. Ever since then, to my own private self, I had
liked to classify people as " more " or " less " alive. It
has not much to do with physical fitness, and even still
less with " temperament or vivacity." Some, though
quite fit and strong, are quite dead inside. Others have
differing degrees of aliveness. I suppose completely
" dead " people are only to be met with among the
insane. Not the violent ones, but those terribly quiet
ones, those poor souls who shuffle about in the gardens of
asylums, who see yet seem not to see, engrossed in their
dreadful misery, who suffer yet cannot even shout their
misery any more, and seem to live in some bottomless
depth which is even beyond suicide. I had seen them
once on a tour of a big state asylum and they haunted
me for days afterwards. Yet how many of us so-called
normal people have " dead spots." . . . It is perhaps
only the question of degree ; with one or two spots, or
even a half a dozen, you can jog along in life and adjust
yourself more or less. With a flock of them you land
in an institution.

To return to the story, the " most alive " people
among the many hundreds I have known in my life
were my grandmother, Isadora, a social worker—a
hunchback who did the work free, because he liked it,
and not as a professional—an old Texas cowboy, a

T

society woman who also did social work, and two physicians. All of them were selfless, had a great sense of humour, and were spiritual. An old word, yet I don't know any new one that could replace it.

I stayed in Lodz for about two months. As soon as my health improved I became very restless and started to look for work. A friend of my father's knew of an Englishman in Warsaw who needed a secretary. I left for Warsaw and got the job.

The Englishman was a director of the famous English boiler factory of Babcock and Wilcox. Tall, blond, lean, well-groomed, he looked the typical British upper-middle-class business man. This was a far cry from Isadora or even the *Musical Courier*, but I was glad of any work and my employer proved pleasant. The work was utterly uninteresting. I could never become excited over boilers or rivets or plants. The six months I spent with the firm are now covered with a sort of patina of boredom. The work was easy, the tempo was English. We had two hours at noon and I recall taking long walks with the two Polish stenographers, telling them endless stories about America, Russia, Switzerland. A good audience always used to stimulate me. Outside of work I read a great deal, mostly Polish. Comically enough, Mr. Metcalf, my employer, thought me very good, and the letter of reference he gave me when I left is one of the best I possess. The touch system I used did the trick again, I think, for he liked the speed with which I turned out his letters and the fact that I really knew English quite well. At 5 P.M. religiously, we were all served tea. At six the office was closed.

The most pleasant recollection of that long winter was my friendship with Pan and Pani M., which I renewed. As luck would have it, they had a large flat and a spare bedroom, and, as I could not find a room anywhere and living in an hotel was too expensive, I moved in with them as a paying guest. I recall going to bed almost daily with a book in my hand and the sound of M.'s playing coming through the door, which I always left ajar. He played with gusto, trying to be the whole orchestra.

Toward spring my health became worse again, for the winter had been wet and raw and I had frequent colds. My sister, with whom I corresponded quite regularly, urged me to come to America, and when spring came I decided to go.

I left Poland in May, with a mingled feeling of regret and hope. I travelled through Germany and embarked in Bremen on one of the cabin steamers of the Dollar Line.

Part IV

AMERICA

A DIFFERENT AMERICA

THE America I came to in 1923 was so different from the America I had known in 1916 that it might have been a new country. I stayed in New York only a couple of weeks and then went straight on to Chicago to join my sister and brother-in-law.

I arrived there on a day in June, and it was as hot as hell. I beg your pardon. At the station I was met by my sister and her sister-in-law. One of them was blue, the other red. What I mean is that each was dressed in one colour from top to toe, including shoes, hose, hat, bag, and the minutest accessories. That, it seemed, was the mode of the day. I stared at them, completely flabbergasted. But they, too, did their own staring. They said :

" Look at her hair ! You must have it bobbed. At once ! With your curls, it will look swell. Look at her eyebrows ! Did you ever see anything like it ? We must teach her to tweeze them. And look at her coat ! "

Thus I was introduced to that everlasting American preoccupation with fashion, with fashion in clothes and in hair and make-up, the continuous beautifying and primping. I protested vainly, I tried to defend my clothes, which were rather tailored and expensive and not at all old—not more than a year or so. " But what can be wrong with this ? " I said. " Even Isadora liked this dress and she dressed wonderfully. She had one, made by Patou, almost exactly like it."

"It's two years old in style. Look at these sleeves. You can't do it. Not in America. You must be up-to-date."

And so it went on and I submitted. I cried when the barber cut off my beautiful hair, but when I saw that the bob made me look like eighteen, I dried my tears. I had things done to my face and my hands and my clothes, and I bought many pairs of shoes, for shoes had to match. I got into the American habit of having loads of shoes, loads of bags and gloves, for everything had to " match." . . .

That, I remember, was my first impression. The second was the climate. The people in Chicago referred to all its infernal changes very quaintly as " a spell." . . . " It's nothing," someone would say, " just a hot spell. They don't last very long," or, " You will get used to it." Later, in winter, I was to hear similar expressions about the frightful cold : " A cold spell," or, " It's the wind from the lake ; it never lasts more than three days."

That first hot " spell," however, which I ran into on the day of my arrival, lasted more than a week. At my sister's house they had devised various amusing ways of counteracting the heat. We walked about naked, with kimonos lying around handy in case of callers. Every room had a fan which whirred the hot air incessantly. Every now and then we took a bath. At first we took cold baths, but soon found that getting out of the cool water into the hot air was not pleasant ; then we hit on the idea of taking hot baths, as hot as we could stand, which was better. The air, by contrast, seemed quite cool for a while. We drank quarts of hot tea with lemon, which is a Russian trick and rather good. It makes you perspire, and when you perspire you cool off. Often we went to the movies, which had a cooling system. We would sit through two shows and cool off ;

then emerge into a street which was like a Russian sweat bath. What amused me most was the way we spent the nights. We lugged some blankets and pillows to the park and slept on the lawn. Hundreds of other people did the same. Big, fat policemen walked around, keeping an eye on public morals, keeping an eye on all the couples, lest they should forget that they were not in their own bed at home, but on a public lawn. . . .

The third great impact in this new, strange America was the *milieu* in which my sister now lived. It was the *milieu* of musicians and the movie theatre, for Victor was a concert master in one of these. The theatres themselves overwhelmed me with their rich and splendid vulgarity. Louis XIV, Louis XV, baroque, silks, brocades, velvets—everything was there and everything screamed with newness and ostentation. And the toilets! The lovely, lovely toilets! The dainty and exquisite lounging rooms with the dim lights, fragile mirrors, and chairs covered with pastel silks. To my surprise no one ever seemed to sit on them; all the women and girls rushed right past them into the toilet-room proper, where the lights over the mirrors were bright and glaring and where they could see their well-groomed, hard faces clearly and restore their awful, yet exquisite make-up.

The music in these vulgar palaces, however, was surprisingly good. Far better than in the European cinemas. These were the days of the silents, when every large movie theatre had a full orchestra and scores were made up specially for and synchronised with each feature, and each week was ushered in with a new overture. Usually it was a hodge-podge of classic and semi-classic music, but occasionally, as when Victor made the arrangement, a movie overture was a fine, harmonious job, written with taste and finesse.

As to the musicians themselves, they exemplified the
real American melting pot : French, German, Italian
Bohemian, Russian, Jew, Gentile . . . every race and
creed seemed to be represented, and they lived, or
rather worked, in an atmosphere of their own, a unique
world of tense work and odd relaxations.

2

CHICAGO'S SEAMY SIDE

" You want to take a ride with me, Lola ? " asked the
doctor. He was a friend of the family, a small man with
a fine head, kind brown eyes, and a humorous mouth.
" Oh, thanks. I do," I replied.

As we drove off, the doctor seemed to recall something and asked if I would mind if he were to drop in at
his old office for a few minutes. I didn't mind at all.
It was always exciting to go with the doctor somewhere ; he was an eccentric, cheerful fellow with a
passion for music almost as great as his passion for
surgery, and a temperament that didn't seem to go
with any exact science.   Besides, I had heard about his
" old " office. It was in that part of the West Side
where coloured folks, and the " hunkies and dagos,"
lived. It was his first office, which he opened in this
cheap neighbourhood when he had just got through
college and did not have much money to start on. And
now that he had a nice office in a big down-town
building, he still kept the old place and went there
occasionally.

It was a hot, dusky summer evening. We were
making our way rather slowly, for the streets here were

poorly lighted and dirty and ragged children still played outside. Flitting across our road at the most unexpected moments, they would materialise suddenly, like little dark shadows, in front of our headlights and disappear as swiftly into the gloomy obscurity of the street. The noise they made was the only thing that broke the stillness of the night, and by contrast it made the murky quiet still more impressive.

The dark houses seemed utterly deserted, the street lights were small and dim, and only once in a while the blazing electric sign of a corner drug-store made a little sudden pool of light which seemed to float by as we drove along. We were approaching the office and the doctor slowed down, when a low, high-powered roadster purred up at our side, and the driver, a jaunty young man in a soft felt hat, waved his hand and shouted :

" Hello, doc ! Got some work for you to-night "— and was immediately swallowed by the dark street.

" Who was that, doctor ? " I asked.

" Bunny, a gangster."

" You mean a criminal ? "

The doctor looked at me with a quizzical smile. " Well, you could call him that if you like."

" What did he say ? "

" Now don't ask so many questions. . . ." The doctor parked his car. " Let's go up and see who is waiting for me."

We went up one flight of steps to his office. In the first room, bare and poorly furnished and full of that peculiar sadness which pervades some waiting-rooms, three negroes sat in various attitudes of dejection. The doctor passed on to the other room and I sat down on one of the hard, stiff-backed chairs, covertly observing the three men. They seemed motionless : sprawled and somehow utterly relaxed on those small, hard chairs, they looked more like some strange mummies that had been slumped down carelessly. Only the white flicker of their eyeballs, as their eyes followed the doctor, betrayed that they were alive. Their hopeless immobility and the sadness of that bare room affected me so strongly that, unable to sit quietly, I got up and started to pace the room, wishing the doctor would get to work. Presently he poked his head through the door, and called one of the men.

I went to a window, leaning close to the pane and trying to pierce the darkness without. On the opposite corner there was a small drug-store. The sign was quite high up and the light it shed was not strong. However, I soon distinguished the familiar shape of the long roadster which had passed us earlier that night. It was parked close to the kerb. And presently I saw the door of the store open slowly and in the light which filled the open space there came distinctly the silhouette of the jaunty young man with the felt hat. With his back to the street, he stood for a moment, evidently talking to someone within the store ; then he turned slowly, got into his car, and drove off.

He interested me. I made a mental reservation to find out some more about this " gangster " from our friend, the doctor, Then I turned, facing the room. The second negro was gone now, and after the lapse of a few minutes the third and last one was called. With the absence of these silent, dark men, the bare little room became still more barren and lifeless.

Finally the doctor emerged, smiling cheerfully, rubbing his hands. " That was quick work, eh ? Three patients in twenty minutes. Now we had better decide where we shall go to-night. Shall we go to the dog races ? "

" We can decide that in the car," I replied rather rudely. " I am not going to stay in this dreadful room another minute."

" I must stay here for a little while longer, Lola. I am sorry," said the doctor, " but someone may turn up yet. . . . It may not be long. I have to wait . . ."

He seemed of a sudden anxious and bothered, as if some persistent thought had overlapped his habitual, happy-go-lucky cheeriness.

I turned wearily to the window and, recalling the jaunty young man, I said :

" I saw your elegant gangster across the street at the drug-store a minute ago."

" You did ! " The doctor seemed a bit excited. " Is he there yet ? "

" No, he drove away. By the way, what did he really mean by saying he had ' work for you ' ? Is he your patient ? "

" No, but sometimes——" The doctor stopped abruptly, standing tense and absorbed, as if listening to some sounds. " There—they are bringing someone up the steps. Go and wait in my office. I may need you." And with this he rushed out into the hall.

Through the open door I heard slow, heavy footfalls as if of men carrying a burden, and, rooted to the spot in a sudden rush of anguished excitement, I waited breathlessly.

The heavy footsteps came nearer and nearer and presently the little procession appeared at the head of the landing. The doctor came first, supporting a man's head ; the rest of the large, inert body was carried by two men, obviously working men. An ugly gash in the forehead of the wounded man was bleeding and the blood dripped methodically on to the cheap linoleum rug of the hall and the room as they carried him to the operating table. The doctor bent over the man in an instant of close scrutiny. Then he lifted his head.

" Where did you pick him up ? "

" Right around the corner, doc. Is he hurt bad ? "

"No. He will come out of it all right. See anyone round him?"

"No, doc," said one of the men. "We was just going home and found him on the sidewalk, on his face."

"Bunny must have done it," said the other in a low voice. "I seen his car at the drug-store. Will you tell the police, doc? So we can go?"

"Go ahead. I'll attend to that," said the doctor.

They left, visibly relieved, and the doctor became exceedingly busy about the wounded man's head. Within a few minutes the man began to groan heavily as the doctor dressed his wounds, then he opened his eyes and started getting up, but was pushed back gently and told to be still. The doctor then telephoned the police station and, having done that, asked the man's name.

"Joe Mlavin."

"Russian, are you?"

"Yes, sir."

"Can you remember how it happened, Joe?"

"He came up and aska da match. Not remember much."

"This young lady here knows Russian; you can tell her about it when the police come."

They came within a few minutes—two husky six-footers. You did not have to wait until they spoke to know they were Irish. The small, wiry physician looked like a boy next to them. But his manner became very official. Did it just seem so to me, or was there a tiny sly twinkle in his eyes?

"You want a report, don't you, officer?" he said. "He is Russian. Working man. His name is Joe Mlavin. This lady here knows Russian well. She can translate for him."

But the two policemen did not seem at all interested. In fact, they almost disregarded the doctor's speech.

One of them bent perfunctorily over the Russian and asked :

" How much money did he get off you ? "

The heavy, stolid, bandaged face grinned and the man said : " Just zee change in ma pocket. Ozer money I hid in coat lining. Forty-eight dallers."

" That's fine. You are a smart fellow." Then he turned to his companion. " Let's get going. We can make out that report at the station."

" Don't you want the description of the fellow that held him up ? " asked the doctor. And again I had the impression that inwardly he was smiling. He seemed to be having fun.

" That will be all, doc," said the Irishman gruffly. And they both left.

After the man was sufficiently recovered from his shock to go home, the doctor told him to come for a dressing in a couple of days and then we, too, went.

Again we were picking our way through the dark and deserted streets. Only there were no children's voices to break the silence. The night was still warm and oppressive. The scene in the office became a little unreal, as if it hadn't happened.

" Doctor," I said after a while, " you knew that this Bunny was going on a hold-up when he passed by us an hour ago ? "

" Sure I did."

" And when he said he would have ' work ' for you you knew he might hurt someone ? "

" I could not be sure. He doesn't always get his man. But it wouldn't do to disregard a warning like this. The nearest hospital is miles away ; sometimes it may mean saving a man's life."

" Good Lord ! But if you knew, why didn't you go to the nearest policeman and tell him about it ? "

" Why, that wouldn't have done any good."

Though I couldn't see his face in the dark, I could imagine him smiling. " The policeman wants to live, too. Do you blame him ? "

" What do you mean ? "

" I mean that if any policeman in this district went after Bunny, his life wouldn't be worth two cents from then on. Most likely he would be found dead the next day. You see, Bunny is a big gangster and he has a whole organised gang behind him."

" And is this why those two officers did not want to take the description of the hold-up man? They knew?"

" Sure they knew. But they didn't want to get involved. They will probably say in the report that the ' victim could not describe his assailant,' and leave it at that."

" You think they are paid by Bunny ? Bribed ? "

" I don't think so. They are just nice big Irish boys who don't want to get bumped off. If they catch an individual criminal, they probably do their best. But when they are up against a big gang, they are just frightened."

" But it is wrong, all the same. A policeman is supposed to be a hero, like a soldier. If ten policemen to-day would arrest ten gangsters and be bumped off the next day, and then ten more would do the same the following day, the gangs couldn't exist."

He looked at me as if I were suggesting something fantastic and bizarre ; in fact as if I were " talking through my hat."

" But this, really, means that there is here in Chicago no law or protection," I said, womanlike and obstinate, in one more effort of protest.

" Now why worry your head about it ? " said the doctor kindly, as if talking to a child. " I took you out to give you a good time. . . . Shall we go to the dog races and see the nice doggies ? "

THE AUTHOR

Chicago 1923

And we went to the dog races. They were run by a
man called Al Capone, I heard ; it was one of his
" rackets." . . .   " What is a racket, doctor," I asked,
" and who is this Al Capone, anyway ? " . . .   The
doctor grinned and hushed me up while some people
around us looked both scared and amused. . . .

" You'd better not mention his name here, Lola
darling," the doctor said. . . .   Thus I was learning
about the Chicago of 1923.

3

A POKER GAME

I KNEW the game. I learned it at the age of twelve
when we lived in Switzerland.   A cousin of mine, of the
riper age of seventeen, had taught it to me and we used
to play it secretly in the nursery with a limit of five
centimes and two jokers (a stiff game), until we were
caught by my mother and I was summarily deprived of
my monthly allowance of five francs and forbidden to
play it. . . .

Perhaps because of this early experience, the game
had retained a certain fascination, and now, in Chicago
I was glad to find that I could play it again.   It was one
of the favourite games of the boys and was played in
the musicians' room along with hearts, pinochle, and
such.   The stakes there were pretty high and occasionally some mild cut-throating took place.   On occasion,
however, when the game was played at someone's
house, it took on a more social aspect.   The limit was
lowered to a quarter or less, the " girls were let in on
it," with gracious condescension, for girls are

U

notoriously rotten players and rotten losers—or so the legend goes anyway—and we had a generally hilarious time.

One memorable night—for the game never started before 1 a.m., after the last show—I remember we played until eight in the morning, but the exhilaration of having won twenty-five dollars seemed to compensate amply for the loss of a night's sleep.

However, this was not the game I meant to tell about. There was nothing exceptional in this game excepting perhaps, the streak of luck which pursued me all night. The game I remember most was the one after that. It all started from a fishbone which got stuck in my throat at dinner time. None of the home remedies, such as swallowing dry bread and thumping on the back, seemed to help, and we called our good friend, Dr. S. He arrived promptly, took one look at my throat, and said : " Well, well, it got stuck in your tonsil. Pretty deep, too. I think you had better come along with me, Lola darling. I have nothing here I can pull it out with."

" How about my eyebrow tweezers ? " I suggested hopefully.

The doctor gave one of his comical grins, lifted his eyebrows, and said :

" Oh, no. Tweezers won't do. I need something else for that. Come on, let's go."

We got into his car and drove off. To my surprise he did not go to his office, but drove to a wholesale house for surgical instruments, where he got admittance by some mysterious pull of his own—it being nearly 8 p.m. There, from trays of brilliantly shining, sharp-looking things, he selected a few which looked like tiny round silver spoons, had them wrapped, and took me to his house. He boiled the little spoons in a small pot. spread them carefully on a white napkin on the kitchen table, screwed in a powerful bulb in the centre light which hung from the ceiling, and made me sit down on a hard kitchen chair. His wife, a pretty young thing, was putting their baby to bed when we arrived, and now she came and cast a surprised glance at the arrangement in the kitchen.

" You are just in time, darling," the doctor said to her, and to me he said :

" Now, Lola dear, I am going to take out your tonsils."

" But why, doctor ? " I asked, amazed.

" Because they are rotten through and through. They don't do you any good and they might do you a lot of harm. We will take the little fishbone right along with them."

" But isn't it quite an operation ? " I asked again, remembering dimly that some people went to hospitals for it.

" That's all nonsense. Of course if one of those high-toned specialists does it, he has to make it look important. Besides, he might cut a vein or something and there would be trouble. But not with me . . ." he added modestly.

" Really ? "

" Of course. Don't you trust me ? "

" Yes, of course I do," I said quite truthfully, yet I was still a little shocked at the suddenness of it.

" Now look," he said. " I am going to give you a little local anæsthetic. You won't feel a thing. Not a thing." Then, seeing that I still felt doubtful, he added with a smile : " Why, you could even play a game of poker to-night. How about it ? "

This assurance perked me up considerably. " Are you sure ? " I said.

" Sure as I live. I will fix up a little game right now, and then we will take out your tonsils. Helen has just

put the baby to bed and she will be my nurse."
Whereupon he went to the phone and called up Victor
and Rita and another couple, telling them to come for a
little game "specially for Lola." The telephone was
in the hall right off the kitchen, so I heard what he
said.

After this he injected novocain into my throat and
with the help of his wife, who held down my tongue
with a tea-spoon, he cut out my tonsils. He put them
in a saucer and danced about the kitchen singing lustily :
"A five hundred-dollar job! No bleeding! No
dissection! Perfect!" I looked at them, and though
I didn't know much about such matters, the little grey,
cheesy things looked as if they had long lost their period
of usefulness. Everyone had arrived by that time and
we went to the dining-room for our game. It was a
very nice game. I found I could not laugh much on
account of the wooden feeling in my mouth, but I had
enough voice to make my raises and I enjoyed the jokes
just the same. Also I enjoyed the little feeling of
importance with which the operation seemed to have
invested me, the anxious and covert glances of my
sister, the way they all lowered their voices when I
made my bid, so I should not have to speak too loud.
Also, I was winning. It was nice. This lasted for a
while, perhaps an hour or so, and then it was not nice.
The wooden feeling had almost disappeared and my
throat began to hurt. I wanted to tell the doctor about
it but found all of a sudden that I couldn't speak at all.
I took a piece of paper and wrote on it :
"You are a pig! It hurts! Why didn't you tell
me?"

"Why, what's the matter, Lola darling?" the doctor
asked with his smile which was both kindly and
mischievous. "Can't you talk? Didn't you enjoy
the game?"

Everyone laughed excepting myself, for I couldn't laugh or talk. The game broke up and the doctor's wife suggested I should spend the night at their house.

It was a miserable night. And I remembered that poker game for a long time afterward.

4

I CHOOSE A LANGUAGE

I WENT up the steps of the Chicago Public Library. The building was big, reassuring. There would be many books there for me to read, I thought. . . . There were more steps, then halls, and then at last I went through the door marked " Fiction " and stood spellbound in the huge room filled with thousands of volumes ! . . .

Of course, a lot of it would be no good, I thought, an awful lot, for I knew even then that there is more third-rate stuff written and published in English than in all the other civilised languages combined, but I was sure I should know the wheat from the chaff—I had a nose for the very best. . . . Gingerly, slowly, inwardly excited, I began to walk between the rows of alphabetically arranged books. It happened to be the row with the *C*'s . . . I thought of Conrad. . . .

Up to 1923 I knew only three of Conrad's books : *Lord Jim, Victory,* and a Tauchnitz edition of *Chance.* The Tauchnitz was a Continental's only access to English books in those years after the war. Importing books from England or America was simply prohibitive. As I walked along by the shelves, I wondered how many other books Conrad had written. Surely he had

written some others. I was quite excited at the prospect of finding some new Conrad books and then, rather
suddenly, I stood in front of the row, a big long row . . .
Conrad, Conrad, Conrad . . . more than twenty volumes,
it seemed, and I still recall the thrill of it. But the
librarian who had issued my card said I could only take
five. Five books altogether, she said, and after choosing five at random I left the library with my first feeling
of warmth for America. A country which gives its
people all the best books in the world to read free is a
marvellous country—whatever its other faults.

All through that summer I kept going to the library,
getting my fill of English books, reading, reading, reading all the time—at home, in the parks when it was hot,
in the elevated, and in the library itself. " How can
you read all the time ? " my sister would say. " Now
you've discovered the library, you don't know the
world exists," or some such comment, and I would
reply ecstatically : " I have discovered a new writer.
Her name is May Sinclair." Or, " I've discovered
Swinnerton," or " Zona Gale," as the case might be.

All these were discoveries in a much more literal sense
of the word than a native Englishman or American
would imagine. For names of writers have a way of
penetrating into the public consciousness even though
their works may not be read. These names are somehow in the air : on the jackets of books in the shops and
stalls, in the daily Press, in conversation ; and with
them goes a certain accepted reputation or flavour. An
American may never read Zona Gale or Hergesheimer
because he may not like their style, yet he would know
approximately what they stand for. To a European
most of such names were a complete blank. From my
last years on the Continent, I had carried away with me
only such well-known names as Shaw, Wells,
Galsworthy, Eugene O'Neill. Elmer Rice's plays were

just being translated.   And most of these writers I had
read in Polish. Dozens of other important English and
American writers were totally unknown.   The same,
of course, holds true conversely of Polish and Russian
writers.   Who, in England or America, knew in 1923 such
Polish writers as Zeromski, Wyspianski, Sieroszewski,
or the Russians Sologub, Chukovsky, and many others ?

Thus I " made discoveries " and revelled in them and
read and soaked myself in English, and the more I read
the more clearly I saw how deficient my own English
still was.   It had no roots.   It was the rather perfect,
grammatical, but colourless English of a foreigner.
True, I knew a few strictly English idioms which I had
picked up from my English friends in Petrograd, and
some dated American slang I had learned from contact
with the Americans at the J. D. C. Mission.   But I did
not know, not deeply, not familiarly, the idiom of a
single class or group.

The realisation, I recall, came as a sort of shock.   I
had just discovered Sheila Kaye-Smith and was learning all about Sussex.   Somewhere in the middle of the
book I stopped short and, for some obscure reason,
began taking stock of myself.   I have always had a
dim but persistent conviction that some day I should
write tolerably good books—that is, books which people
would want to read over again at least once.   This feeling was quite apart from, and not in the least influenced
by, the encouragement of my " literary talent " I had
received as a child, in school and so forth.   I knew I
was not ready.   Though I took a certain pleasure in the
process of writing and was, at times, a profuse correspondent, I knew quite well that this had nothing to do
with creative writing.   What I did not realise until
that day in the Chicago library, at least never with such
terrifying clarity, was that I had not even a proper
instrument, no tools to work with, *no language.*

To be a linguist has its advantages or, shall we say, satisfactions—the enormous satisfaction of reading various literatures in their original form, the pleasure of travelling unhampered by the barrier of a language. For a writer, however, it has equally enormous drawbacks : by using many languages, one is apt to become an amateur in all of them, a master of none.   In 1923, in Chicago, I was—though I did not know it then—at a sort of culmination point in my erratic, cosmopolitan existence.   I had been moving continually since I was a child and had first left Russia in 1910.   I had lived in :

Russia (with occasional stays in Poland)	Up to 1910
Switzerland	1910–1912
Germany	1912–1914
Russia	1914–1915
U.S.A.	1915–1916
Russia	1916–1918
Poland	1918–1921
Austria, Germany, Italy, Belgium	1922
U.S.A.	1923

I spoke at that time, fluently and thoroughly, Russian, Polish, and English.   I had a good knowledge of German and spoke French of a sort.   I could write in all these languages, printable stuff at that, but I could not have written the simplest short story in any of them, at least not one dealing with a definite locale, or a definite class of people.   I had become that truly horrible, volatile creature—a *cosmopolitan*, a creature that feels at home everywhere because it is not at home anywhere.

How I hate that word now !   It seems to epitomise all that is shallow, footloose, and superficial.   Ten, fifteen years ago, as a young girl settling down in some new country—always temporarily of course—I used to have a slight feeling of superiority to the natives, the provincials, the people whom you could identify instantly with a certain place. I thought I was worldly, more objective. It was not until that day in the Chicago library, reading about the Sussex peasants, that I first thought what cosmopolitanism meant in relation to writing, when I first saw all its disadvantages. Could I ever write like this about Russian peasants? Or Polish peasants, whom I thought I knew well? *No!* Could I write about the middle classes, the people I came from? Yes . . . perhaps . . . But in what language? Russian, Polish, or English? None. For I knew none as a writer should know them.

On that memorable day the die was cast and I chose English as my writing language. There would be no other ever again. The choice was really between Russian and English alone, for I had never written much in Polish, which I liked more for sentimental reasons. It was the language of my parents. Russian has always been closest to me ; it was the only language in which I wrote poetry, and its literature was dearer to me than any other, but I knew that I should probably never return to Russia to live and that meant that I should never use the language for writing. For I knew then, as I do now, that, cosmopolitan that I am, I could keep a language alive and flexible only in the country in which it was spoken.

5

MANNERS

THE summer was over. I had had a good rest— swimming, loafing about the town, and reading. And now I was ready to look for a job. I wanted it to be writing of some sort and tried to get on a newspaper, but was refused. Then, one day, scanning the " want ads," I saw one from the advertising department of a furniture factory. The style of American advertisements seemed to me rather marvellous, and I thought it might be good training to work with them for a while. Besides, the ad promised a job " with a future." I applied for it and got it. . . . I was to learn many things about America in that place.

One day, after I had been there for about a week, I was working at my desk, making clean copies of an ad. . . . A hand came down on my curly head and a thick, jovial voice said :

" So this is our new stenographer ? "

I jumped up, pushing the hand away. " How dare you ? "

A fat, elderly, Jewish-looking man was standing at my table, looking rather flabbergasted. The eyes of the whole office staff were on us both. . . .

" Well, well. . . . I happen to be the boss—curly-head."

" That may be, whatever it means. . . . I don't like familiarities from strange men. . . . You haven't even been introduced to me."

A suppressed giggle seemed to fill the room. I sensed that something was wrong somewhere, but couldn't put my finger on it.

" What's your name, girlie ? "

" Kinel. Miss Kinel."

" Say, I mean the first name."

" Lola . . ." I said doubtfully.

" Well, Lola, I hope you will like it here." He turned about and left the room before I could say anything further.

Then the noise burst out—they laughed and giggled and talked.

" Who is this fat man ? " I asked.

" One of the owners, Mr. Hartwig. We call an owner ' boss ' in America."

" He is very ill-bred. Why should he call me by my first name ? "

" Oh, we always do in America," said the department head. " I was just going to ask you your first name myself. You have been here more than a week."

" But . . . but . . . I don't understand. . . . It's all right socially, of course, but in an office ! I wouldn't call him by his first name."

They laughed. " Oh, come on, who wants to be so formal ? " said one of them.

" Well, then, why should he do it ? Socially he may not even be my equal."

They were all puzzled, almost as much as I. . . .

" What do they call each other in offices in Poland ? " someone wanted to know.

" They call me Panna Kinel (Miss Kinel) ; then if they get really intimate and friendly, they would call me Panna Lola. They would never call me by my first name. Only a brother, cousin, or fiancé would call me by my first name in Poland. And, of course, no one would ever put his hand on me, or clap my back or fiddle with my hair. We shake hands when we come to the office and when we leave. If you are a married woman, the men on the staff kiss your hand on coming or leaving."

" Kiss your hand ? In an office ? "

" Yes, it's merely a token of respect to any married woman. Of course, if you are really friendly with some of your colleagues and give them permission, they can kiss your hand even if you are single."

They laughed and were very much amused.

6

THE SECRETS OF WORDS

THE advertising department of the furniture factory was divided into two sections by the filing cases ; on one side was the advertising section proper, on the other the art department.   In the advertising section, the manager and assistant and I did the copy ; in the other half of the room the artists made the sketches for the ads.   The art director, Mr. Lowry, was a tall, lanky Scotchman with a wide, humorous mouth.

Often, when we were through with our copy, there was nothing for me to do.   At such hours, I tried my hand at writing.

One day I was walking the length of that big room, for I was thinking of a plot for a story.   I like to walk when I write—and I like to have enough space to take at least a dozen or more steps.   As I passed the filing cases in the centre of the room, I felt something against my ankle, very lightly, but went on walking ; on making the turn I felt the impact again, slightly tighter.   In fact, I almost tripped.   A roar went up around me.   I was startled out of my dreams and looked round stupidly. . . .

" . . . What is it ? "

There was a string tied loosely across the floor about ankle height and it had caught me.   They all laughed. . . .

" Say, why do you walk like that ? " the art director asked.   From his eyes I guessed that it was he who had pulled the trick on me.

" I do it unconsciously—when I concentrate on something. . . .   It doesn't bother you all, does it ? " I asked, getting a bit mad.

"Not at all—go ahead—enjoy yourself. We were just curious." They did all stare at me.

"What are you writing, anyway? A love story?"

"*O, do licha z wami!*" I said, swearing in Polish.

"What was that?" they asked.

"A Polish swear word. I did not want to hurt your feelings."

"How do you swear in Polish?" the art director asked.

"Oh, variously. . . . You say: '*Psia krew* (dog's blood); *psia noga* (dog's leg); *psia jucha* (dog's . . . h'm).'"

They were convulsed. "Is that how the Poles swear?" one of them asked.

"Yes," I replied, "it relieves your feelings very well."

"What was that third dog's something?" asked the art director.

"I can't translate that one. It is a bad one, anyway. I should not have said it."

"Say it again in Polish."

"I can't—not in cold blood like that," I said. "I would turn red."

"But we don't understand it anyway," one of them said.

"But I do. . . . Now in English I could swear like anything," I said reassuringly.

"I bet you don't know any swear words," one of them said provokingly.

"Sure I do—let's see. . . ." I gathered them all in my mind, all those I knew, and then I let go: "Jesus Christ—God damn—son of a bitch—son of a dog . . ."

"Stop, stop!" they all shouted and laughed.

"Why, what's wrong?" I asked.

"Why, a nice young girl like you mustn't use these words."

" Oh !   Oh, I see . . . I know. . . ."   And then I let
them in on my secret.

The words didn't mean anything to me.   They were
just words—American words.   For me they did not
carry the same portent that they do to Americans and
English people.   For the truth is that in a foreign
language all words are at first merely words.   They
remain just that until you have learned to associate
with them the same emotional content that they have
for the natives.   That takes years.   I remember in
Italy " *Porca l'oca* " and " *Porca la Madonna* " were
just beautiful, beautiful Italian to me.   They sounded
beautiful, anyway, but they mean " pig goose " and
" pig Madonna "—they're *fierce* swearing.   And even
now, after ten years in America, I can still use the
coarsest English words in mixed company without
blushing, whereas a much milder word in Russian or
Polish could not be forced through my lips.

7

A WRITING JOB

AFTER I had worked in the furniture factory for a few
months, I realised that the " future " promised in the
ad was rather ephemeral and one day in the spring I
left the place and began to look for a different job.

This time I was more lucky.   I got on the staff of a
magazine.   The editor of the magazine was what I used
to call privately a Homo Puritanicus.   He was the
second Homo Puritanicus I had come in contact with ;
the other was on my first trip to America when I met an
American missionary who was returning from Persia.

Even physically these men were alike ; so much alike
that if, suddenly, I were to come across one of them on
the street now, I am sure I should not know which one
of them it was. . . . The editor's face was also long and
narrow and lean, with a strong, jutting chin and
straight lips which were practically non-existent. . . .
But I did not realise this all completely—not until the
day I was fired. . . .

The magazine was called *Visual Education* and I was
doing the movie reviews. I also helped in making the
lay-out, did proof-reading and some editing. But
movie reviewing was my main concern and I got full
credit for it and thirty dollars a week. I enjoyed it
immensely. I had no special office hours, I went to see
all the important movies, but especially those which
were good for children and for parents, those that were
" educational " ; I wrote them up in my own style and
had the little thrill of seeing my name regularly in
print. . . . And it was on the question of what movies
are " good for parents " that the editor and I
disagreed. . . .

It was the movie " Λ Woman of Paris," which
Charlie Chaplin had directed and which I happened to
see. I saw it again. I talked of it to all and sundry
and I wrote a glowing review : " It was a milestone in
the making of movies . . . movies were becoming real
art . . . etc. . . . etc."

The editor glanced at the review, said : " Well . . .
well . . . well . . ." and went to see it himself. The next
day I was working on the lay-out, figuring where to fit
in my write-up of " The Woman of Paris " so it would
stand out most prominently. The editor came in ; he
bent over the table, glanced at it sharply, and said :
" Er—we won't use that, Miss Kinel."

" What ! " said I. " The best movie ever made ? "

" It isn't fit to be recommended," he said, or

something to this effect. " What on earth were you thinking of when you wrote that up ? "

" But you can't mean this ! It *is* a beautiful movie—so true to life, so beautifully handled, without sentimentality or exaggeration." . . . I went on and on. . . .

" Well, we won't argue about it," he said shortly. " It's immoral. That's what it is and I won't have it. This is a magazine for teachers and parents. It isn't fit to be recommended."

But I couldn't give in. It was not merely a piece of work—my judgment as a critic was involved. It was the age-old question of morality in art !

" It is very moral—if truth is moral," I retorted hotly. " It shows life as it is, sad and tragic and hap-hazard ; anyone with sense can draw the right conclusions from the picture, just as you draw them from a good novel or story. . . . The woman has been punished enough—if that's what you are driving at— she deserves nothing but pity and sympathy, for she is not bad. . . . It is the most educational movie I have yet seen in America, for it is artistically truthful. I insist that it should be printed."

I tried to say more, but the editor's neck and face got very red, he glared at me with his small, hard eyes and told me to shut up. And the following day—it was pay day—I got my weekly cheque and with it a short printed notice of dismissal.

Thus I sacrificed a job for the sake of truth and art and a moral principle. I returned home to my sister's with a feeling of both shame and pride. . . .

8

RANCH

" WHY don't you go ? " my sister said.   " The change
will do you good."

We were entertaining our aunt and uncle from
California.   They had stopped in Chicago on their way
back to Los Angeles after a trip East and had invited
me to go with them.

" You come with us now, darling," said my aunt.
" You can stay as long as you want to and make your
home with us."

" Come whenever you want to, little Gussie," my
uncle added, using the old nickname he had given me
eight years ago.

" Thanks very much.   I just want to think it over."

Nothing held me in Chicago.   I had just been fired
from my reviewing job on the educational magazine
and for the moment was too sick even to think of job,
hunting again.   On the other hand the memories of my
first visit in California eight years ago were not very
pleasant.   I recalled the bridge parties and inane clubs,
the big house, my aunt fussing and ordering people
about. . . .   I hesitated . . . then, in a flash, I remembered the week spent on the ranch.   I said quickly :

" If I come, may I stay on the ranch ? "

" Why, of course you can visit the ranch.   You can
go up with your uncle any time.   But you won't like it.
You will soon get tired of it."

" Oh, no, I won't.   And I don't mean to ' visit.'
. . . I thought . . .   Could I stay there for a while ?   I
could wash dishes or something."

" Oh, stuff and nonsense ! " Auntie said with her

W

former decisive briskness. " You don't need to do
anything. You can stay as long as you like, but there
is nothing to do out there; you will soon get tired
of it."

I thought of the mountains, the wild orchard and
garden, of riding horseback on the hundreds of trails,
only a few of which I knew. . . . And, by contrast, of
auntie's town house : bridge games and luncheons full
of doilies, the gossip of " nice " old ladies. . . .

" Thanks, auntie. I think it will be lovely."

Uncle was rather flattered by my preference for the
ranch :

"So you want to live with the cows, little Gussie?"
he asked with a chuckle. "You like the country,
do you?"

" I love it. I have never had enough of it."

" Well, then you come along with us and we will put
you on the ranch. Out with the piggies."

We all laughed and the following day I left with them
for California.

And thus I returned again to the ranch, the memory
of which had for years constituted the high spot of my
first American trip ; the story *par excellence* in my
reminiscences. Often when telling of America to
people in Russia or Poland or Germany, I would say :
" Out in the West, in California, you know, they have
big ranches. One ranch is as big as a hundred farms.
And the country is wild and all the cattle are wild, and
even the horses, too. My uncle has a ranch like that
and I stayed there once. It is very very beautiful—
bare brown hills dotted with groves of trees, fields
surrounded by sycamores, and huge live oaks. And
all the old trees are covered with moss. Spanish moss,
it is called. . . ." And if this conversation happened
to be in my own apartment, I would get out an old,

small cardboard box in which I had carefully preserved some of the Spanish moss I had once picked on
the ranch. I would take it out tenderly and spread it
before my guest : it was grey, brittle stuff and didn't
look much like anything. The guest would look at it
politely, curiously, or indifferently, as the case might
be, and I would put it away in the old box, along with
the old rattle from a rattlesnake. For me it was not
just a bit of grey dry weed. It was a talisman which
conjured up the landscapes and smells of a country
which was both very old and very new. . . .

The box with these " relics " was still in my old
steamer trunk when we arrived in Los Angeles. But
since then I have somehow lost it. I dimly recall
throwing out the moss into a waste-basket ; I didn't need
the talisman any longer. Two days after my arrival I
went up with my uncle to the Alisal Ranch. There
was plenty of moss on the trees there.

As we drove through the big old wooden gate into
the main yard, I had a curious feeling of apprehension :
would it all be as I had remembered it, or would it
appear smaller and shabbier and disappointing as so
many places do when one hasn't seen them for
years ? . . .

The car stopped in front of the old ranch house : it
was the same. The garden was the same and the old
orchard. So were the bunkhouse and the old chicken
coops. At the far end of the huge yard, across the
creek which divided it into two halves, there loomed
the old barns and the stables, the smithy and the
corrals. . . . A deep peace seemed to pervade the little
valley and the air was even more delicious than I had
remembered it.

That afternoon when I went riding with uncle in his
favourite old cart to " look at the ranch," as he called

it, eight years seemed to have vanished completely. Even Pomp, the old black horse which drew uncle's cart, seemed the same, though he was very aged now as horses go. He was twenty years old, but he didn't look any different except that now he stumbled a bit. . . . I had a curious feeling that I had come " back home." . . .

Save for two or three brief visits to the city, I stayed on the ranch for eight months. It was one of the happiest periods of my life.

" What do you do all day ?   Don't you get lonesome out there ? " my aunt would ask on my rare visits to the city.

" Not a bit, auntie.   I ride and I hike and sometimes I go sketching . . . and I drive Pomp to Solvang for the mail, and the other day I helped the boys drive the cattle up to the mountains. . . .   The days pass so quickly."

" You will soon get tired of it, I know.   Why don't you stay here for a while, play bridge, and meet some people ?   You can't bury yourself on the ranch, a young girl like you. . . .   You stay here now, this time— for two weeks anyway," she would add with the suggestion of her old-time authority.   " I will see if I can get some of the young people to come for a game ; we will have two tables."

" Oh no, auntie, please," I would say with a feeling akin to panic.   " Thanks ever so much, but I would rather return to the ranch.   I am quite happy there."

" Oh, go away," the old lady would say in a sort of grumbling.   " How can you be happy—without a proper bath, without any comfort, with no one to talk to but cowboys ? "

I could never explain to my old aunt what the ranch

meant to me. I could not tell her that the evenings spent around the big fireplace with some of the cowboys smoking pipes and swapping tales, spitting long juicy spits which sizzled on the burning logs, while others grew hilarious over a cut-throat game of hearts, were far more cheerful and homey and interesting than the bridge games of her circle. Nor could I explain the fascination of riding horseback over the narrow cattle trails hugging the steep sides of hills, hanging precariously over deep wooded ravines, skirting creeks framed in the white spotted stems of ageless sycamores and huge, dark live oaks. Auntie was over seventy and never rode horseback. . . .

Neither could I tell her of my adventures in the hills, for they were of the kind that are not tellable. They had to do with the California landscape and my ever-growing love for it : the sight of the undulating brown hills under a deep blue sky, the smell of the sage and the brush in the noon sun, the sound of the crickets at dusk, and the lowing of the cattle as they went slowly up the trails to bed themselves for the night—all this was in it and more. Not since the days of my child hood, when I used to spend occasional summers on an old Polish estate, had I fallen so completely under the power of the earth and trees and sun and wind. And here, in the American West, I had found this power in a combination that was extraordinarily beautiful and new. . . .

As soon as I got used to the saddle, I spent five and six hours a day riding. Often, when setting out for the day, I would not even know where I was going. The ranch was so huge and there were so many places to go. I liked just to wander. I would follow a trail for a mile or so, then plunge into the woods, or cut across a valley or climb a hill that looked full of promise. Often the promise would be fulfilled, in lovely landscapes etched with a soft precision in the trembling clean air against the distant blue mountain ridge, or unexpected glimpses of the ocean from a high spot, or thick wooded groves near the creeks which masses of Spanish moss made into settings for mysterious fairy tales. . . .

After a while the landscapes got me completely. A desire to catch some of them for myself possessed me rather fiercely. I had never drawn, except in school, where I was supposed to be "talented." I knew no technique. In my desperation I wrote to a good friend, a commercial artist, explaining my predicament and asking for help. She sent me a pad, a box of good water-colours, and a set of brushes. One of the cowboys rigged me out with what we called my " set." It consisted of a wooden grocery box to which two leather straps were attached, which, in turn, I tied to my saddle strings. On the other side of the saddle I tied an old leather pouch with all my painting paraphernalia. I carried water in a canteen. Thus equipped, my mare and I took on a strange aspect. She was very sweet about it and never rebelled. I would drift about looking for subjects. So little did I know about sketching that when I tried it the first time, I actually sat on my box facing the sun and wondered why the colours all seemed wrong. . . . Presently I turned about and found the colours lovely, but of course the subject had disappeared. Soon, too, to my sorrow, I discovered that in California there is no dusk, no long period of twilight ; the sun sets very fast and to catch the lovely evening colours one has to work like fury. The same thing holds true for the dawn except that its unearthly transparence is even harder to catch. . . . Often I would sketch late in the afternoon until it was too dark to see, then complete the thing the following day from memory. . . .

Sometimes there were odd little adventures, as on the day, while sketching, when I discovered a huge hairy spider, fully eight inches across, sitting placidly on a stone about two feet away. . . . The sight of the creature filled me with a cold dread. For a minute I could not move ; then I did move, rather fast, though quietly. I packed, climbed into the saddle, and loped away as fast as I could.

"Why didn't you kill him ? " the cowboys laughed when I described the dreadful thing. "That was a tarantula ; there's lots of them in that part. Them are poison."

"I knew they were poisonous," I said ; "that thing looked it."

Another time it was a rattler which I missed by a few inches as I set my precious box right near him. I grabbed the box and ran ; it was all I had by way of weapon and I was not sure I could kill a snake with it. And again, just as I had unpacked and sat down on my box, with my pad on my knee, I heard the mare stamp her feet. She was tied to a tree and seemed restless ; her ears twitched nervously. I had a feeling that someone was looking at me, turned around, and faced two beautiful wolves standing across a little ravine, not fifty feet away, and looking at me steadily. Again I was frozen, but this time not badly. . . . I knew they were not wolves, merely large coyotes, two grown fellows in their full winter fur, but they did look like wolves and since the days in Russia I had always had respect for wolves. . . . Besides, why did they stare so persistently ? Slowly I got up and moved towards them. . . . The coyotes followed me with their eyes, retreated a few steps, then stood still, staring. . . . I repeated my motion and they did the same. . . . For the third time I walked towards them ; they both turned, as if tired of the game, and disappeared swiftly in the thicket.

" Jesus Christ, I wisht I'd been there with my new gun ! " one of the boys commented that night. " I would of gotten both of them. That's ten bucks. The Government pays us five bucks for each coyote we get— except they would never have come that near to me."

" Why ? " I asked in surprise.

" Because they can smell a gun a hundred yards away. They knew you didn't have one, so the rascals got curious."

It seemed fantastic, but the boys assured me it was true.

There were deer in those woods, and wildcats and skunks and hundreds of birds, and in the southern part of the ranch there were boars in the thick brush—wild hogs, the boys called them—and flocks of quail. The deer I saw often, for my uncle did not allow anyone to shoot them and they did not try to hide. . . .

There was all this on the ranch besides the special events, big times when the boys rounded up the cattle and there was branding, and driving herds to the station for shipping, or when they broke young horses or went hunting the wild hogs. . . . But in the city, when I came on a short visit, auntie would ask with surprise : " What is there to do on the old ranch ? Aren't you tired of it ? . . ."

9

COWBOYS

It was the third or fourth day on the ranch and it was the third or fourth dinner I had eaten all alone in the main dining-room of the ranch house. The square table, not very large really, seemed immense in its desolation, with only my cover at one end ; the massive old pieces of furniture seemed oppressive ; the fireplace too big. It was horribly lonely. . . .

One door led from this room to the kitchen. Beyond the kitchen was the mess-room, the place where the cowboys ate. When both doors of the kitchen were open, I could hear their voices, their hearty guffaws, and occasionally a high squeal of delight from the cook. She was a large, stout, motherly woman with a sense of humour, and a hearty laugh which often ended in a squeal. When she walked between the two rooms, for she served both me and the boys, she let the doors slam or banged them, and this noise, and the noise of men's voices coming from across, emphasised my formal isolation. It was on the fourth day, I think, that I rebelled. I said :

" Mrs. Sprague, from to-morrow on I am going to eat in the other room with the boys."

" Why, Miss Lola, what would Mr. Murphy say if he heard of this ? "

" I don't care what uncle says. I hate to eat alone. I don't enjoy it."

" But them men are just plain cowboys, miss, and you aren't used to such," she said, looking at me with curiosity.

" Oh, I shall get used to them —as long as they won't

mind me . . ." I said lightly, wondering just how I could convey to the good old soul that I was a cosmopolitan and a woman of the world, though, what with my short bob and my general slightness of person, I probably looked to her very insignificant and young.

" They do swear an awful lot," she said, bending towards me.   " Not that they ain't gentlemen, every one of them, nice boys and all, but they do talk rough and all they know is horse."

" That's just fine.   They can talk just as they please, Mrs. Sprague.   Don't you worry," I assured her, inwardly delighted at the prospect of watching these uncut diamonds of the West.

" Well, now, I reely don't know what to do.   Your uncle wouldn't like it. . . and the boys themselves might be embarrassed. . . .   Not being able to talk the way they are used to."

That aspect of the situation had never entered my head.   But I dared even this.

" I am sure they will get used to me very quickly ; people always feel at home with me. . . .   Don't you ? "

" Why, sure I do, honey," she replied.   And then, with a wicked gleam in her eyes, she tried her last argument :

" Why, you know, Miss Lola, you will have to eat everything off of one plate."

" What do you mean . . . meat and vegetables . . . and desert ? "

" Sure," she said, with a sly giggle, " beans and meat and hot cakes and pie.   When they get through with the meat and the beans, the boys mop off the gravy with their bread and they are ready for their pie. . . .   I just can't spoil the men with a lot of extra dishes, what with the wood stove and heating all the dish-water.   I got enough to do cooking and baking."

" But, but, Mrs. Sprague—couldn't I get just one
small extra plate for my pie, just one saucer ? "

She grinned at my discomfiture.

" Well, I guess I can do that.   You see, if I served
you all them extry plates, the way I do here, the boys
would want the same for themselves—they are that
selfish—and now that I got them trained to one plate,
I would hate to give in to them."

And so the problem was solved and I had my meals
with the cowboys.

The slightly romantic and synthetic picture of cowboys, as based on old Western films, Bret Harte, and
even the dim memory of the first visit to the ranch in
my teens, was squelched completely at that first meal.
One and all, they were a bit bow-legged ; they were
dressed in coarse blue trousers, with shirts open at the
neck and cowboy boots.   And though they washed
their red-brown leathery faces and hands rather carefully before each meal, they did not bother to change
their clothes, and so brought with them into the dining-
room the pungent aroma of horse and cow.   I like these
odours outdoors and in the fields, but they don't go well
with food, though in time I got used to them.   Their
table manners were very good, better than those of the
average German burgher, who blows in his soup,
swathes his neck in a napkin, and gathers samples of
food on his beard.   Their language and their stories, to
which I had looked forward particularly, were a little
disappointing.   They talked fast, slurring the words together.   The swear words they used were in certain
staid patterns which after a while became monotonous ;
it was always either : " Gosh darnit," with " Jesus
Christ " at the more dramatic points ; or " Some day
I'll show that son of a bitch "—usually referring to a
horse ; or, " that durn' cow, gosh darn her."

At first they would intersperse their recitals with an

occasional " Pardon, miss," in my direction, but after I told them that I really didn't mind, and to go ahead and be at home, they relaxed.

It is true that this was merely their ordinary, moderate style, for, as the cook explained to me, they were " careful in my presence " not to talk " too rough." And so my desire to delve more deeply into the American language was not fulfilled, and I did not learn anything beyond what I knew already. Their talk was all shop—horses, their work, and horses again. In their cosmos, I gathered, a horse was almost as important as a man ; sometimes more. The cowboy entertained rather varied emotions about horses, from love and affection to anger and contempt and mere respect. The cow was not regarded at all. The cow was cattle and cattle was beef—eventually, anyway. All cattle were simply the material with which the cowboy worked, but the horse was a helper in his work and therefore on a par with man. Cattle were divided into steers and bulls, cows, heifers, according to their various categories, and though the cowboys who rode the range often knew nearly every single animal in the huge herd, comprising as many as two or three thousand head, never did they regard them as individuals, the way they did the horses. They had none of the affection a farmer has for his dairy cows ; in fact, they regarded all ordinary farming and dairymen with contempt, and the suggestion that one of them might milk a cow would lacerate their pride beyond expression. For this reason they used to regard the man who did the chores on the ranch, including the milking of the few dairy cows, with pity and sympathy. One had to be indeed down in this world to stoop to milking. . . .

The talk, as I said, was shop ; all about their work of riding, of little things that happened while they were riding the range, for that was their most important job.

It was their daily routine. Twice a year they rounded up the cattle, cut out those to be sold for beef, and did the branding.

If, occasionally, the talk veered to other, foreign topics, it usually petered out sorrowfully. I recall one instance when we talked of Edison. I think it was on the occasion of his illness and a rather miraculous recovery. There was something about it in the Sunday paper which I used to get from Santa Barbara. Commenting on the item, I said :

" There is a really great man. No nonsense about it."

Said one of the boys :

" Who, him ? Why, he ain't great ! "

" Why, Charlie," I retorted hotly, " how can you say that ? Don't you know all the things he invented ? The electric bulb, the victrola, the movie film, and a hundred other inventions ? "

" He didn't do that. That's just advertising. Them papers all lie," Charlie said with a show of assurance.

" Sure," another one said in his support. " He got men in them laboratories that does the stuff for him and he just gets all the credit. That's always the case once a guy gets a big name."

True, the ranch did not have any electricity and could not boast of any of the modern gadgets.

I could not argue against such concerted opposition and ignorance. I capitulated.

" The way them papers lie," said a third, " I don't never read them because you can't tell what's true and what ain't. If I want to read, I take a book. Give me a book like Zane Grey—that's what I read."

Later I found out that with the exception of Zane Grey and a couple of other writers like him, the boys really never read anything. That is, aside from one other important book—the Seers, Roebuck mail-order catalogue. That was thumbed over frequently all

through the month, but around pay day it was particularly in demand, was pored over reverently, the
pictures gazed at minutely, and all the descriptions read
carefully.   Sometimes, I know, the whole of a cowboy's
monthly salary, forty dollars, was spent on a gun and a
hat, a pair of chaps, or some such thing.   I asked
Mother Sprague once : " Don't the boys ever try to
save ?   Don't they try to make a home, or get somewhere ? "

" Not them ; they ain't half grown up, Lola.   They
just remain boys all their life."

Cowboys rarely got married, I found, and still more
rarely, even if they did, did they settle down somewhere
for good.   Like sailors on the sea, they roamed the
West, changing ranches whenever they got tired of one
place, moving from state to state.   Their private life, if
any, was discharged on week-ends, when they shaved,
donned their brown shoes and ready-made suits, and
went to town. . . .   The town, on Sundays, was their
port of call.   Late Sunday night and occasionally not
until early Monday morning, in time for the first bell,
they would be back on the ranch—back to their horses,
the range, and the cattle, their inarticulate communion
with nature, their articulate swearing, their evenings
when they played hearts, smoked their pipes, and spit
long spits into the fireplace. . . .

I am committing a crime, I know, writing like this,
debunking the heroes out of Zane Grey, both the white
ones, those with practically all the virtues, and the black
ones, those cattle thieves and murderers and seducers.
Perhaps the reason why cowboys now like to read about
these imaginary ones is that their real life in this modern
age has so little glamour.   Perhaps that is the real
tragedy of their life.

10

MARIAGE D'AMITIÉ

I MET my future husband on one of my flying visits to the city. We liked each other at once and he began to come down to the ranch for week-ends. It was nice to have someone to ride with besides the cowboys ; it was nice to be with someone congenial and to share all one's delights in the ranch. It was nice, above all, to have a good friend and to be mildly in love. . . . There would never be another D. in my life, I thought, then why not . . . why evade life eternally ? . . .

My friend was much surer of everything. Why not marry ? We were congenial and very happy when together. That was what a good marriage meant : companionship and friendship, and love, of course—the pleasant kind, not the searing, tearing emotion. No high romance. Romance was all right for other fools ; didn't we both know better ? It tore at your heart and burnt you out. . . .

We talked it all over, rationally, as all modern young people do nowadays, and we were sure of it all—except, for odd moments, when I felt frightened for fear it was all wrong. Once, during one of those panicky flashes of insight, I tried to back out. He overrode all my objections. In the end I had only one argument left : " But suppose, darling, one of us stumbles against someone else, another ' great passion,' as you call it. It might happen, to you or to me—what then ? "

He looked at me quickly : " I hope not. Anyway, why suppose ? If we stay as happy as we are now, all of our lives, wouldn't it be enough ? "

It seemed enough. More than enough. And we planned.

" You know, darling, business is so good that next year we may go to Europe. It would be nice to see it with you ; you would help me with all your languages. I have always wanted to go to Italy and to France."

" And I have always wanted to see America, real America—all of it, not just the big cities."

" We can do that too. That's easy. Every summer we will go somewhere else and explore. I can easily take off a month or six weeks. This summer we'll do California. That will be our honeymoon. We will start with Tia Juana and wind up in Frisco."

" Oh, how nice ! "

" We will drive whenever we feel like it and stop wherever we want to. For as long as we want to. No plans."

" How lovely ! I hate plans."

" We will stop at the ranch."

" Of course."

It was exactly what we did. In his big racing roadster we drove up the old El Camino Real. We took a week going north. On getting to old Monterey we stopped. When the month was over we returned to the little coastal town where my husband lived and where I spent the four years of my married life.

II

THE BIGGEST THING IN LIFE

. . . IN a woman's life, I should add, for a man doesn't react that way at all. A man has to " get used to it," so to speak—at least, my husband did.

It was, of course, the moment when the nurse put the little bundle near my pillow on the bed and said with professional enthusiasm :

" It's a little girl, Mrs. S. Did you want a little girl ? "

" I did. I knew it would be a girl."

" Well, isn't this nice ? . . . It's an awfully sweet baby, too."

I looked at my tiny daughter. I had just wakened from the anæsthetic and everything had the quality of a dream : the tiny round face and the dark hair and blue eyes were those of a dream I had always had, ever since I played with dolls who were my children, and later when I played with real babies whenever I could, and still later when, as a sophisticated young lady, I rarely passed a baby carriage on the street without peeking in to see the baby. . . . And this was my own, my very own baby. . . . Then I caught the nurse's eye. This was stern reality.

" Why is she so pink ? "

" Why, bless you, she isn't pink at all. You ought to see some of the others."

" Will that go away ? "

" Why, of course. She is quite perfect ; look at all the lovely hair—some are bald ; and see how plump and sweet she is. And her head is nice and round. . . ."

x

" Why shouldn't it be ? " I asked, amazed.

" Oh, sometimes it isn't—not at once," the nurse replied enigmatically.

" When can I nurse her ? " I presently asked.

The nurse laughed. " Not for a few hours yet. There is no hurry ; you had better rest now."

" But won't she be hungry ? "

" Oh, no, she won't. We will give her a little water. Now you rest. Mr. S. will be here in a couple of hours ; then I will bring her in again."

The rest of the two weeks in the little hospital was spent in a maze of schedules and rules and regulations. It was the first time I had been in a hospital and that is why, perhaps, the routine struck me all the more forcibly. A 6 a.m. I nursed the baby, which, to my chagrin, was instantly taken away ; then I was told to nap, but at 7.15 was awakened rudely and washed from top to toe without my even sitting up—a procedure which never failed to amaze me ; then I was combed, powdered, I brushed my teeth, my temperature was taken, and by then it was breakfast-time. At nine came the second nursing and so on all through the day, by the clock, by hours, half-hours, and even minutes, without the slightest deviation.

Needless to say the only hours I was interested in were the nursing ones. There were six nursings, the last being at midnight, and always the baby was taken away almost immediately, though in the daytime, or when my husband came, we were allowed about ten minutes' grace. . . .

" Why, please, nurse, this is crazy. . . . It's my baby and I want to play with her a little bit."

" Oh, go on. You will play with her enough when you are home," the nurse would reply teasingly.

" But I haven't seen her toes . . . not since yesterday.

My God, aren't they heavenly . . . so tiny and so perfect ! ''

" If you aren't going to mind, I will tell the doctor on you," the nurse would say with mock severity and carry the precious bundle away. She was my private nurse, or " special," as they call it in hospital language, and devoted all her time to me. She was young and gay and we got on well. As my health at that period was quite perfect, she had really not much to do, and in the long hours between nursings or meals she would amuse herself by curling my hair, giving me manicures, facials, and what nots. She gave me an alcohol rub and massage in the morning, per regulation, and one at night for good measure. On her hours off duty she used to run down to the main street and shop, and on returning would show me all her new finery. She was a good nurse, though, as regards her duties, and nothing I said could ever move her when it came to regulations.

" Couldn't I read a bit this afternoon ? " I would beg. " While you are off duty . . . just half an hour ? ''

" No. The doctor said no ; it's bad after a confinement. You can't sit up yet and you couldn't read lying flat on your back.''

" Well, why can't I sit up yet ? It's been a week now. I am tired of being on my back, doing nothing, and I feel fine.''

" Doctor's orders.''

" Oh, heck ! . . . Too many orders. Look here, just do one little thing for me. Please.''

" Yes ? ''

" When you bring baby for her noon nursing . . . well . . . just forget to take her back to the nursery for a while. . . . You know you are off duty, no one will notice, and I will watch over her here.''

" Now, look here, Mrs. S. . . .''

" Oh, please. I won't keep her more than an hour. She always goes to sleep at noon, so I will let her sleep here, next to my pillow. Mr. S. will come in at one, and after he has seen her we will send her back to the nursery."

" Is that a promise ? "

" Yes, yes. . . . Oh, thanks."

Towards the end of my stay, however, I made her break one hospital rule. She enjoyed it as much as I. Her frequent comments on my baby's perfection began to have a strange effect on me. Once I said rather crossly :

" You say that to every mother, I bet. To make her feel good."

" No, I don't. I tell them their babies are nice, but I don't call them perfect."

" Is she really exceptional ? "

" She is very fine, one in a hundred. Do you know, I heard Dr. B. say to another doctor in the nursery the other day : ' Here is a perfect specimen,' and he showed him your baby. Why, all the nurses know it."

" Is that true ? " I asked, glowing inside with the fiercest sort of pride.

" Cross my heart," she replied. " Why, if you had seen as many babies as I have, you would know it's the truth."

A tremendous thought struck me. " Nurse ! "

" Yes ? "

" Let me see all the babies in this hospital ! "

" But you can't get out of bed yet. You mustn't be on your feet. . . ."

" Bring them in here ! I want to see them ! "

" Why, Mrs. S. . . ." Then, suddenly, her face broke into a smile. She bent towards me and, lowering her voice, as if in fear that someone might overhear us, she whispered : " Very well, I am going to sneak them in, one by one, so you can see. . . . Now don't you give me away. I am not allowed to do this."

" I won't. How many are there ? "

" Eleven, I think. Just you wait."

" Not many," I thought regretfully, but was deter-mined to see them all. It took us a couple of days, I recall, for she had to sneak them in as occasion permitted, and so I saw all of them. Most of them were red; some were very thin ; some had oddly-shaped heads, narrow and comical ; the only well-formed baby was a fat boy, but even at this miniature age he showed coarse features and his small eyes were dull and lifeless. Compared with all of them, my baby daughter was really beautiful. In my heart I knew that even if she had not been as bonny and cute, I should have loved her not a jot less, perhaps even more. But I was very glad all the same. . . .

" You know, most of them grow out of it," the nurse said, carrying away a strange infant. " In the first few weeks few babies are beautiful."

My husband laughed when I told him of the experience. Though later he loved and adored the baby not less than I, his attitude toward her during those first early days was a sort of quizzical amusement. " I have to get used to her," he would say. . . .

12

MARRIAGE AND BOOM

" You will have to sign here, darling," my husband would say on bringing home with him a huge, legal-

x*

looking document which I would never bother to read,
for it was full of incomprehensible technicalities. I
did ask questions, however, before signing, and the
answers usually made me feel small, petty, ignorant,
and—for want of a better word—Old-Worldish.

" What is it ? " I would ask.   " Does it mean we are
borrowing ? "

" Yes.   I need a bit of cash for number two.   You
know the new little store. . . .   Here . . . on this dotted
line."

" But didn't you say something about your not
having quite paid up for the first store ? " I would
ask, signing the paper.

" Yes.   But that has nothing to do with it.   The
first store is doing marvellous business and this is the
time to expand.   We need more stores—more of
everything.   Our town is growing.   I will explain it to
you to-night, so you can understand.   I have to rush
back to the bank now, honey."

And in the evening my husband would sometimes
try to explain to me this marvellous American thing
called a " boom."   And all about a " cycle " and
prosperity.   " You see," he would say, " we are on the
upswing now and we have to take advantage of it.
When I opened the first store we took in one hundred
dollars a day ; now we are taking in two hundred and
thirty on week-days and three hundred on Sundays.
Do you realise what this means ?   Within one year
business has almost trebled."

" But we do have to pay it all back sometime," I
would interpose weakly.

" Of course we do.   I am paying it up now, right
along with the interest.   Don't you see, the two stores
are both paying for themselves and making a profit on
top of it."

" But suppose they don't always take in so much

money every day ?   What then ? " I would ask with
a woman's habitual distrust of debts and borrowing.

"But they will for a while.   We are having a boom,
I tell you.   And this one is going to be the biggest in
history.   And besides this our town is growing on
account of the oil fields.   We have ten thousand more
people to-day than we had two years ago.   In the store
I constantly see new faces. . . .   And listen—after all,
the bankers know what they are doing and they are
more than willing to give me credit.   They all want to
help us young business men to boost up the town and
make it bigger and better.   The old-timers here just
sit on their money and draw interest.   We make things
go."

This last argument used to convince me completely.
It was a common refrain : "The bankers have faith in
me."   From time to time there appeared in the local
paper short articles and other Press comments on
business trends, usually after a Chamber of Commerce
meeting, and my husband's name figured quite
prominently ; he was mentioned along with the most
enterprising and progressive young business men.   It
made me proud.   And I signed the papers with less
and less hesitation each time.

This was in 1926, and between then and 1929 I must
have signed quite a few, most of them without reading,
for there were those bankers who liked to lend money,
and my energetic husband's unbounded optimism, and
this mysterious American thing called a " cycle and
boom and prosperity "—it was all part of this new
American magic, in the country where everything was
possible and people became rich overnight.   After all,
who was I but a young, timid European woman, without the least notion of business or economics or how
money was made ?   I just signed.   Christ, how I wish
I hadn't !

Of course there was the pleasure of acquiring things, and the glow of expansion. Within two years there were three stores instead of the original one ; we built a house, we had two cars, and, as a fitting climax, my husband bought the most expensive corner in the little town, the one on which his first drug-store stood. The price was $75,000 and the transaction made local history. The little newspaper had a huge article about it and I had to sign another paper. This time I felt a bit shaky doing it. Why did we have to rush things so ? I asked. And how many years would it take to pay up all these debts ? " Five or six, not more. This isn't much. Every business man does things on credit. All big corporations do it," he explained to me.

" You mean they don't pay cash when they buy things ? " I asked naïvely.

He laughed. " My dear, in this country there isn't one-third, not one-tenth of the cash it would require to have everything paid up at once. These transactions are all on paper and they are based on confidence. The bankers have confidence in me as a good business man ; business is splendid, and so they know that I shall have ample money to pay it back."

It all seemed a bit mad, but then so many things in America seemed a bit mad, and there, on the other hand, were all the lovely surprises. My husband liked to give surprises : there was the Steinway concert grand shortly after we moved into our new house ; and the Brunswick panatrope which greeted me on my arrival from the hospital when baby came. It was the strains of Kreisler's " Liebesfreud " which came through the door as I walked in, and the sounds were so pure, so true, so full, that it was like a miracle. The panatrope had just been invented and anyone who knows how perfect it was in comparison with the old-time phonographs will understand how I felt. I stood on the threshold, enthralled. If I had closed my eyes, I could have believed that it was Kreisler and Rachmaninoff in person, playing in the next room.

Then there was the ranch. One day, while I was still in the hospital with the baby, my husband walked in, and, kissing me, said :

" I've bought a nice ranch. It's going to be for baby."

" What do you mean ? When ? Where ? " I asked in surprise, for I knew he had not been out of town at all.

" This morning. It's six hundred acres, down in M. County. Good land and we've got half the oil rights."

" But when did you see it ? "

" I didn't see it. I don't have to. It's a good buy and dirt cheap and I know the country down there. I know there is plenty of oil there. How would you like baby to be an oil heiress some day ? "

Baby, who was just six days old, was sleeping in the crook of my arm after a nursing session.

" Goodness, baby," I said, kissing her little downy head, " if you knew how many things your daddy is planning for you. . . ." And then, turning to my husband : " Do I have to sign anything again this time ? "

" Yes. Just a mortgage. We will fix the papers up to-morrow." And on the following day I signed another paper. I was not quite sure what the term " mortgage " meant, but it had a nicer sound than the word " promissory note " . . . for by that time I had a distrust of the word " note."

A couple of years ago, when I first began to take some interest in economics and started to read people like Stuart Chase and Arthur Salter and Veblen and others,

I learned the meaning of many words. My husband's explanation of its being "all on paper and based on confidence" came back to me often and roused a sardonic smile. But all this enlightenment was in the nature of a post-mortem. By that time my husband's financial dreams, his whole future, built on real business talent, hard work, a boundless optimism, and the "confidence of bankers," had crashed about him in ruins.

13

DIVORCE AND DEPRESSION

THE crash, when it came, was a double one for us. My husband's elaborate financial structure began to topple almost at the same time that the one eventuality which I thought might some day break our marriage cropped up. It, or rather she, walked into my husband's office one day looking for a job. She was the last one of about a hundred girls who replied to his advertisement for a girl at the cosmetics counter. He liked pretty, well-groomed girls in his stores so that when the dowdy, weather-beaten wives of the ranchers came to town to shop and stopped in at the drug-store, they might be encouraged to buy a lot of beauty stuff in the hope that they, too, could look as fresh and as pretty as these girls. . . .

"I hired an awfully cute girl to-day," he said to me that night at dinner. "Very small—you can just barely see her head peep from behind the counter—but as pretty as she can be. And," he added with enthusiasm, "what I liked about her most was the fact that she seemed so willing. Modest, and sweet, not like most of the girls you get nowadays."

At the first opportunity, when I dropped into the store, I talked to the new girl. I liked her immediately : she was small, graceful, had tiny feet and hands, and a sweet face with big brown eyes. Moreover, she was quiet and rather reserved. Perhaps because I am rather talkative myself, I have always liked quiet women, especially if they are pretty. Later, much later—in fact when it was too late—I found that she was not really quiet or calm. Underneath her apparent quietude, there was a seething emotional turmoil. . . .

However, she was charming and I was susceptible. So was my husband. We began having her about the house. She was very helpful. She knew so many little practical things about housework which I did not know ; she knew all about gardening, how to prune rose trees and bud carnations and many other things. And it was one Sunday in our garden, while Baby played with our big white bulldog and I was picking flowers for the house, and my husband and the girl were trimming the rose bushes, that I discovered they were in love. It was not anything that they said or did, or even looked. It was simply that they seemed so cheerful and happy when together and there was between them a little electric current, and, being a wife, I had a sixth sense. . . . All wives have. . . .

My husband did not know it yet himself. Most nice men are never aware of these delicious preliminary stages. He simply thought he " liked the girl." He talked of her often, praised her industry and willingness, and once or twice said : " She is such a quiet little thing, too. . . . I wonder why she interests me."

I did not wonder. I knew. What I wondered

about was what I should do. What should a girl do
when her husband is falling in love with another girl
and doesn't know it yet ? Should she open his eyes
and precipitate matters ? Preposterous ! Should I
talk to the girl ? She knew, of course. Girls always
do. But so far there was nothing one could take
exception to. What could I possibly say or do at this
stage ? Nothing.

I waited. I waited and watched, worried, shocked,
and somehow amused, for that part of me which
habitually registers everything that is dramatic in life,
whether it happens to me or to some stranger, was
amused. I thought : " So this is how it feels . . . this is
how it is . . . some day when I shall have to write about
a triangle, I shall know exactly how to describe it . . .
exactly "

Then, presently, I heard that the girl had a " steady
boy," a fiancé, and a little while later they were
married, and I thought : " This will put an end to it
and everything will be all right." . . .

But it wasn't all right and it wasn't the end. There
came a day when my husband stopped talking about
the girl, when he hardly mentioned her at all, though
she still went on working for him. And I knew what it
meant. And then came another day, and many more,
when he would be late for dinner or late from work, and
I knew what that meant, too, but did not ask any
questions because I did not want to hear any wrong
replies. And then came another when I could not
stand the strain any longer and I made him face things
and we talked it out. . . .

It wasn't the end, because here was Romance—high,
searing, emotional passion, the sort of thing my
husband thought did not make for a good marriage.
It can certainly break one, though. In this case it
broke up two and we all had to go through a little hell,

Iris Now

each one of us through a little private hell of his own : the boy, the girl, my husband, and myself.

My own hell was the smallest of them all, I ought to admit, for as the thing went on I realised, at first rather slowly, then very clearly, that my baby was the thing that had mattered most in my marriage, more than husband and home—more than anything had ever mattered in my life. And so underneath all the pain and worry and strain, there was also the exultant thought : " I am going to have her I am going to have her all for my own—I shall be both daddy and mother to her." . . . And on the day when baby and I left the little town, baby and I and the coloured maid, driving in my coupé behind the huge truck which bore all the furniture, all the lovely surprises, the Steinway and the panatrope and the sets of books—in a regular little exodus—I felt besides the tiredness and sadness of it all a sort of feeling of relief and a sense of life's being a ceaseless adventure. . . .

All this was just a few short years ago. Yet the memory of the town is already dim. It has that pleasant, faded quality which we sense on seeing old photographs. On the rare occasions when I pass it, I am not touched or stirred in any way. Rather I catch myself in a sort of naïve surprise : why, this is Main Street . . . and there is our street . . . where our house stands . . . how steep it is . . . I used to have such a hard time backing out of that garage. . . .

It is as if someone else, not my present self, had lived in it and had told me of it, and I have a vicarious thrill of recognition, the thrill of a second-hand emotion. . . .

14

ON THE FRINGE OF HOLLYWOOD

THE years since my divorce have been so quiet and uneventful that I can compress them all into one sketch. At first I moved quite often : I lived near the beach ; then in the mountains ; then with my sister in New York.   There were, of course, very " sensible " reasons for moving : the beach was " too foggy " and the mountains were " too dry " and New York was " not good for baby and far too expensive."   But underneath all this was simply the fact that I was restless and it took me time to get adjusted.   In the end I settled down in Hollywood.

When I say Hollywood, I mean, of course, the fringe of it.   I do not know any directors or writers or stars. On the boulevard, or in the restaurants, I run into some of them occasionally ; I mean I recognise them with the reaction which all of us outsiders probably have of : " Why, he looks exactly the same as on the screen," or " I should never have thought that this was she," as the case may be.   I do not know the studios very well, either.   At various intervals I have bombarded them all with letters of application, trying to get work, but each time I got only a few meagre replies.   At first I used to think that perhaps my letters went astray or the department heads were not very well-bred. . . .   I did not realise that most letters of this kind are tucked away into the waste-basket by the office boys. . . . Twice I actually got an interview, but was told that it was merely because my letter was " so interesting " that they wanted to meet me, for there was no work, not even that of a reader. . . .

After that I did not write letters to the studios any more, and by and by, of course, I heard all the hackneyed advice which the natives-who-know give to innocent newcomers : " You've got to meet them socially—mingle with them—try to meet all the big shots—at parties, you know—that's how you get in." However, not knowing any " big shots " socially or otherwise, I could not very well " mingle," and that was that.

Since then I have settled down to writing in all earnestness and to a sort of routine. My routine, I imagine, is rather different from the kind other writers have. Other writers, I have a feeling, are either bachelors or bachelor girls writing in great comfort in lovely apartments or penthouses, going out at night, meeting interesting people, travelling about gathering material. Or, if they are married, they seem to be living—judging from newspaper stories—in nice farm-houses where they work in peace and quiet, creating characters and atmosphere. My routine is different, for I am not really a writer yet. I am primarily a mamma. A divorced mamma. Being a divorced mamma is rather different from being a mamma with a daddy in the house. For one thing the mamma has to attend to so many things which are usually done by daddies, such as paying all the bills, taking care of the car, fixing broken toys, putting in a new fuse when the lights go out and leave one in terrific darkness, opening bottles—cider jugs are especially bad—and a host of other things. When you consider that all these are merely an addition to the regular duties of a servant-less American mamma, such as marketing, cooking, cleaning, washing, ironing, sewing, and that a divorced mamma has less money to do it all with than a regular mamma, you can perhaps understand why the writing is merely squeezed in, so to say.   There are so many interruptions.

In the mornings when the child is in school and there is supposed to be peace and quiet, there are all sorts of calls.   People come to buy gold and to sell cookies. Before the dole there used to be sometimes as many as four or five door calls each morning—in spite of a sign, " No peddlers and agents," drawn up elaborately by my little daughter on a piece of paper and glued suggestively below the door bell.   They disregarded it.   They rang the bell and offered anything from safety pins and dishcloths to stationery and home-made candy. Occasionally, when the people seemed shy and especially un-agentlike, my social conscience arose and I bought things I did not need.   For I realised that, except for the grace of God, or, to put it more concretely, for the fact that I still get monthly cheques from my husband and from my sister, I, too, might have been peddling from door to door. . . .   Then there are phone calls, there is marketing to do. . . .   I write in between. . . .

In the afternoons there are other interruptions—the children.   My little daughter and her friends.   The street is full of children and, this being the West and not New York, we are all very sociable.

" Mammy, can Virginia and I play dress up ? "

" Yes, but first you must practise."

" All right.   But after I practise, can we have some of your old evening dresses ?   And some slippers ? "

" Yes.   Now run along.   Mamma is working." . . .

I work for a while.   I don't know how long.   Then I hear a voice :

" Mamma !   Wake up ! "

" What ?   What is it now ?   Can't you see I am writing ? "

" You weren't. You were dreaming. You looked
far away."

" I *was* far away. I was in Russia."

" We want to play theatre. Will you put up the
rope ? "

" Get it, darling, and I will put it up."

" But I don't know where it is."

" Go and find it [very sternly]. Now listen, honey :
mamma is working. You ought to understand this.
You are a big girl."

" Oh, I do, mammy. We won't make much noise,
either. And we want two sheets so we can be
ghosts."

We get my old finery, the sheets, and a rope. I tie
the rope across the room, throw a bedspread across it,
and the theatre is ready. I go back to my table. I
don't hear a thing. I am really missing a lot of fun,
for I also like playing theatre, but then I am trying to
finish a story, or a scene in a play, or a sketch in this
book. . . .

Of course it is not always just like this. Often the
children play out on the street, or they draw quietly
while I sit diligently at my typewriter. Occasionally
my little daughter is curious :

" What are you writing, mammy ? "

" A book."

" Is it going to be published ? "

" I don't know. Perhaps it won't."

" Then why do you write it ? "

" Oh, just for practice. Now run along."

But she isn't through yet. She sees a book that's
lying open on my desk. It's been lying there for a
few weeks. It's Max Miller's *I Cover the Waterfront*.

" Ooh, mammy, you mustn't copy. You must write
yourself."

" I do write myself," I answer irately, wondering just

how I can explain. " You see, this helps me to stick to a certain style. You know what ' style ' is ? "

" Oh, sure. It's the way things are written. Like *Alice in Wonderland* makes you laugh—the way it's written."

" That's right, honey [inwardly I am thrilled at this display of intelligence]. Well, this man knows how to write things with very few words. Now sometimes, when mamma feels that she is using too many words and writing too much, so that people may get bored, she just reads a bit in this book and gets the right inspiration."

" Oh, I think I know. Just be sure and don't copy. Because then it won't be yours."

" I won't, cross my heart," I promise, and my little critic goes away. I should have really a great respect for her, for she too is a writer. Or, rather, a poet. And she has arrived ! She started at the early age of two, though of course she doesn't do her own writing. We call it " making up poems " and it usually occurs in the mornings when she crawls into my bed, together with the cat, for a little visit. Then, if the inspiration seizes her, she begins to improvise, waving her chubby arms in rhythm with her rhymes, and I grab a pencil and a note-book and jot it all down. I have to use shorthand, for she singsongs quite fast and can never repeat anything. I have an old fat envelope full of these " poems " and think some of them delightful. One day, as an experiment, I gathered a few and sent them to *Playmate*, a children's magazine. They chose the four worst and sent her a year's subscription free as payment. This was worth $1.50—exactly one dollar and fifty cents more than I had earned in these years of writing. . . .

To go back to the afternoons and my work.

Towards four or five I have to think of dinner, and although I am a good cook I have never so far been able to combine good writing with good cooking ; one or the other suffers invariably and more than once I have burned my carrots in Hollywood while I was in Danzig or Vienna—figuratively speaking.

The evenings differ. Sometimes I write and sometimes I am too tired. Sometimes we go to the movies, which we both adore, but mostly we read. The books I read differ vastly from the kind I used to read years ago. I used to read mostly fiction. Now I read biography, economics, everything that's being written on Russia, from Don Levine to Walter Duranty, and some of the lastest fiction. The latter has a queer effect on me. It either spurs me to harder work or leaves me in despair. If only I could write one beautiful book, I think, one book like *S. S. San Pedro*, or *February Hill*, or *Tortilla Flat*. . . . But I never shall— it will take me at least another ten years to know English as these people do, and to learn how to write. . . . Then I go through one of my bad moments. . . .

Some of these moments last a few days and even longer. They get particularly bad when a story returns with a rejection slip—a story which I thought rather good—or when I have wrestled too long with the second act of a play and I feel that, perhaps, I can never write a good play, or, perhaps, like Hergesheimer, I shall have to wait for recognition for fourteen years. I do not feel like waiting for fourteen years. On days like that I take an old envelope which has all my old letters of reference and I go down-town to call on the agencies.

They are strange places. The ladies in them have yellow hair and hard faces and they give you sheets covered closely with small print and blank spaces which

you have to fill in. On these sheets, in addition
to all kinds of personal questions, are also stated
your supposed qualifications. There is an empty
space left against each for your mark.   You are
to put a cross against those that you possess
and leave the others blank.   There are spaces left for
" foreign languages and other qualifications " which
are far too small for me to fill, so that I usually have to
mess up the margin of the paper, and, again, there are
others like " comptometer, multigraph, Burroughs,"
and other mysterious words that I cannot fill in at all.
And as I make out my application I always feel sadly
that I do not fit into this commercial pattern of work.
I know that these different gadgets are installed in
American offices for the sake of speed and I have no
doubt that I could learn to manipulate them in time,
but for the moment I feel that I have to be truthful.

Worse than these printed sheets, however, are the
personal questions.   The yellow-haired ladies shoot
them at you, looking indifferently straight ahead,
answering their everlasting telephones and marking
down messages.   Some of them even manage to chew
their gum.   Like Napoleon, they can do four things at
a time ; for they have shot these same questions at
hundreds—no, thousands—of young women and men
and they do not care much what you answer.   They
accept and sift your replies much as a machine would—
a machine in good running order which knows just
" yes " and " no " and " white " and " black " and
" how fast."   " How fast " is very important :

" How fast do you type ? "

" About eighty words a minute . . . depends on the
typewriter."

" What's your shorthand ? "

" I don't quite know now . . . used to be a hundred
and twenty or so."

" When did you work last ? "

" Oh, eight or nine years ago. In Chicago."

Here they usually stop for a moment. I stop too. I never explain this long interval. I never tell of my marriage or my divorce or my having a little daughter. I feel that for this job-hunting it is better to appear single and unattached. . . . Then comes the worst question :

" Any local experience ? "

" No . . . but I am sure . . ."

" No local references ? "

" Character references ? "

" No."

" Business ? "

" None, I am afraid. But I have my references from abroad : Petrograd, Warsaw, Berlin. . . . You see, I travelled a great deal," I say eagerly.

But the yellow-haired women don't care about these names. They never look at my references. Possibly none of them have ever been in Europe. It is far from California. Maybe Chicago is as far as they have ever travelled—the Fair in Chicago. They say in their tired, dull voices :

" We will let you know if there is anything," and the filled-out sheet disappears in the filing-case and one has the feeling that it is now buried for-ever.

Sometimes I feel like shouting that, though I may not know how to use a multigraph—I don't even know what the damn thing is—or a new-fangled switchboard, I do know a whole lot of other things that are more useful: I can write better letters than most of my employers; I can mix with all kinds of people from snobbish aristocrats to simple cowboys or poor emigrants ; I orient myself quickly, and—finally—I could even learn to use all these gadgets if necessary. But when I see the faces of the yellow-haired ladies, I find I cannot shout, for it would be like shouting against a machine, a well-oiled, efficient machine which knows its routine and which knows only routine people : " Book-keeper with Burroughs " ; " stenographer with P. B. X." ; " multigraph and fanfold biller." They have never, never handled people who have worked on a paper in the midst of a revolution, done social work during a famine and a typhus epidemic, and translated poetry for a genius who was an alcoholic. . . .

And so I go away. I go home and put another yellow sheet into my typewriter. . . .